FROMMER'S
GUIDE TO
HAWAII

by Faye Hammel

1981-1982 Edition

Published by Frommer/Pasmantier Publishers
A Simon & Schuster Division of
Gulf & Western Corporation
380 Madison Avenue
New York, New York 10017

ISBN 0-671-41430-5

Manufactured in the United States of America

*Although every effort was made to insure the accuracy
of price information appearing in this book
it should be kept in mind that prices
can and do fluctuate in the course of time.*

CONTENTS

Chapter I	Whys and Wherefores	1
Chapter II	Honolulu Logistics	8
Chapter III	Most-for-the-Money Hotels	14
Chapter IV	Dining Discoveries	43
Chapter V	Adventures in the Cosmopolitan City	76
Chapter VI	Honolulu After Dark	95
Chapter VII	A Honolulu Shopping Bonanza	100
Chapter VIII	Circling Oahu	114
Chapter IX	The Big Island: Hawaii	122
Chapter X	The Valley Island: Maui	157
Chapter XI	The Garden Island: Kauai	192

MAPS

Hawaiian Islands	4
Honolulu: Major Areas and Streets	9
Central Waikiki	25
Ewa Waikiki	54
Downtown Honolulu	78
Oahu	116

INFLATION ALERT: We don't have to tell you that inflation has hit Hawaii as it has everywhere else. For this reason it is quite possible that prices may be slightly higher at a given establishment when you read this book than they were at the time this information was collected in late 1980. This may be especially true of hotel and restaurant prices. Be that as it may, we feel sure these selections will still represent the best travel bargains in the islands.

Chapter I

WHYS AND WHEREFORES

TO GET THE MOST for one's travel dollar in thriving, prosperous (and inflationary) Hawaii, the tourist today must be more *akamai* (smart) than ever before.

For Hawaii is no longer the remote, end-of-the-rainbow place it once was. Waikiki once knew only the sound of the surf. Today it bustles with over a million tourists a year, scores of hotels, literally hundreds of eating spots, and a wealth of sightseeing, entertainment, and sports activities. It is the most popular vacation spot in these United States.

Hawaii has something for everybody. It has luxurious $400-a-day suites with broad lanais (balconies) and views of the Pacific, and plain $20-a-day rooms with views of somebody else's kitchen. It has $25 luaus and 95¢ bowls of Japanese noodle soup. It has some of the most breathtaking vistas in the world, some of the most exciting cultural activity, and some of the most splendid stretches of sand and surf anywhere. And it has, like any other center of such attraction, its tourist traps.

That's where this book comes in. It takes know-how to get the best accommodations for the price, no matter what the price; to find the most delectable and adventurous food for the money, the most authentic Polynesian entertainment, the most thrilling Hawaiian sights. It takes know-how, too, to make every day count in Paradise. And what we intend to do in these pages is to give you that know-how, to let you in on the inside tips that separate the *kamaainas* (old-timers) from the *malihinis* (newcomers). We'll show you the best way to enjoy the major sights and take you, too, off the beaten path to surprising places that most tourists never hear of. We'll show you the best way to escape to this best of all escape places. In short, we'll tell you how to get such good value for your dollar in Hawaii that you'll have enough money left over to come back again next year. And the year after that. For Hawaii is one of those places that, once experienced, has a way of getting in the blood.

Some Elementary Hawaiian Geography

The Hawaiian Islands were spewed forth from the bottom of the Pacific in great volcanic explosions that occurred many thousands of years ago. The entire archipelago includes some 122 islands, most of them merely tiny mountain peaks of a submarine mountain range that stretches for 1,600 miles. The eight largest islands make up the Hawaii we know: the four major ones of Oahu, Maui, Hawaii, Kauai—which belong to the world of the visitor; Lanai, a plantation island totally owned by the Dole Pineapple Company; Molokai, the place where Father Damien made history at Kalapaupa by caring for the lepers (there is still a sanatarium there, but the island is also gaining fame as a retreat for those who really want to get away from it all); Kahoolawe, which is a target range for American planes and ships; and Niihau, where the old Hawaiian way of life is still maintained and which is kept *kapu* (tabu) to all but those invited by its owners, the Robinson family.

Contrary to popular belief, the Hawaiian islands are not in the South Pacific; they are much closer to the U.S. mainland, 2,500 miles away, and lie in the northern Pacific Ocean at a latitude about even with the southern part of the United States. With increasing technological advances, the time of a journey from the West Coast to Hawaii takes only about five hours by plane and four days by ship.

What Hawaii Is Like

Hawaii is at once like everything you dreamed it would be and totally unlike anything you imagined. It is both a tropical paradise and a cosmopolitan boom town, a place where the old island gods still hold sway and where speculators and builders and real-estate men are riding high. It is one of the most fascinating paradoxes of old and new, of beauty and razzle-dazzle, of serenity and show business anywhere. It is an island world that went from the Stone Age to monarchy to statehood in less than 200 years. It is a place where Japanese and Chinese and Polynesians and Americans and Filipinos and Koreans, merchants and missionaries, whalers and working men from all over came together to form a new world. And where, despite everything, the old Hawaiian gentleness, the warmth and hospitality that have come to be known worldwide as *aloha,* still pervades all. This is what makes Hawaii someplace special: no matter how many new hotels and condominium apartment buildings rise above the Waikiki skyline, it will never be as cold and commercial as Miami Beach. The spirit of the Hawaiians still holds forth.

The Hawaiians—A Brief History

To know the Hawaiians of today, it helps immeasurably to know a little bit about the Hawaiians of the past. The very earliest settlers to these volcanic islands arrived from various parts of Polynesia, probably Tahiti and Bora Bora, about 750 A.D. Guiding themselves by a primitive and probably intuitive navigational science, they crossed thousands of miles of ocean in pairs of large outrigger canoes, connected by long bamboo poles that supported a tiny hut between the canoes. They brought with them their animals and plants, introducing such foods as the sweet potato into a climate that had never yet supported it.

They settled primarily on the largest islands of the Hawaiian archipelago—Hawaii, Kauai, Maui, Molokai, and Oahu. The islands were fragmented into little kingdoms, each ruled by its own chief, with its own *kapus* and particular customs. Power belonged to the strongest, and the bloody overthrow of leaders was quite common. But life was stable, and very probably even comfortable. None of the settlers ever made any attempt to return to the tribes from which they had come. In the warmth of the sun, these Stone Age men, living primitive lives, worshipping their own gods, and keeping the old ways of life, remained undisturbed and untouched by outsiders until the 18th century.

In 1777, Captain James Cook, who was really looking for the Northwest Passage, stumbled on the island of Kauai. The natives, who had long believed that their great god Lono would one day return to them, mistook Cook and his crew for the god and a full entourage of lesser deities. At first he received a god's reception, but soon fighting broke out between the natives and the sailors, and eight months later, on another voyage, Cook was clubbed to death by natives and drowned off the Kona shore of the island of Hawaii. But from that time on, the Sandwich Islands, as he had named them in honor of the Earl of Sandwich when he claimed them for Great Britain, became part of the modern world. By 1790, King Kamehameha the Great, operating from his home island of Hawaii, conquered the other islands in the chain in a series of bloody forays (except for Kauai, which

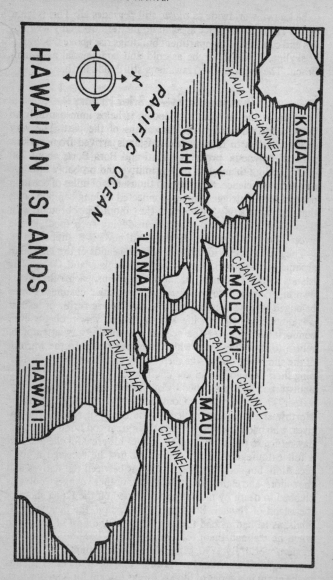

surrendered) and united them under his rule. Hawaii was already one nation when the first emissaries from the Western world—merchants, fur traders, whaling men—started their invasion of the islands.

In 1820, a band of New England missionaries arrived in Hawaii, determined to save the heathen islanders from the devil. They brought piety, industry, and the Congregational religion to the natives; their coming speeded the end of the old Hawaiian life. (Their story is told eloquently in James Michener's *Hawaii*, in both the novel and the film.) They smashed the idols and continued the destruction of the rigid *kapus* (already weakened by the king prior to their arrival), taught the people to read and write, and "civilized" the natives. And although they undoubtedly did an enormous amount of good, many of the natives here have never forgiven them, as the island saying goes, for doing so well. Some of the missionaries' children turned into businessmen, bought up the land, started industries, and it is their descendants who are still among the ruling forces of Hawaii's great corporate empires.

The native Hawaiians never really adjusted to the white man's world, refused to work his plantations, died from his diseases in horrendous epidemics. Today, just a few thousand pure-blooded Hawaiians remain. The rest have disappeared or become intermingled with the other races—mostly Japanese and Chinese—that came to do the white man's work.

The Orientals began to arrive around the 1850s, when the whaling trade was dropping off and the sugar plantations were becoming big business. The Chinese came first to work the plantations, then the Japanese, lastly the Filipinos. The Hawaiian melting pot began to simmer.

Meanwhile, the reign of the second Kamehameha, Kamehameha II, had been short. He and his queen died of measles in London in 1824. Kamehameha III reigned for 30 years, during which time the independence of the islands was declared from Britain. An English-language newspaper was started and a public school opened at that time, both in the islands' capital, Lahaina, on the island of Maui. But the capital remained there only until 1845, when the king and his court moved to Honolulu. Commerce was picking up in the Honolulu harbors, and in 1850 that city was declared the capital of the 19th-century kingdom.

The line of the Kamehameha descent ended after Kamehameha IV and V had passed out of the picture, by 1872. William

Lunalilo was elected successor by the legislature, but he died within a year; David Kalakaua succeeded him. Queen Emma, the widow of Kamehameha IV, appeared to have a rightful claim to the throne, and it was to this end that many riots were staged. American and British marines were called in.

In the latter part of the 19th century, industry continued to boom, with sugar the leading crop and coffee a close second. (Rice, now of small importance in the state, was once the number-two crop.) Finally, in 1875, the Hawaiian sugar planters worked out a reciprocal agreement with the U.S. government, by which Hawaiian sugar companies were assured an American market, and the Americans were given the freedom to use Pearl Harbor as a coaling station. The American Age was arising in Hawaii; the annexation of the Republic of Hawaii took place in 1898, but statehood would not be achieved until more than half a century later, in 1959.

King Kalakaua, "The Merry Monarch," was followed by Queen Liliuokalani, the last reigning monarch of the islands. When her plans for a new constitution were violently opposed, she was removed from office in the bloodless uprising of 1893 and replaced by Sanford B. Dole, a *haole* (white man) representing American commercial interests. It was while she was under house arrest that she wrote the poignant "Aloha Oe," now a song of good-bye to those leaving the islands. But it was also a lament, a farewell to the days of the past when kings and queens, and even an occasional god, walked the earth.

The 20th-century history of Hawaii began with the booming of the pineapple industry, a boom that has never stopped. The U.S. Armed Forces moved into the area and made Hawaii an independent army department in 1913. Although Hawaii was not directly involved in World War I, many islanders had volunteered for the French and German armies before the U.S. entered the conflict. The depression of the '30s blew through the islands with the relative calm of a trade wind, compared to the hurricane-like devastation on the mainland. Big business was not yet too big, industry not yet well developed.

But Hawaii felt the impact of World War II more than any other American state. Because the U.S. had developed the harbors and military installations on the islands so greatly, they were a prime target area for the enemy. After the dreadful bombing attack of December 7, 1941, Hawaii entered a period of martial law. Liquor consumption was regulated, curfews were imposed, and blackouts were common. Fortunately, the islands'

Japanese population was not herded off into concentration camps as it was in California. In fact, a group of Nisei volunteers became one of the great heroic regiments of the U.S. Army fighting in southern Europe. The 442nd Regimental Combat Team has been called "probably the most decorated unit in United States military history," and one of its members, Daniel K. Inouye, is the senator of Watergate fame. This participation in the war did a great deal to break down race lines in Hawaii. Today, the Japanese are the largest single ethnic group, and one of the most powerful, in the state.

After the war, increasing lines of transportation developed between the American mainland and Hawaii. Tourism became a major industry and the already existing industries grew at phenomenal rates. Years of labor disputes in the 1940s, spearheaded by the militant ILWU, raised the standard of living for the Hawaiian working man to an all-time high. Finally, in 1959, after a 30-year struggle for statehood that began with Hawaii's first representative to Congress, Prince Jonah Kuhio Kalanianaole, delegate John A. Burns (later Hawaii's governor) effected passage of the bill that made Hawaii the 50th American state. Dancing in the streets celebrated a goal long promised and arduously won.

Since statehood, Hawaii has blossomed and boomed and burst forth into a new era. Now largely Democratic in politics, with a mostly Japanese legislature, it is liberal in its outlook, proud of its ability to blend the races, to let the newcomer "do his own thing." Garment industries, steel mills, and cement factories are growing. Agriculture uses the most advanced techniques, and pineapple and sugar are still big business. So are tourism and the military. Technology has moved in and made Hawaii the mid-Pacific outpost in America's space efforts and oceanography research. The University of Hawaii and the East-West Center for Cultural and Technical Interchange have raised the level of education in the state remarkably, bringing in scholars from all over the world. Population swings near the three-quarters-of-a-million mark; over a million tourists are expected annually. Despite economic uncertainty here as everywhere, it looks as if Hawaii is still on the way up.

Chapter II

HONOLULU LOGISTICS

YOU'RE OFF THE PLANE and standing in the Hawaiian sunshine. If you're lucky, some doting friend—maybe even the representative of your hotel—has greeted you with an aloha kiss and draped a fragrant lei around your neck. If not, don't worry; there are lei stands all over the islands and you'll have worn dozens by the time you're ready to go home.

Your biggest problem, right now, is getting from the airport to Waikiki, where you'll most likely be staying, a distance of about 10 miles. You could, of course, grab a taxi (they're always waiting at the airport). The tab to Waikiki is about $8. It makes much more sense for the individual traveler to catch one of the comfortable Gray Line buses that shuttle between the airports and several large landmark hotels in Waikiki. Buses meet all flights until 1 a.m. The fare is $3.50, and they can't be beat for economy and convenience.

Although we are great believers in the City Bus System, "TheBUS" (as it is called) is not ideal for baggage-laden tourists. Buses do operate from the terminal into Waikiki, but they have no provisions for your luggage. If, however, you can contain all your belongings in the seat, the price is certainly right—50¢ a ride. And you'll get a head start at meeting the local population.

Transportation Within the City

BUSES: Once settled at your hotel, however, you should definitely learn how to use TheBUS. They run all over town and maintain frequent schedules between Waikiki and downtown Honolulu. The best way to figure out how to go where is to pick up one of the bus schedules available at the Ala Moana Shopping Center Bus Information booth. If you get into something really complicated, a phone call to the customer service department at 531-1611 will provide the answers. The fare, again, is 50¢; have

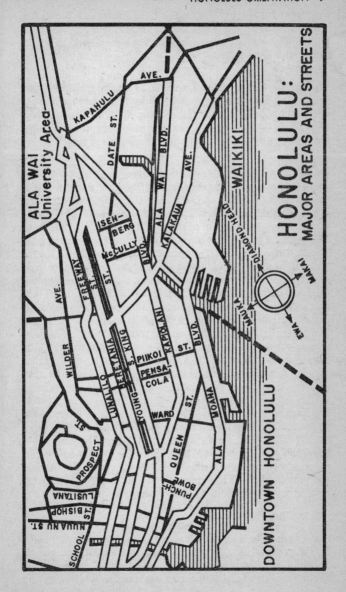

exact change ready. If you want a free transfer to a connecting bus, ask for it as you board. Senior citizens can get free passes after a four weeks' processing period (phone 524-4626 for details). Kids are charged 25¢.

TAXIS: They're available all over the city, although they do not cruise looking for passengers, which means that you have to call one on the phone. (See the Yellow Pages of the Honolulu phonebook for listings.) They are quite expensive, but could be cheaper than renting a car if you only have to do minor traveling.

U-DRIVES: At some time or other during your Hawaiian stay you'll probably want to get behind the wheel of a car, maybe to tour around the island of Oahu, or for a sightseeing excursion over on the windward side. The car-rental business (or U-Drive, as it is called here) is one of the most competitive in the state. The best idea is to check the companies out on the scene, since prices change so quickly; the tourist newspapers will give you the leads. If, however, you know in advance that you're going to do a great deal of driving (and especially if you're going to the neighbor islands where your own set of wheels is a must), you should reserve your car in advance from one of the reputable island companies. All of them offer "flat rates," which means that mileage is included; they usually turn out to be less than the regular rates plus mileage for extensive driving. **Hertz** (2424 Kalakaua Ave., Honolulu), **Avis Rent-A-Car** (Honolulu International Airport) and **Budget Rent-A-Car** (2379 Kuhio Ave.) all offer lots of discount coupons to major attractions, and charge slightly higher prices than do operations like **Tropical Rent-A-Car Systems** (2918 Ualena St., Honolulu), a highly recommended island firm; **American International Rent-A-Car** (3049 Ualena St., Honolulu), and **Dollar Rent-A-Car Systems** (2270 Kalakaua Ave., Suite 1010, Honolulu). Depending on the car, the company, and whatever special deals are available at the time you're there (be sure to inquire about "all-island" specials), expect to pay from $13.95 to $28.95 daily for your car.

Camping

If you must be on wheels, but can't afford both car and hotel, here's an idea that just might work for you. If you have a camper's adventurous spirit, a group of two or three, and a minimum of three nights, you can save considerably by carrying your own hotel—and fully equipped kitchen—around. You can rent some surprisingly comfortable campers in Honolulu and on the neighbor islands, from about $25 to $35 per day for two people, $1.50 for each extra person. Some units can accommodate up to six people; others are just for two. Two companies rent recreational vehicles: **Beach Boy Campers,** 1720 Ala Wai Blvd., Honolulu (phone: 955-1849), and **Holo-Holo Campers Inc.,** P.O. Box 11, Hilo, Hawaii (phone: 935-7406 or 961-2001). Camping is very much the thing to do among island residents, and the public campgrounds, usually on the shore of a secluded beach, are quite beautiful. No reservations are required, and they are seldom crowded.

Island Geography

Now that you're navigating around the city, either on foot or by bus or car, you should know something about where you are. Honolulu is, of course, the state capital, and the only major city on the island of Oahu. But before we get you oriented, we have to tell you that people here have no use for such terms as "north" or "south" or "east" or "west"—not even "uptown" or "downtown" are much help. For the Hawaiian Islands sit in a kind of slantwise position on the map, and the only reference points that are used are either place names or directional signals meaning "toward the mountains" or "toward the sea."

Here's how it works. Let's suppose that you are standing on Waikiki Beach, looking at Diamond Head crater; this means you are facing in a Diamond Head direction. You are, of course, at the beach area, but just a few miles away from this Pacific Riviera the water is deep enough for ocean-going vessels to dock in Honolulu harbor, which fronts on the downtown business district. (It was, in fact, that harbor's depth that made Honolulu a logical center for international commerce.) The downtown area is in an *ewa* (eh-vah) direction, toward the village of Ewa, from Waikiki, and further out in this section of the island low plains of rich, red volcanic earth give birth to tons upon tons of sugar and pineapple. Anything toward the ocean is *makai.* Over to your left from the beach area, in a *mauka* direction, are the striking Koolau Mountains, which form the dramatic backdrop for the city. On the other side of the Koolaus is windward Oahu, miles of verdant countryside bordering on the water's edge. This is fast being transformed into suburbs, the bedrooms of Honolulu from which commuters speed into the city's offices every day via tunnels bored through the mountains.

The Weather and When to Visit

Hawaii is one of those rare, blessed places on earth where the weather is always—well, almost always—wonderful. Any time of the year that you can get here is the right time to come. Most people come during the summer months of June, July, and August (mostly mainland families and young people); or during the dead of winter (the Christmas to Easter "high season" when prices go up), when the crowd is older and as much Canadian as it is American. But the weather is always good. An average temperature throughout the state would probably settle at about the 74-degree mark; in the summer it's usually in the 80s. Leave your warm coats at home; bring a sweater or light topper for some mountain areas at night; pack a light raincoat, too, just in case.

During the summer, a Hawaiian "rain" will probably be a 10-minute light shower during which nobody bothers going inside. During the winter months, there may be an occasional thunder-and-lightning storm, and sometimes it rains for several days in a row. Some winters it hardly rains at all. The varying amounts of rainfall can be explained in terms of northeasterly winds bringing rain clouds that are subsequently blocked by the main mountain range on the northern side of each island. Each island, therefore, has its windward side (where the rain falls) and leeward side (to which the storm clouds seldom get). Most tourist centers are, naturally, leeward. The gentle tradewinds keep the weather on a pretty even keel.

Average Monthly Temperatures in Hawaii			
January	72.2	July	77.7
February	71.9	August	78.4
March	72.2	September	78.3
April	73.2	October	77.4
May	74.9	November	75.4
June	76.8	December	73.3

A Matter of Language

You don't have to go to Berlitz before you go to Hawaii. English is the one language spoken everywhere in the state, although many first- and second-generation immigrants still use their native languages at home, and the Chinese and Japanese even have their own daily newspapers. But some of the old Hawaiian words have become charmingly intertwined into the language, and it's fun to know and use them. So that you'll know your *kanes* (men) from *wahines* (women) and your *kamaainas* (old-timers) from *malihinis* (newcomers), here are some tips.

Remember, first, that Hawaiian is a very simple language, much simpler than English. It contains only the five vowels plus these seven consonants: h, k, l, m, n, p, w. Vowels are sounded as they are in Spanish; consonants, as they are in English. The written language was the work of the missionaries who wrote down the native oral language. Mary became *Malia*, John became *Keone*, Britain turned into *Beretania*. Remember that every syllable ends in a vowel, and that you pronounce every syllable, and it all becomes quite simple. You always put the accent on the next-to-the-last syllable. For example, *kamaaina* is pronounced kah-mah-*eye*-nah, *wahine* is wah-*hee*-nay. Don't worry too much about the details, though.

Everyone will think you're pretty *akamai* (smart) if you know that a *haole* is a white man (Caucasian), a *hapa-haole* is half-white, *kau kau* is food, a *keiki* a child, a *luau* a feast, a *hukilau* a fishing festival. *Pupus* means hors d'oeuvres (they're usually served free with cocktails during Happy Hours), a *punee* is a couch, and *lomi-lomi* means massage (lomi-lomi salmon is literally "massaged"). If you want something done fast, it's *wiki-wiki*, and when something is finished, it's *pau*. The *alii* were royalty, the nobility of old Hawaii, and breaking their *kapus* (tabus) could get a man into plenty of *pilikia* (trouble). You'll most likely have a hotel room with a *lanai* (a porch). A pregnant woman is *hapai*. Everyone, of course, knows that a *lei* is a garland of flowers, a *muumuu* a long, loose-flowing Mother Hubbard-type dress (actually, the nightgowns of the missionary ladies—the only clothes that would fit the ample frames of the old Hawaiians). *Kokua* means cooperation or "take care" (you'll often see road signs saying *kokua*) and *mahalo* is the island way of saying thank you. And once you've been in Hawaii for a couple of days you'll have no need of definitions of *aloha*. The warmest greeting you can give in the islands: *aloha nui loa*.

Chapter III

MOST-FOR-THE-MONEY HOTELS

SOMEWHERE IN HONOLULU there is a hotel that is exactly right for you—whether *you* are a budget-conscious family counting pennies or a retired millionaire clipping coupons or, like most of us, the average tourist who wants a good time and a good deal for his money. For the Honolulu hotel scene covers an incredible variety of accommodations, everything from bohemian haunts as run-down as you'd expect, to hotels where the bedrooms are as big as ballrooms and where presidents, movie stars, Arabian princes, and Greek shipowners feel right at home. And the price range is just enormous. You can rent a suite for $300 a night at one of the seaside palaces, or a cute little kitchenette apartment a few blocks from the beach for about $15.

What I have attempted to do in this chapter is to pick out what I consider the best accommodations in whatever price category you choose. If you want to pay anywhere from $56 to $100 and up for a double for the night, make your selections from the first category, "The Great Ladies." If a nightly tab of $30 to $55 suits your fancy better, stick to the second category, "The Moderately Priced Hotels." And if you're watching your pennies, turn to the third category, "Budget Discoveries." Here I've described clean, comfortable, and sometimes surprisingly lovely accommodations where the nightly tab will run lower than $30 double.

You'll notice that most of my hotel recommendations are in Waikiki, rather than in downtown Honolulu or other parts of the island of Oahu. To my mind, Waikiki and the areas near it are the best places for the typical visitor, who wants to stay close to the turquoise waters and sparkling sands that have lured him perhaps thousands of miles from home. And Waikiki is ideal because it's so small. Bounded on one side by the Pacific, on the other by the Koolau Mountains, it's small enough so everything important is within walking distance, or just a short drive or bus ride away.

To help you get your bearings geographically, you should know that there are three major arteries in Waikiki, all of which run parallel to each other. Fronting on the beach is **Kalakaua Avenue,** Waikiki's main street and its choicest location, full of big hotels, shops, restaurants, thousands of tourists. About three short blocks *mauka* (toward the mountains) is **Kuhio Avenue,** a bit quieter and less crowded. And a few more blocks *mauka* of that is the **Ala Wai Boulevard,** next to a peaceful waterway close to the mountains, created back in 1920 when a brilliant entrepreneur got the idea of draining the swampland that was Waikiki. It is adjacent to the public and inexpensive Ala Wai Golf Course.

As you read the hotel descriptions below (and remember there are many other good hotels in Waikiki; these are simply my choices), you'll become aware that, regardless of price structure, there are two general categories of hotels in Hawaii: the big, lively, resort-type hotels that are ideal for active singles and unencumbered couples; and the usually smaller, apartment-type hotels that are better suited for families with children or for anyone who wants to stay in the islands more than the usual week or two. These smaller apartment hotels all have a money-saving (and child-pleasing) advantage—a kitchenette, perfect for making breakfast coffee, storing Junior's chocolate milk, and fixing a quick snack when you don't want to eat out. (Most of the large hotels do not have kitchenettes, but some will furnish you with small refrigerators if you request them.) By and large, the apartment hotels are on the side streets that run between the three major thoroughfares, and on the Ala Wai Boulevard. Remember, all the hotels are within easy walking or busing distance of each other, and all are near the important attractions of Waikiki. In general, prices are higher the closer you get to the beach; rooms get bigger and tariffs lower as you head toward the Ala Wai.

Note: the area code for all phones in the state of Hawaii is 808.

Hotel Know-How
Now, a few words about some miscellaneous matters.

RATES: You should know that many hotels have different rates for high season (usually mid-December to April 1) and low season (the rest of the year). High-season rates add an average of $5 to $7 to your bill per day. During slack periods, rates may come down considerably, especially in the smaller establishments. And many hotels offer special considerations for weekly and monthly stays.

Also note that we cannot be responsible for any change in the rates quoted here. The prices listed are those supplied by the hotels as we go to press at the end of 1980. Even though prices may rise in these inflationary times, I feel these hotels will offer the best value for the money.

PRIVATE BATHS AND MAID SERVICE: Every hotel described below offers private baths; note will be made of those that do not offer daily maid service.

AIR CONDITIONING: Most of the newer hotels offer air-conditioned units; where this is not so, trade winds and cross ventilation will usually offer enough comfort. If you suffer a lot from the heat, though, you may find an air conditioner important, especially in the warm summer months, July through September.

RESERVATIONS: It is always advisable to reserve a hotel room in advance. This way, you can be sure of getting the type of accommodation you prefer at the rate you want to pay. Even without reservations, you will probably find a room in Waikiki; there are usually more hotel rooms than there are guests, unless a big convention is in town. A few week's notice is usually adequate, but remember that the more popular the hotel, the more essential is a reservation a good deal in advance—perhaps even several months. And reservations are particularly important in the high season, from December through Easter and from June until Labor Day. Some very popular hotels request that one reserve at least *a year in advance* for the Christmas–New Year's holidays. The general rule is this: as soon as you know you're going to Hawaii, start making reservations.

BABYSITTERS: The desk clerks at any hotel can put you in touch with qualified people who will look after Junior while you're out seeing the town.

The Great Ladies: Expensive

If anyone were to ask me to name my favorite hotel in Honolulu, I would have to go right out on a limb and say the **Kahala Hilton**. About a 15-minute ride from the razzle-dazzle of Waikiki, in the beautiful Kahala residential area, it is a rare combination of island tranquility and jet-set sophistication, a place where the warmth and graciousness of the staff perfectly match the charm and serenity of the surroundings. Little things like having your name remembered, a pineapple waiting in your room when you arrive, and an orchid on your pillow add up. So conducive, in fact, is the Kahala to relaxation that about one-third of the guests are repeat visitors who never leave the grounds. I don't blame them.

One could, in fact, spend days here just celebrity-watching. Was that really Sammy Davis, Jr., or Carol Burnett or Hugh Hefner? Or you can concentrate on more mundane things, like watching the trained dolphins dance the hula in the lagoon; lazing on the gentle beach; tooling around in a pedalboat or kayak; taking a plunge in the pool. If you have an eye for beauty, take a stroll inside and outside the hotel, and bring your camera. Inside, note the immense multicolored glass chandeliers that suggest the driftglass of Hawaii's beaches; the 2½ acres of teakwood parquet flooring from Thailand; the Polynesian-inspired circular rug masterpieces; the paintings by artists like John Young; the circular staircase leading to the Maile Restaurant with its lava rock wall covered with orchid plants—as a start. Outside, study the architecture, the acres of beautiful gardens—with their bamboo groves, waterfalls, rare plantings—in which the hotel is set. There's even a lagoon stocked with fish, giant turtles, penguins, and dolphins.

Where to stay? You have your choice of 369 spacious guest rooms, all with elegantly tasteful appointments, including a large seating area, a lanai in many of the rooms, quiet air conditioning, color television, and knockout his-and-her bathrooms with two separate bath vanities and a small refrigerator. The price range depends on whether you face the mountains ($95 to $125 for a double) or the lagoon or ocean ($175 to $185). Magnificent suites run from $290 to $600 a day. There is no charge for children of any age sharing their parents' room, and there are daily activity programs for them during the high seasons and at holiday times. An extra person is charged $8. If you're alone, deduct $2 on the price of the doubles.

This, however, is not the place to be alone. You should be here with someone you love—the better for enjoying the romantic nights on the seaside **Hala Terrace** where Danny Kalekini presents one of the last authentic Hawaiian shows on the island; for enjoying the lavish Sunday-night buffet; for candlelight dining *à deux* in the *Travel-Holiday*-Award-winning **Maile Restaurant;** or just for the sheer beauty of being in a place that combines the charm of the old and the excitement of the new Hawaii.

Reservations can be made through Hilton Reservation Service or any Hilton Hotel. The local telephone number is 734-2211.

The most spectacular hotel in Waikiki itself? That accolade might go, perhaps, to the four-year-old **Hyatt Regency Waikiki at Hemmeter Center,** 2424 Kalakaua Ave. (phone: 922-9292), a $100-million caravanserai by the sea that already ranks as one of the great showplace hotels of the country. Occupying an entire city block, the 1234-room hotel accomplishes the seemingly impossible: creating an oasis of calm and tranquility and lush tropical beauty in the midst of the most bustling, heavily trafficked area in town. Christopher Hemmeter and his team of architects and designers created the effect by placing all the public areas around a lushly landscaped, huge atrium or Great Hall, above which the guest rooms rise in twin, 40-story towers that afford maximum views of ocean and mountains, and maximum amounts of privacy and peace. The Great Hall, one of the most beautiful spots in Honolulu, replete with tumbling waterfalls, fountains, cascades of greenery, South Seas-scented flowers and plantings everywhere, magnificent sculptures, and dotted with art, antiques, and intimate conversation areas, is, quite naturally, one of the most popular shopping (see Chapter VII), restaurant, and promenade areas in town.

The guest rooms have also been designed with an eye to the utmost in both comfort and glamor. Among the largest in town (425 square feet), each has a lanai with outdoor furniture, a sofa, huge closets, wall-to-wall carpeting (even up to the edge of the bathtub), TV, air conditioning, and either twin beds, doubles, or double doubles. Grasscloth-type wallpaper, cheerful color schemes (either green and yellow or orange and brown), and quality art works everywhere (original paintings or good prints) create a harmonious feeling. These units rent from $65 to $105, depending on the view and floor. The oceanview Parlour Suites have all this plus a spacious living room and rent for $180. And the incredible two-bedroom Presidential Suites, veritable mansions in the sky, complete with living room, library, and no fewer than six lanais, are $550 per night. All suites are located in the

Regency Club, which embodies a personalized approach that makes everyone feel like a VIP and also offers penthouse rooms at $100 to $105.

The beach is directly across the street, but guests can also swim and sun at home at the third-floor pool and enjoy drinks at the Elegant Dive poolside. All told, the hotel has five restaurants and seven cocktail lounges including the **Terrace Grille,** an indoor-outdoor restaurant overlooking the ocean, and **Harry's Bar,** tucked into a corner of the open-air atrium, with the mood of a European sidewalk cafe: international newspapers are available at the counter. **Bagwells 2424,** the ultimate in continental dining; **Spats,** a Roaring '20s speakeasy; **The Colony,** a steak house; and **Trappers,** a fashionable club with stylish entertainment, deserve detailed reviews in themselves (see Chapter IV).

Hyatt Hostesses are on hand to advise visitors on sightseeing, restaurants, sports, babysitters, or whatever. During school vacations, they plan special activities and trips for children. Like everyone else here, they're intent on treating visitors well and with aloha.

Reservations are easy: call 800/228-9000, toll free.

As much a landmark on the Waikiki skyline as Diamond Head is the pink-stucco, six-story, Moorish-style hotel called the **Royal Hawaiian,** 2259 Kalakaua Ave. (phone: 923-7311). Standing on the site of King Kalanikapule's home by the sea of a century and a half ago, it was Hawaii's original luxury hotel and has been the subject of newspaper and magazine stories, the scene and site of scores of television shows and movies, since it opened back in 1927. Now under the Sheraton banner and with all its rooms refurbished, the Royal Hawaiian wears its regal heritage like a proud mantle. You can't help saying, "They don't build hotels like this anymore."

Surrounded by acres of lush tropical gardens (note the splendid monkeypod tree) and fronting on a handsome stretch of beachfront, the hotel exudes that unmistakable aura of regality —in the black terrazzo marble of its lobby floors; the coral-toned, handloomed Hong Kong rugs; the high-ceilinged splendor everywhere. Its **Monarch Room** is one of the famed dining rooms of the world, and one of the best places in the islands for top-name entertainment.

Despite its regal bearing, the Royal Hawaiian has become quite democratic now that it's part of the swinging Sheraton hotel chain. From December 21 to March 31, double rooms go from $65 (garden view) on up to $93 for ocean view double, $3 less for a single; the rest of the year, they range from $58 to $88 double. And all are beautiful, immense, and in the old style, even to the double doors. Views are superb, and service via the white telephones is immediate and gracious. As you would expect, suites are splendid, ranging from $115 to $300 during high season, $105 to $280 the rest of the year. You can stay either in the older original hotel building or in the new high-rise wing, where all rooms overlook the pool and the Pacific. Guests at the Royal can use the facilities of the four other Sheraton resorts in Waikiki —the Moana, Surfrider, Sheraton-Waikiki, and the Princess Kaiulani—and charge them to their bill. Reservations can be made by phoning 800/325-3535, toll free in the continental U.S.

The newest skyscraper directly on the beach, the **Sheraton-Waikiki** was an instantaneous success from the moment it opened its doors in the summer of 1971. And it's not hard to tell why. It's a light, gay, vibrant place where everybody seems to be having a good time. The lobby has a wonderfully open feeling about it, and the breezy summerhouse mood extends into all the public rooms and the 1900 air-conditioned bedrooms as well. The "standard mountain view" rooms here—$60 and $70 double from December 21 to March 31, $52 to $80 the rest of the year—are quite large as hotel rooms go, and the appointments bespeak charm. Flower murals in blues and greens dominate the color scheme, bathrooms and closets are roomy (so are the private lanais), and, of course, there's color TV. The oceanview rooms are dazzlers. Most nearby hotels have a view of the Sheraton, but at the Sheraton your views are of a vast expanse of blue Pacific, the sun dancing on the waves in daytime, the lights from Diamond Head to downtown Honolulu glistening under the night sky. These rooms go for $80 and $90 double in high season, other times, $72 and $82. Suites range from $120 to $340, and some, fit for diplomats and royalty, boast a vast 20-foot living room with an outdoor lanai, and can easily accommodate four people. No matter what room you choose, though, you're welcome to use the coin-operated laundromats, hair dryers, automatic irons, and lounge with vending machines, TV, and chairs to relax in while your wash gets done!

You'll probably find you're spending a lot of time right at the hotel, what with all those great little shops in the lobby, that vast expanse of beach at your doorstep, and one of the biggest and sunniest pools in Waikiki on the beachfront. When you're hungry, there's the pretty **Ocean Terrace** for casual meals, the glamorous **Hanohano Room** for gourmet dining in a spectacular setting 30 stories up (take the glass elevator just for the view), as well as the **Kon Tiki Restaurant, Safari Steak House,** and **Oahu Bar** for drinks, steaks, and entertainment. If you decide to leave "home," you can, of course, "play and charge" at the other Sheraton hotels on the beach. Reservations: phone 800/325-3535 toll free in the continental U.S.

While all of Hawaii seems to be going high-rise, there is, at least for the time being, one last survivor of the truly Hawaiian cottage hotels on the beach at Waikiki—the **Halekulani,** Kalia Road at Lewers Street (phone: 923-2311). Those who know the Halekulani are hoping its owners can also resist economic pressures to build up-up-up. Meanwhile, it's still there, 40 cottages, housing 200 rooms, nestled in a five-acre tropical garden and boasting some 500 feet of ocean frontage. In Hawaiian, Halekulani means "House Befitting Heaven," and generations of the hotel's guests have found the name an apt one. Here is Hawaiian hospitality at its best, where a gracious staff (many of whom have been with the hotel for more than 20 years) treats returning guests like old and welcome friends.

There is a wide range of accommodations at the Halekulani. The choice locations, of course, are near the oceanfront, but you'll look out into a garden wherever you are. For the standard twin bedroom and bath (if you can call anything at the Halekulani just standard), prices are from $45 to $75 for two. Add a sitting room, and the tab goes to $75 to $110. For an ocean view, the rate is $80 to $130. Kitchenette suites, also with sitting room, are priced at $75. Add $12 for a third person. There are also some family cottages that run from $115 for a two-bedroom, two-bath cottage for four, to $285 for a four-bedroom, four-bath cottage that sleeps eight. Add 10% to the above rates from December 15 to April 15.

Wherever you eat at the Halekulani, you'll be looking out over the sea: in the **Coral Lanai,** the more sheltered dining room; the **Surfside Lanai;** the informal **Diamond Head Terrace;** or the **House Without a Key** (how do you lock a palm tree?) where the bar opens at the crack of ice. Every afternoon around 6, join the *kamaainas* to sip a mai tai, watch Hawaiian entertainment, and see the island sun go down. The toll-free reservation number is 800/367-5660.

To use the word "hotel" to describe the **Hilton Hawaiian Village,** 2005 Kalia Rd. (phone: 949-4321), is really an understatement. With 1556 rooms, 20 acres of grounds, three swimming pools, a man-made lagoon, its own U.S. post office, supper-club theater, acres of shops, and almost a dozen places for wining, dining, and catching the celebrities, it's a swinging little world of its own. Henry J. Kaiser built it, Hilton bought it, and the visitors love it.

If you're a guest here, you may not find it necessary to leave the Village during your entire stay. You can surf, take outrigger-canoe rides, or just plain swim off one of the finest stretches of beach in Waikiki, with acres of white sand even at high tide. During the day there are free hula and ukelele lessons. Come nightfall, you can have your drinks under the stars in the beach-side Garden bar, dine on Cantonese cuisine in the **Golden Dragon Dining Room,** feast on prime ribs of beef in the **Rib Room,** or enjoy continental food in the luxurious **Mahahiki** dining room. Then on to the Jim Nabors Polynesian Show in the **Hilton Dome** or a nightcap in the **Pot O' Gold Lounge**—among other possibilities. You could spend your entire vacation shopping; there are some 100 regular stores here plus a slew of exotic Oriental ones in the Rainbow Bazaar.

There is also a wide choice of accommodations. You can live in either the Rainbow Tower (which has possibly the finest rooms in Waikiki), the Ocean Tower, or the Diamond Head Tower. View is the main factor in determining price. You can have a good-size double room in the Ocean or Diamond Head Towers from $54 and up, with only court or garden views. Broader mountain and garden views start at $60; yacht-harbor and ocean views begin at $66. If you can go to $80 and higher, the world of luxury is yours—ocean views, private lanais, refrigerators, color TVs, etc.; complete apartments and penthouse suites run from $100 to $425.

An extra person in a room is $10; single occupancy is $8 less. There is no charge for children regardless of age staying in the same room with their parents. If you want to eat your meals "in"—and there are so many restaurants that you won't get bored—you can choose a modified American-plan arrangement (two meals) for $30, or a three-meal American plan at $37.

Another self-contained resort community that provides enough glamorous diversion for weeks of Hawaiian living is Western International's **Ilikai,** 1777 Ala Moana (phone: 949-3811). Inside this unique island-within-an-island, you can choose from more than 800 of Waikiki's largest luxury accommodations housed in two buildings overlooking both the Waikiki Yacht Harbor and Ala Moana Beach Park, with its acres of green lawns shaded by huge monkeypods, banyans, and coconut palms. Your vacation here can be as lazy or as lively as you wish: there's sunning and swimming in two pools or the nearby blue lagoon; for the more adventurous, there's sailing, surfing, or scuba diving in the waters beyond. One of the rare hotels in Waikiki with tennis facilities, the Ilikai now has seven courts. You can shop until you run out of traveler's checks, eat your way through a variety of fun restaurants, watch top island entertainment under the stars, and stay in some of the nicest hotel rooms in town.

I am a great believer in hotel apartments, and here the Ilikai really shines. The typical room in the main building is the largest in Waikiki, offering all the conveniences of a full apartment. A large sliding glass door opens onto magnificent ocean and mountain views. Closet and bathroom are liberal, and the kitchen and dinette are both fully equipped. Now for the prices. Based on view, rather than height (the hotel is right on the beach, so ocean views are unobstructed), rooms in the Tower Building run $74 to $78, double. There is no charge for children under 18 occupying the same room; over 18, the extra charge per person is $10. Yacht Harbor Building rooms start at $54, but are sans kitchenettes and smaller, although elegantly furnished.

Much of the Ilikai's excitement is in its restaurants and nightclubs. Its coffee shop, **Pier 7,** long one of my favorite mood spots in the islands, looks out over Waikiki Yacht Harbor; its chowder, with chunk after chunk of succulent clam, is unbelievable. You can lunch outdoors under the shade of palm trees and umbrella tables at the **Centre Court,** or enjoy one of the best buffet spreads in the islands at the **Canoe House** (see Chapter IV). When night falls, everything goes into high gear, for sunset signals the start of the hotel's traditional torchlighting ceremony by the Lilikoi Sisters. Then you must choose between Opus One cabaret for the sounds of music or the **Top of the I** for dinner, dancing, and gazing at the lights of Honolulu blinking 30 stories below. For reservations and information within mainland U.S.A., call toll free 800/228-3000.

If what you crave is elegant living, glorious views of the ocean, and plenty of room to stretch out, then the **Colony Surf,** 2895 Kalakaua Ave. (phone: 923-5751), is an excellent choice. It's located in the quieter Diamond Head section of town, across from Kapiolani Park, and the size of the rooms is matched by the splendor of the vistas; would you believe a 25-foot windowed panorama of ocean in many of the rooms? There are two buildings: the **Colony Surf,** whose elegant one-bedroom suites have fully equipped kitchens, two double beds, color TVs, every nicety, and cost from $90 (single or double occupancy) on the limited-view lower floors, all the way up to $130 to $165 for direct ocean frontage; and the **Colony East Hotel,** whose studio rooms go from $65 to $70, single or double, to $75 to $85, depending on the view. Although they are smaller than the immense suites in the hotel building, they are luxuriously appointed, have kitchenettes, air conditioning, two double-size beds, plenty of closet space, and large bath vanities. You can't go wrong in either building.

The Colony Surf is also the home of the famed **Michel's,** which I'll describe later in the section on restaurants. Elegant and expensive haute cuisine is served here at dinnertime, but breakfast and lunch are both reasonably priced, and the mood and views are superlative. The **Colony Surf** is a *kamaaina* hangout, a spot where the knowledgeable locals go just to get away from it all. It's that kind of place.

Although it's in the midst of the Waikiki madness, at 2552 Kalakaua Ave. (phone: 922-6611), there's an air of retreat about the **Hawaiian Regent Hotel.** It's wrapped around a cool, lush inner courtyard and the architectural details are striking. The third-floor swimming pool and sitting area, with glorious views of newly widened Waikiki Beach just across the street, is a stunner. The good looks continue in the rooms, which are large and exquisitely furnished in teak and rattan, with divided baths and vanitorium and tub-shower combinations. Breathtaking views of sea, mountains, or Diamond Head are enjoyed from spacious and private lanais. There are TV, radio, air conditioning, direct-dial phones—the works. Prices begin at $47 double for mountain view rooms, and go to $81 for oceanfront. Deduct $2 for a single; add $8 for an extra person in the room. One-bedroom suites are $185; two-bedroom suites, $360; there is no charge for children under 12. There is a $5 winter supplement December 19 to March 31. You can eat at the attractive Summery Coffee Shop or dine on fine continental cuisine in the multiaward-winning **Third Floor.** The Library is a contemporary wine bar and lounge overlooking Waikiki Beach, and the Garden Court Lounge is a relaxing, open-airy spot for tropical drinks and entertainment. For a cup of expresso, try the Cafe Regent, a Parisian-style cafe set in the gardens of the hotel courtyard. For beef and seafoods, it's the **Tiffany Grill** on the third floor. Reservations and information; call 800/421-0530 or 800/421-0734 toll free in the continental U.S.

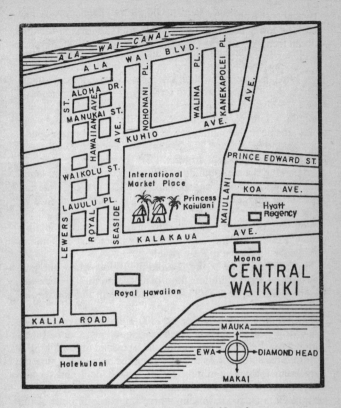

The Moderately Priced Hotels

Most of the hotels described below offer accommodations ranging in price from approximately $18 to $42 for double occupancy. So that you'll know where you're at, I've divided them into three major categories: those fronting on or very near Kalakaua Avenue, Waikiki's main drag and the street closest to the beach; those along or near Kuhio Avenue, which runs parallel to Kalakaua; and finally, those on or near the Ala Wai Canal, a five- or six-block walk *mauka* from Kalakaua Avenue.

ALONG KALAKAUA AVENUE: The veteran classic South Seas hostelry on the beach at Waikiki is the **Moana Hotel,** 2365 Kalakaua Ave. (phone: 922-3111), a handsome white colonial building in the Sheraton family. Old Hawaii hands always like to say, "I remember Waikiki when just the Moana was here," and, indeed, some seven generations of visitors have danced and dreamed under the stars and twinkling lights of the huge banyan tree on the beach that, along with the hotel, has become a Honolulu landmark. The hotel's decor is colonial, for the Moana Hotel bridges the monarchy to territory to statehood periods of Hawaiian history. Rooms are larger than the standards of contemporary hotel construction. Rates at the Moana go from $41 to $57 double in the main building (ceiling fans but no air-conditioning), and for $64 and $72 double in the air-conditioned ocean lanai from December 21 to March 31; the rest of the year, it's $39 to $49 in the main building, $52 and $63 in the ocean lanai. Take $3 off for single occupancy and add $10 for a third person. There is no charge for a child occupying the same room with an adult.

You will, of course, want to dine in the oceanside Captain's Galley Restaurant and take in the Banyan Court Polynesian Spectacular, a festive nightly ritual.

The Moana is one of the few old-time spots where the graciousness of the plantation days of Old Hawaii still survives. Reservations: phone 800/325-3535, toll free in the continental U.S.

The **Waikiki Beachcomber** at 2300 Kalakaua Ave. (phone: 922-4646), located as it is between Seaside Avenue and the International Market Place, sits astride the heartland of Waikiki. It's an attractive hotel, across the road from the beach, with smartly Polynesian lobby and dining rooms, plus a pool and terrace looking over the avenue. This is the site of Don the Beachcomber and the Bora Bora Showroom, where you can catch one of the best Polynesian shows in Waikiki. Considering their luxurious appointments and generous size, the rooms are a very good buy. You can count on TV, air conditioning, dial-out phones, refrigerator, divided bathroom, and a furnished lanai for your $44 single, $46 double. At this price you'll look toward the mountains or toward the ocean, the latter view partially blocked by the Royal Hawaiian Hotel across the street. Higher up, it's higher up—$51 and $57 single, $53 and $59 double; with a third person, an extra $6. Rooms are $5 less April 1 to December 20. I like these rooms, especially the grass-textured wallpaper with its floral designs and the welcome spaciousness. Reservations: Island Holidays Resorts, P.O. Box 8519, Honolulu, HI 96815.

A striking 37-story, 495-room Tower has recently been added

to the popular **Pacific Beach Hotel,** right across from the beach at 2490 Kalakaua Ave. (phone: 922-1233), making it more exciting than ever—especially since the Tower boasts a fantastic, three-story, 250,000-gallon saltwater Oceanarium, from which lobby and restaurant viewers can observe the marine life of the Hawaiian coral reefs without ever having to take snorkel in hand! Both glamor and practicality are available at the Pacific Beach: glamor in the good views in all of the 850 rooms, whether they face ocean, mountain, or Diamond Head; and practicality in such conveniences as the kitchenette-bars, color TV, air conditioning, shower-tub combinations, double-double or king-size beds throughout in the large and luxurious rooms. The decor is elegant green and brown, the furniture ultramodern. Rates begin at $48 for a standard double and go up to $70 for those rooms in the front of the building that have the ocean just outside and a sunset spectacular such as few hotels can boast of; singles are $3 less. From April 15 to December 20, rooms are $6 less. The hotel also boasts three professionally designed tennis courts, a large heated pool, and a bevy of restaurants and lounges that include, within view of the Oceanarium, the Oceanarium Restaurant (see Chapter IV for details) for light dining, Neptune for continental fare, and Shogun, a Japanese steak and seafood restaurant.

The Pacific Beach Hotel is part of the Best Western chain; call them toll free at 800/528-1234.

Walking into the lobby of the regal **Queen Kapiolani Hotel,** 150 Kapahulu (phone: 922-1941), is like walking back in time to the Hawaii of a century ago, when royalty was in full bloom. This towering hotel overlooking Queen Kapiolani Park, less than a block from the beach, is the representation of all the elegance that Queen Kapiolani, the consort of Kalakaua, Hawaii's last reigning king, meant to her people. A bubbling fountain surrounded by tropical plants on the outside of the building leads the way to the lobby, which is worth a visit in itself, lavishly done in green wallpapers and accented by magnificent chandeliers of kerosene lamps, reminiscent of the days of the whalers in Hawaii. The bentwood wicker chairs are stunning replicas of Old Hawaii furniture. The Kalakaua Dynasty decor carries over to the rooms, too; they are almost royal chambers in themselves, decked out in gold and royal blues. The door to each room, in fact, has a full-color reproduction of the seal of the state of Hawaii over it. The views, too, are splendid, since the hotel is across the street from Queen Kapiolani Park, and there is no new construction to block the view from here to Diamond Head or the ocean. Besides the elegance, there are such modern creature comforts as air conditioning, an open-air restaurant and pool on the third floor, and a full dining room. Single rooms start at $34, twin-bedded ones at $37. Prices go up to $44 and $47 for more luxurious accommodations, and there is a charge of $7 for each extra guest. Kitchenette rooms are available at $49 single, $52 double; suites, $100 double. The feeling of a royal Hawaii of long ago pervades all. For reservations, write Hawaiian Pacific Resorts, 1150 South King Street, Honolulu, HI 96814, or phone 800/367-5004, toll free.

Since its takeover by the New Otani Hotel Corporation of Japan, the **Kai'mana Beach Hotel,** Diamond Head way at 2863 Kalakaua Ave. (phone: 923-1555), has been totally refurbished and looks very good indeed. The open-air lobby, with its wicker bucket chairs and sofas, looks out on the Hau Tree Lanai cocktail lounge and a beautiful view of the Pacific. There's an Andrade boutique in the lobby and another in the little shopping arcade outside, which also boasts an antique shop, Of Things Past, and an ice cream parlor, Scoop du Jour. Rooms are spacious and well appointed; the corner rooms have lanais on two sides for a stunning view. Furniture in the guest rooms is dark rattan, and the color scheme is soft green. There is a tremendous variety of types of accommodation here. I'll cover a few to give you an idea of what's available. Standard rooms go from $30 to $35 single, $35 to $38 double, depending on the floor. Then you get into the type of view: Diamond Head is $38 single, $41 double; Ocean and Waikiki $45 single, $48 double; Penthouses $47 single, $50 double. Junior Suites, with one bedroom, are $95 or $100, single or double. Garden Apartments are $35 single and $40 double for the studio kitchenette and $45 single and $50 double for the one-bedroom with kitchenette. From December 20 to March 31, rates are $5 higher in all categories. An additional person is $6. Naturally, all accommodations are air-conditioned and have color TV.

Now that we've gone in a Diamond Head direction about as far as we can go, let's head back along Kalakaua Avenue, into the center of Waikiki. Here, about a block away from the beach, at the corner of Kalakaua and Lewers Road, you'll find the **Holiday Isle Hotel,** 270 Lewers St. (phone: 923-0777), a nicely appointed hotel with a superb location smack in the middle of everything. Many of your fellow guests here will be spending $40 and $42 a day for a double, but they're paying for the glorious views; if you're willing to forego that view, you can have the same rooms they have—on the third and fourth floors—for just $37 a day double, $35 single. Rates are $5 lower April 1 to December 20. Each extra person is charged $6 a day, but there's no fee for children under two, unless they need a crib. A cool, blue-green color scheme runs through the hotel; all rooms are air-conditioned and nicely laid out, and all have refrigerators. There are color TVs and radios in every room, and the staff is hospitable and charming. For those too lazy to get themselves to the turquoise Pacific less than a block away, there's a nice-size pool on a deck outside the hotel lobby that offers a beautiful view as well as privacy. Downstairs, you can get good food and modestly priced drinks at either Gus' Steak House or Shipwreck Kelly's. Reservations: Island Holidays Resorts, P.O. Box 8519, Honolulu, HI 96815.

One of the newer hotels in the Waikiki area is the big, beautiful, bustling **Waikiki Village** at 226 Lewers St. (phone: 923-3881). The enormous lobby boasts several shops and a swimming pool located just behind the reservations desk! The staff members are very attractive young people who clearly like their work and enjoy being helpful and dispensing aloha.

The hotel is air-conditioned throughout, and there is a television set in each of the attractively furnished rooms. The decor is modern with a Polynesian flair. Double-room rates start at $30 to $40 per day for rooms without a kitchenette. Two-room suites with kitchenette are $56 and up for up to four persons. Add $8 per day for each additional person. The kitchenette units here consist of a unit with a sink, half-size refrigerator with cupboard and counter space, and hotplates—perfectly adequate for light meals. Waikiki Village also boasts an attractive coffeeshop and a cocktail lounge, and one of the prettiest stretches of Waikiki Beach awaits you just across Kalia Road.

If there is a "heart" of Waikiki, the **Cinerama Reef Towers** must be it. Located at 227 Lewers in Waikiki (phone: 923-3111), half a block from the beach in one direction and half a block from busy Kalakaua Avenue in the other, it is right in the midst of everything, as well as being the home of the Don Ho Show at the Polynesian Palace. Accommodations here lean toward the living-room-by-day, bedroom-by-night feeling; most rooms are equipped with refrigerator and coffee-maker, and some—at higher price levels—also have kitchenettes. "Standard" rooms are a good buy at $26 for a single, $28 for a double. Don't expect much in the way of views here, or in the "superior" rooms ($30 to $32 double), since the Cinerama Reef Towers is really socked in by big hotels. Be satisfied with a glimpse of the ocean or mountains or the pool of a nearby hotel. "Deluxe" rooms go for $34 to $36 double, $2 less for singles, and $9 more for an extra person. Lanais are small but private, bathrooms have just a stall shower, and closets are adequate.

One of the first high-rise hotels to be built in Waikiki, and still one of the largest (885 rooms), is the **Cinerama Reef**, right on the beach and in the center of things at 2169 Kalia Rd. (phone: 923-3111). Now that other hotels have climbed around the Reef, panoramic views are hard to come by unless you have an ocean-front room. You might make it in a superior-class room at $42 to $47 for a double, but chances are you'll have to go deluxe at $50 to $61 double. Standards begin at $34 to $36 for a double ($2 less for a single), and these are quite adequate in size and comforts with sliding glass doors to the furnished lanais and sliding shoji doors to the spacious closets. Bamboo motifs are featured on the mural-type wallpaper, and color schemes are on the bright side.

Lots of interesting shops line the extensive lobby and the lower-level walkway to the beach. Restaurants include the inexpensive Perry's Smorgy and the Reef Broiler, and, at poolside, Rudy's Italian Restaurant II is a popular spot for hearty eating. Reservations from Cinerama Hawaii Hotels, 2169 Kalia Rd., Honolulu, HI 96815.

The newest addition to the Cinerama Reef empire is the **Waikiki Tower of the Reef Hotel,** 200 Lewers St. (phone: 922-6424), and very pleasant it is. The back of the attractive open lobby looks onto the pool area of its sister hotel, the Edgewater, whose pool it shares, and the beach is a very short walk away. Just off the lobby is the attractive and moderately priced Waikiki Broiler Restaurant, which is not just the usual hotel coffeeshop. The rooms are smartly decorated in brightly colored floral schemes, bathrooms have full tub and shower, and all rooms have direct-dial phones, color TV, and air conditioning. Most rooms have lanais; corner rooms have two lanais; and to create a suite, two corner rooms can be opened up so that you have three lanais and two TVs! All corner rooms have kitchenettes (they are the only ones that do). The one thing that determines whether rooms here are standard, superior, or deluxe is the height of the floor (not the fact that it has a kitchenette, special view, etc.). Rates are $36 to $28 single and $28 to $30 double for standard accommodations; $34 single, $36 double for moderate;

and $38 single, $40 double for deluxe. A third person is charged $9. Junior suites for up to three persons are $48.

In this era of high-rise Hawaii, it comes as a shock to find a low-slung, two-story hotel cozily nestled into a tropical garden, complete with pools, plantings, and that old-time Hawaiian feeling you weren't sure still existed. And that's the kind of pleasant shock you'll get when you walk into the courtyard of the **Hawaiiana Hotel,** 260 Beach Walk (phone: 923-3811). Located on a side street, half a block from the beach on one side and Kalakaua Avenue on the other, the Hawaiiana is not well known among tourists since it doesn't go about blowing its own horn; but those who know it treasure it and wouldn't dream of going anywhere else. All of the units are attractively furnished as studio rooms or suites, with complete electric kitchens; all catch the trade winds, most have lanais, and all have views of either the garden or one of the two pools (there's a shallow one perfect for kids). The studio rooms run from $32 to $43 single, $34 to $45 double (the lower-priced ones are closest to the street and office); a third person in a room is $8 per day; the lovely two-room suites run $50 for one, $55 for two, $60 for three, $67 for four, $75 for five.

But the comfort and charm of the rooms is just the beginning of the story here; the hotel believes in doing extra little things for its guests, like serving them free coffee and pineapple juice out by the main pool in the morning; placing a pineapple in their rooms when they arrive; giving them leis on departure; presenting two Hawaiian shows and one movie a week (free); and leaving a newspaper at the door every morning. Use of the washing machines and dryers is free, and so is parking on nearby Saratoga Road. The Hawaiiana is the kind of place where you get to know your neighbors, and many couples who have met here now plan their vacations together and reunite at the Hawaiiana every year! Mapuana Schneider, the hospitable manager, suggests advance reservations, especially during the busy midsummer and midwinter seasons.

After you've seen the Hawaiiana, it's almost a case of déjà vu when you see **The Breakers,** 250 Beach Walk (phone: 923-3181). The mystery is cleared up when you learn that the same architect designed both. Like its neighbor, it has that low-slung, relaxed, Hawaiian-garden feeling. There are about 66 rooms in the five ranch-style buildings, all of them nicely appointed, with complete electric kitchenettes, modern Oriental decor, air conditioning; many have lanais. The studio rooms go at $32 and $36 single, $34 and $38 twin. There are also 15 garden suites that rent at $47 for one or two, $52 for three, $57 for four, and $6 for an extra rollaway bed. You'll enjoy the large pool, the leis on departure, the beach facilities down the road, and the lovely garden setting.

A real find, one you'll not see advertised anywhere, is the **Waikiki Shore Apartments,** 2161 Kalia Rd. (phone: 923-3283). This is a condominium apartment building, with each unit privately owned; in fact, it is the only apartment building I know of right on the beach at Waikiki. Many of the owners have purchased their apartments here as investments, and make them available year round for short-term rentals.

Studio apartments start at $42 regular, $32 off-season (May 1 to December 15). One- and two-bedroom apartments start at $55 and $72 respectively, $45 and $62 off-season. Two-bedroom oceanfront apartments begin at $99 ($77 off-season). Prices advance a few dollars depending on the floor. All rates are for two people; add $7 per day for each extra person. If you have kiddies under 12, leave them home; and if you're traveling alone and are under 18, you'd better look elsewhere, since those between 12 and 18 must be accompanied by an adult.

The rooms are spacious. Each apartment has its own private lanai that runs across its entire width, so you have views of both sea and mountains, and of the green, spacious lawns of Fort DeRussy, next door. Each apartment is furnished and decorated differently, of course, but all are attractive, and all have complete kitchens with garbage disposal and laundry facilities, as well as private telephones. Alas, there is no air conditioning. The beach is one of the loveliest around, and dozens of restaurants and shops are just a few steps from the front door of the cool, inviting lobby, decorated in rich shades of turquoise. You get the feeling of apartment living here, not of a tourist hotel. Ample parking is available in the basement.

The cool and peaceful **Holiday Inn Makai-Waikiki,** 2045 Kalakaua Ave. (phone: 955-6363), is outstanding among the newer hotels. I like the location, near Fort DeRussy and the good beaches in that area. The two-level lobby gives a feeling of coolness, with its terrazzo floors and tasteful furnishings. And you certainly won't go hungry or unentertained here. The Makai Sugar Company Restaurant on the mezzanine floor offers excellent food impeccably served. There's cocktail and sandwich service at the pool. And at night, the Sugar Mill Lounge features entertainment of high quality.

The rooms are quite lovely, all air-conditioned, with color television sets, telephones, and private lanais. And every room has a fine view of either ocean or mountains, not too common in many Waikiki hotels. Most rooms have two double beds or a king-size one. Depending on the season (the lowest rates apply from April 1 to December 19), one-room accommodations go from $30 to $45 for singles, from $36 to $50 for doubles. There is a charge of $8 per extra person when using the existing equipment, $6 more if a rollaway bed is required. Children under 11, free. Two-bedroom suites are $85 for up to five people.

Located at the entrance to Waikiki, adjacent to the Ala Moana Shopping Center and overlooking the Ala Wai Yacht Harbor, is the **Ala Moana Americana Hotel,** 410 Atkinson Dr. (phone: 955-4811). This 1194-room luxury building is a beauty, certainly the closest to the "mostest"—for shopping as well as to downtown Honolulu. Ala Moana Beach Park is within walking distance, but the main action of Waikiki beach is about a 10-minute bus ride away.

The handsome lobby is the ideal place for talk and a drink. The second-floor level is worth a look for the outstanding examples of art of the islands, including a mural of the King Kalakaua era executed by Juliette May Fraser, and some charming paintings from modern Hawaii. And despite the wealth of shops and restaurants in the adjoining Ala Moana Shopping Center (you need only cross a footbridge to be smack in front of Liberty House), there are more shops lined up in the lobby, plus four restaurants, five lounges, and a show room in the hotel. The Plantation Coffee House is a shopper's haven during the day and a celebrity hangout after hours; it's open around the clock. The **Ala Moana Americana's** luaus are always good fun. And there's the **Whaler's Broiler** for steak and seafood, **Mon Cher Ton Ton** for Japanese cuisine, and, on the 36th floor, **The Summit** for romantic rooftop dining and dancing.

Every room in this tallest of Hawaii's resort hotels has air conditioning, color TV, radio, tub-shower combinations, direct-dial telephones, and automatic wake-up system. The color schemes are attractive; most of the rooms have twin beds and lanais. Singles and doubles go from approximately $39 to $64, depending on the floor and the view. There is no charge for children under 14 sharing the same room with their parents, but there is a maximum of three people in a room.

ALONG KUHIO AVENUE: It's hard to ask for a more central location in Waikiki than the one enjoyed by the handsome **Coral Reef,** 2299 Kuhio Ave. (phone: 922-1262). It's next door to the bustling International Market Place, and the mood here, too, is one of excitement and fun, with shops, restaurants, and a supper-club all holding forth on the main floor. Upstairs are some 243 rooms, each good-size and nicely furnished in island style, with private lanais, shag carpeting, air conditioning, a desk, and a TV set in every room. Rooms have either two double beds or one double and one single. Doubles are $30 to $42 from April 1 to December 20, $37 to $49 December 21 to March 31; deduct $3 if you're traveling alone, add $8 for an additional person. The hotel also specializes in moderately priced suites, eminently suitable for large families.

The attractive new **Waikiki Malia,** 2211 Kuhio Ave. (phone: 923-7621), has a lot going for it—including a rooftop tennis court, a pool, a therapeutic spa, and a wonderfully central location. And right off the colorful, breezy lobby is the Wailana Malia, one of the best coffeeshops in town, open 24 hours a day. And I haven't even told you about the rooms yet! Each of them, cheerfully decorated with cane furniture, crimson carpeting, and printed bedspreads, has a lanai, air-conditioning, and color TV. One entire floor features rooms designed especially for physically handicapped guests, with wide doors to accommodate wheel-chairs and grab-bars in the bathrooms. The Junior Suites consist of a sitting room with two daybeds (or *punees,* as they are called in Hawaii), plus a bedroom. They can accommodate up to four people; rates are $42 single, $44 double, $50 triple, and $56 for four. Regular rooms contain two double beds and have a small refrigerator. Rates for these rooms range from $30 to $37 single, $32 to $39 double, $38 to $50 triple, and $44 to $56 for four. From December 20 to April 1, add $5 per category. For reservations, write Island Holiday Resorts, 2222 Kalakaua Ave., Honolulu, HI 96815, or call 808/922-6111.

The walkway to the airy lobby of the **Sherry Waikiki,** 334 Lewers St. (phone: 922-3771), is surrounded by plant beds filled with lau'e ferns, croton, and palm trees, making for a charming entry into this cozy and friendly little hotel. Off to the left is the sparkling pool, surrounded by a carpeted sundeck and serenaded by soft Hawaiian music that comes out of nowhere. All 100 of the units have kitchenettes, lanais, and full baths with tub and shower. The small studios, which accommodate one to two, go for $42 a day from the end of December until the first of April,

$32 the rest of the year; the larger studios, maximum four persons, go for $52 in-season and $42 off-season, and the deluxe one-bedroom suites, maximum five persons, are $69 and $59.

For toll-free reservations on the mainland, except in California, phone 800/423-2922; in California, 800/272-3282. Sherry Waikiki is a Colony Hotel.

There's a very comfortable feeling about the **Ambassador Hotel of Waikiki**, 2040 Kuhio Ave. (phone: 941-7777). It's neither too large nor too small, has an excellent location in the middle of Waikiki convenient to the beach and shopping, and the rooms are comfortable and attractive. All are done up in studio style in beige and gold tones, have air conditioning, telephones, and sliding glass doors opening onto private lanais. The views are bigger and better in certain locations, but prices are reasonable throughout—from $32 to $44 double. I especially like the one-bedroom suites, which include full electric kitchens, and the corner suites with their great views of the ocean and Diamond Head. Here the prices range from $50 to $66 single or double; add $7 for an extra person. You can have breakfast, lunch, or dinner at the Cafe Ambassador Coffeeshop, or drinks at the Embassy Bar, right on the premises. And if you're too lazy to walk to the Pacific, there's a large pool and sundeck lanai one floor above the bustle of Waikiki; drinks and snacks are at the ready, too.

The **Waikiki Resort Hotel**, 2460 Koa Ave. (phone: 922-4911), has a breezy, open lobby that looks out at the pretty fountains just outside. Rooms here are decorated in golds and browns with dark-green carpeting; all have lanais. The hotel is air-conditioned throughout, and all rooms have the comforts of refrigerator and radio as well as the usual TV. Double rooms run from $34 to $48, depending on the height of the floor and which way the rooms face. The $37 to $48 rooms are on a high floor and face the ocean; the $34 ones are below the eighth floor and face the mountains. Rooms with kitchenettes (as opposed to just a refrigerator) all face the ocean and are $49 per day double. For a touch of luxury, you might try the one- and two-bedroom suites at $85 and $135. Children under 12 are free, provided that additional beds are not required; add $7 per day for an additional adult; and add $4 to these rates between Christmas and March 31. The Falls Coffeeshop is just off the lobby for good and moderately priced food, and there's a lovely swimming pool, too, even though a nice stretch of Kuhio Beach is just down the street.

One of the newer hotels to boast a central location in Waikiki is the **Marine Surf** at 364 Seaside Ave., corner Kuhio (phone: 923-0277), just a block from bustling Kalakaua Avenue. And that's not all it boasts. For $34 single or double you get a studio apartment, not just a hotel room. This means a fully equipped electric kitchen and a dining area. Give them points, too, for color television, sliding glass doors to a furnished lanai, and two double beds. The swimming pool in this 23-story building is 15 stories above Waikiki. The views get better as you go up, and the rates go up accordingly: $38 for superior rooms (single or double); $42 for deluxe rooms (again, a single or double); some penthouse suites available at $75. Rates usually go down during the summer months. No charge for children under 12 unless they require a rollaway bed; extra adults, $5. You'll find a quiet, conservative lobby, but bright, colorful apartments. And Seaside Avenue is a relatively quiet street. Inside the building is Matteo's, for superb Italian food, and Jameson's Restaurant, a cheerful pub. Parking is available.

At the new 625-room **Island Colony Hotel** at 445 Seaside Ave. (phone: 923-2345), elegance begins in the spacious, airy lobby, with its stylish rattan furniture and big, beautiful tapa banners that hang from the ceiling and sway in the breeze. It continues in the pool and sundeck on the sixth floor, the restaurant off the lobby, and on into the rooms, all of which have very large lanais; some of the views are breathtaking. The rooms are lavishly appointed in subdued Polynesian prints with rust-colored rugs, and all have phones and color TV sets. You have your choice here of several accommodations. If you want to do only some light cooking, take the "deluxe hotel rooms," which have two double beds, a large refrigerator, hot plate, cookware and tableware; prices range from $33 a day on the lower floors to $43 on the upper floors. Or you can have a studio with full kitchenette (although the refrigerator is smaller than in the above rooms); these are priced at $38 for the lower floors, $43 for the middle floors, and $48 for the top ones. Then there are one-bedroom apartments with full kitchen—there are four of these per floor—that go for $48, $53, and $58; add $7 for an extra person. Between December 20 and April 10, add $7 per category. There are prints by Allen Akina and Pegge Hopper on the walls of the guest rooms, as well as in the lobby. And a small alcove in the lobby houses several tables of the insanely popular "Space Invaders" electronic games.

The Island Colony is a truly beautiful place, abounding in

aloha. For reservations, write Hotel Corporation of the Pacific, 2299 Kuhio Ave., Honolulu, HI 96815, or phone, toll-free, 800/367-5124.

For comfortable apartment living the **Aloha Waikiki,** 414 Launiu St. (phone: 923-8741), rates high. This is a big condominium building, and at least 35 apartments are always available for rental. These are attractive one- and two-bedroom units with all-electric kitchens. The fully air-conditioned rooms are decorated with cool green carpeting, grass-cloth wallpaper, and tapa-patterned bedspreads and upholstery. There are color TVs and telephones in all units, as well as an intercom and buzzer to admit callers. Price, dependent upon height of floor and view, goes from $47 to $52 double for the one-bedroom suites, from $50 to $63 double for the two-bedrooms. It's $6 for each extra person.

ALONG THE ALA WAI: The **Waikiki Sand Villa** at 2375 Ala Wai Blvd. (phone: 922-4744) looks like a sandcastle. It's made of sand-colored, textured material and is castle-shaped. All of the rooms have lanai, color TV, and tub and shower in the bathrooms. There are no kitchenettes, but the corner rooms on all 13 floors have refrigerators. The guest rooms are good-size and attractively decorated in rattan furniture and printed draperies and bedspreads. And the young staff is cordial and helpful. Rates depend solely on the floor and view, and run $32 single, $35 double for standard accommodations; $36 and $39, superior; $39 and $42, deluxe; $42 and $45, royal. A one-bedroom Junior Suite is $81 for up to four people; an additional person is $6. From April 16 to December 20, these rates go down about $4 in each category. Children under 8 stay free unless they require a rollaway or crib.

For toll-free reservations, phone 800/367-5072; from Canada, 800/663-3602; from Alaska, 800/421-4545.

If comfort and convenience mean a lot to you, then I think you'll be as happy as I was to discover the **Ilima Hotel,** 445 Nohonani St. (phone: 923-1877). Every room in this attractive hotel has a modern, fully equipped kitchen, color TV, private lanai, radio, telephone, double beds, and full tub-shower combinations. Sun-worshipers will love the two sundecks atop the tenth floor, as well as the ground-level pool area with its ample sunning space on one side and tree-shaded comfort on the other.

As for the rooms, they are impeccably clean and attractively furnished in Polynesian style. The studios, which have two double beds and can easily accommodate four, rent for $24 to $42. They're all the same, but the rates get progressively higher as you go up and the views get better. It's $6 for each additional grown-up and $4 for a crib or rollaway. There are also one-bedroom suites: the small ones with two double beds rent from $36 to $52, the larger ones with three double beds go from $42 to $54. The two-bedroom penthouse—which can accommodate eight comfortably—rents at $90 for up to four.

The Ilima is close to the Ala Wai, so it's slightly removed from the hustle and bustle of Waikiki, but just a few minutes' stroll takes you to where the action is.

The **Hawaiian King Hotel,** 417 Nohonani St. (phone: 922-3894), is the kind of hotel one stumbles upon only rarely. Accommodations are definitely superior to many in Waikiki. Each unit, designed with the family in mind, is a handsome, beautifully decorated suite, with large living room, separate bedroom, a full kitchenette (and we mean full, down to the disposal unit in the sink) separated from the living room by a counter, and carpeting in the living room and on the lanai. As further blessings, all the apartments are air-conditioned, and as quiet as they are attractive. There's a minimart, boutique, and laundry at hand. A garden-pool area in the courtyard downstairs is the place to chat with fellow guests. Considering all this aloha, you get good value for your money: standard suites run from $26 to $28 single; from $26 to $30 double (more for deluxe and superior suites), with an extra tab of $5 for each additional person. Special family and weekly rates can be arranged, and rates are $5 higher during the busy seasons—June 1 to September 14 and December 16 to March 30.

At the Ala Wai end of Lewers, the **Waikiki Holiday,** 450 Lewers St. (phone: 923-0245), is about a ten-minute walk to the beach and a block from the busline. From the sweeping entrance and free-form pool outside to the 90 handsomely appointed rooms, lobby, and charming Indian restaurant, Shalimar, the place exudes a quality of charm and comfort that is hard to come by in this price range. All the rooms are air-conditioned and completely refurbished, and parking is available on the premises. Here's the easy-to-take price tab: singles or doubles with kitchens are $29 to $35. An extra person is $5. All the rooms have private balconies with views that get better the higher up you go. For advance reservations, call toll-free 800/367-5176.

A BIT FURTHER AWAY: The **Pagoda Hotel,** 1525 Rycroft St. (phone: 941-6611), comes complete with a scenic floating restaurant right on its premises. The studio rooms are very pleasant, well-set-up for housekeeping with a full refrigerator and stove, and air-conditioned. They go from $33 to $42 double and $30 to $39 single, depending on the floor. You're not too near the ocean here, but your own car or the free shuttle bus will have you in all the excitement of Waikiki in just a few minutes. There's a pretty pool on the grounds.

Closer to Waikiki, across Ala Moana Boulevard from the Ilikai, and equaling it in prime proximity to both the beach and the Ala Moana Shopping Center, is the **Hawaii Dynasty Hotel,** 1830 Ala Moana Blvd. (phone: 955-1111). Rising 17 stories, this 206-room resort is set well back from traffic noise, and since all rooms are air-conditioned, peace and quiet are doubly assured. Entering the grounds, you pass the attractive Dynasty Coffeeshop, part coffeeshop, part dining room, with good food at modest prices. Hawaii Dynasty Hotel rooms are standard size, but the bed sizes are deluxe. When you ask for twins, you get two double beds. Closets, too, are big, and a smart vanitorium extends the whole length of the tub-shower-equipped bathroom. The rooms, done in either beige and green or gold with yellow, have telephones and radios; most have peeks at the ocean; some feature lanais.

Rates go from $24 to $33 for singles, $26 to $35 for double occupancy for the twin double beds. Better views, lanais, and king-size beds add increments, and you can pay as much as $38. There are also penthouse suites for $65. Cribs are free, and there is no charge for youngsters under 12 in the same room. Extra adults pay $7 a night, and up to three people can share one room. From December 21 to April 15, there is a high-season surcharge of $5 per category. Babysitters are at the ready.

Budget Discoveries

NEAR KALAKAUA AVENUE: There's a very friendly feeling about the **Royal Grove Hotel,** 151 Uluniu Ave. (phone: 923-7691), where the Fong family really makes everyone feel right at home. Just a block away from Kuhio Beach, the six-story pink hotel has a pretty pool right on the premises, a tiny grocery shop, health food store, and restaurant off the lobby, an attentive staff, and some 100 nicely-put-together rooms whose prices begin as low as $20 for a single or a double. Comfortable kitchenette units begin at $26.50, and for $28 and up you can have your choice of kitchenette units with their own lanais. The one-bedroom apartments are good buys, too, from $30, and it's $4 for an extra person. Fine value for the money.

The **Kuhiolani**, 2415 Kuhio Ave. (phone: 922-1978), is one of those cozy, at-home kind of places where you can kick off your shoes and really relax. The pyramid-shaped building is just a three-minute walk from the blue Pacific, and service and hospitality are outstanding. The pyramid styling results in larger units on the lower floors (perfect for families that need elbow room), tapering into snuggling rooms on the top floors (great for honeymooners) with appropriately romantic views of the Pacific or Diamond Head. Rooms or one-bedroom suites for one or two people, all with twin beds, kitchenettes, and lanais, run from $25 to $40, depending on the floor and the size of the apartment. One-bedroom units for four or five people run from $42 per day. Prices usually come down during the off-season, from Easter to June 15, and again from Labor Day to December 15. And lower weekly rates are often available.

The **Malihini Hotel,** 217 Saratoga Rd. (phone: 923-9644), occupies an ideal location between beach and town; the beach in front of the Reef Hotel is just a hop across the street, and Kalakaua is a few minutes' walk away. The Malihini is a fine family choice. The large rooms are pleasantly furnished, have either king-size or double beds, fans, full electric kitchens, and some have lanais big enough for dining room tables and a border of plants. Outside, in the brick courtyard, you'll often find fellow guests barbecuing their steaks or throwing a cocktail party for the rest of the crowd. Children are warmly welcomed. There's also a dress shop called the Patio and laundry facilities right at hand. Prices are reasonable: $17 to $19 for a regular studio; $20 to $26 for larger studios with lanais; $30 to $36 for the one-bedroom apartments with lanais for four. Family rates can also be worked out. Prices go up a few dollars during the December 15 to April 15 high season.

Look out any streetside window in the **Waikiki Surfside,** 2452 Kalakaua Ave. (phone: 923-0266), and you're practically within "spitting distance" of Waikiki Beach, which is just across Kalakaua Avenue. Despite its deceptively unprepossessing facade and mini-lobby, all is bright within. The rooms are clean and cheerily decorated, with shag carpets and brown marble tabletops. All rooms are air-conditioned and have color TVs. You can get standard rooms for $24 single or double; slightly better located rooms for $29; and oceanfront rooms with balconies for $35. From December 20 to April 15, add $7 per category. An excellent budget choice. From the continental U.S., the toll-free reservations number is 800/367-5124.

With only 196 rooms, the **Waikiki Gateway Hotel,** 2070 Kalakaua Ave. (phone: 935-3741), isn't one of the "big" Waikiki hotels, but this small charmer is pure Hawaiiana (premissionary). Prominent artist Joseph Feher's pictures depicting the Hawaii of long ago were reproduced as murals and now decorate the bark-cloth walls of each room. They are beautifully complemented by the rich-toned cane furniture and the deep red-and-gold color scheme. Even the bathrooms are beautiful!

Each room has a large lanai (some have two), a direct dial phone, and a television set (color in the suites). Continental breakfast is served free to all guests. One of the island's finest restaurants, Nick's Fishmarket, is in the lobby. And there are laundry facilities on the fourth floor adjacent to the sundeck and the delicious blue pool backed by a wall of lava rock.

The Waikiki Gateway is not at the beach, but TheBUS, which stops right out front, will get you there promptly. Rates start at $26 for a double room and advance up to $34 on the higher floors. One-bedroom suites are $68 for two; add $7 for each additional person. Winter rates—December 20 to April 12—are $7 more. Reservations should be made about two months in advance; the toll-free number is 800/367-5124.

The **Waikiki Prince,** 2431 Prince Edward Ave. (phone: 922-1544), is a small hotel that makes no pretensions, but its studio rooms are clean and comfortable, and go for $26 and up. There are lanais in every room, air conditioning, gold carpeting, attractive furnishings, and either twin or double beds. The rates are the same single or double, but a third person is charged $4 extra a day. A smaller studio unit with only a two-burner stove and refrigerator instead of a full kitchenette is $23 and up, and there are really small studios without kitchenettes for $20 and up. The location is fine, just a very short walk to the blue Pacific and the excitement of Kalakaua Avenue. Alas, no maid service.

For those who like the feeling of a big and coolly efficient hotel, the **Aloha Surf,** 444 Kanekapolei St. (phone: 923-0222), is an excellent choice. Quite new on the Waikiki scene, the hotel looks out on the Ala Wai Canal and is about a 10-minute walk to the beach. A beauty shop, gift shop, outdoor coffeeshop, and pool all adjoin the almost wide-open lobby. The newly refurbished rooms are air-conditioned, have wall-to-wall carpeting, and bright but tasteful color schemes. All rooms have televisions, most have lanais, and some have kitchenettes. As for the views, which start a few floors above street level, they are of the Koolau Mountains and a tiny bit of ocean. The rates remain stable all year round, so don't hope to catch lower prices off-season. Even so, these rates compete well with others in less favorable locations. Standard rooms rent for $26 single or double, superior rooms with private lanai go for $31, and deluxe rooms with kitchenette cost $40. An extra person is $6.

ALONG THE ALA WAI: For my last choice in the Waikiki area, I'll let you in on a little secret. Yes, Virginia, there still is a hotel in Waikiki where you can get a single for $14 a night, a double for $16. And although the units at **Edmund's Hotel-Apartments,** 2411 Ala Wai Blvd. (phone: 923-8381), are small and far from fancy, they are clean and comfortable and adequately furnished with twin beds, kitchenettes, and tile baths, plus a TV set in every room. From the lanai, you look out over the Ala Wai Canal and the public Ala Wai Golf Course, and the refreshing mountain breeze helps keep things cool. Families on a tight budget can choose one of Edmund's plain one-bedroom apartments in the annex, at 308 Liliuokalani Avenue, where there's enough space for the kiddies to let loose in. Prices are $18 for a double, $3 for each extra person. But the biggest asset is owner Mrs. Amy Lau, who makes you feel like an honored guest in her home.

Waikiki Beach and Diamond Head

Chapter IV

DINING DISCOVERIES

DO TOURISTS spend more time eating than doing anything else? Statistics could never prove it, of course, but it has always seemed to me that dining out is one of the most popular pastimes under the Hawaiian sun. And with good reason; although Hawaii is not one of the true gourmet capitals of the world, it embraces a wealth of cultural traditions from all over, and dining here can be more fun—and more adventurous—than almost anyplace else. Honolulu itself has perhaps half a dozen great restaurants, scores of unusual and interesting ones, and many where the food is hearty, well priced, and just what you would expect from a good restaurant back home. Because there are so many restaurants in Honolulu, however, and in so many price categories, I feel that some guidance is in order. You're not going to spend every evening dining out with wine and candlelight and haute cuisine; neither are you going to eat all your meals at beachside burger stands or in the coffeeshop of your hotel. What I've done here, then, is to track down several dozen of what I consider the best restaurants in town, no matter how much or how little you want to pay or what kind of dining experience you're after. And I've divided these restaurants into three categories. To wit:

1. Elegant and Expensive. Here I'll give you the details on a group of restaurants that are at the top of our list, where the cuisine, the service, the ambience, the view—or any combination thereof—all make for a memorable experience. Expect to pay at least $15, maybe a good deal more at those places with an all à la carte menu, for dinner. A few cocktails before, the proper wine during, and a bit of liqueur after will, of course, add up. Not to mention the tip. When it's feasible, I'll also tell you how you can enjoy the same glorious surroundings and superb food for a much lower tab—at lunch. At these places, reservations are a must. And when you phone, inquire about dress; although most

Honolulu restaurants are eminently casual, a few prefer that men wear jackets and ties. (At some island restaurants, "dress" means that men must wear long pants and shoes.)

2. Medium-Priced Restaurants. The bulk of the restaurants I'll describe covers the range from $7 to about $15 for dinner. Many of these offer excellent table d'hôte dinners for reasonable prices. Here you'll continue to sample some of the international cuisines that have found a home in the islands—Japanese, Chinese, Mexican, French, Hawaiian, Italian, continental. And there'll be no shortage of that old Hawaiian favorite, the steak house. (This is the 50th *American* state, remember?)

3. Informal and Inexpensive. Which means exactly what it says. These are casual, come-as-you-are places, a few of them coffeehouses (but in the islands, even the coffeehouses are exotic), where you can expect to get dinner for $7 or under. Some are open around the clock, in case that hungry feeling should strike at an unexpected hour.

You'll note that under each main category I cover restaurants in Waikiki, in the downtown Honolulu area or beyond, or near the Ala Moana area. With one exception, all my choices are a short drive, or bus ride, or taxi ride away. (I'll tell you about a few restaurants in Windward Oahu when we take a later tour around the island.)

Elegant and Expensive

The Third Floor, in the Hawaiian Regent Hotel, has won a name for itself as one of the most fabulous restaurants in town. Many consider it the best. The decor is extraordinary, the service unbelievable (at least six waiters and waitresses served us at a recent meal, all addressing us by name!), and the continental cuisine of a very high order, filled with unexpected touches. Your table setting alone is worth between $50 and $100—bronze cutlery made in the Far East, Arabesque water and wine goblets, brass napkin rings, Camelot butter plates, and Samarkand dress plates, all laid out on a teak parquet table with handwoven moss-green placemats and linen napkins that match the carpeting and the high-back velvet rattan chairs. You dine beneath open beam ceilings, magnificent copper chandeliers, and multicolored Camelot banners against a romantic background of rippling fountains flowing over black river rocks, tropical wall plantings, and koa wall mosaics. You certainly have the right to expect the very best cuisine, and the menu of chefs George Seiffert and Gerard Reversade lives up to expectations.

I said the touches were unusual, and that they are. Instead of ordinary bread, you are served a slice of Indian *naan* bread, made by a master baker from New Delhi in an imported clay charcoal-heated oven. Instead of butter, you are served a combination of butter and duck liver—a whole crock of it. A tray of tiny relishes (miniature baby corn, pickled tomatoes, onions) is yours to nibble on while you study the wine list (the house has an excellent cellar) and order your entree. These range in price from $14 to $21, served à la carte with a crisp Manoa lettuce salad and a choice of vegetables (these are brought to your table and you serve yourself). But do start your meal with the unique iced appetizer buffet, your pick, for $5, of such surprises as blue-point oysters, poached salmon medallions, marinated herring, vinaigrette shrimp, and fresh artichoke hearts. If you're ready for your main course now, you may want to try, as I did, the scampi Provençale, sauteed in garlic butter and tomato with saffron rice, or the splendid seafood casserole. Both dishes were excellent. And one person, instead of the usual two, may order the rack of spring lamb Provençale, served with mint sauce and fresh vegetables. New continental dishes are always being added to the menu, authentically prepared with air-flown imported delicacies. If you have room for dessert, there are European cheeses, French and Viennese pastries, and a very good Polynesian fruit salad flavored with Kirsch wine—plus a dozen different European coffees. But do save some room for the surprise of the evening, as your waitress places a Plexiglas tub on your table with white (dry ice) clouds drifting down from it, like a stage setting of a dream. On it are chocolate cherries and ice-cream-filled chocolates—courtesy of the house. And, oh yes, while you're feasting, strolling musicians wander from table to table to play your requests.

The Third Floor is open for dinner only, 6:30 to 11 p.m. daily. Reservations are a must; so are jackets for the men; validated parking; phone: 922-6611. The Hawaiian Regent is at 2552 Kalakaua Avenue.

Hidden away in the far reaches of Waikiki, down steps, around corridors, and behind doors, is a small restaurant to which the gourmets of the world have beaten a path. This is **Michel's,** in the Colony Surf Hotel at 2895 Kalakaua Ave. (phone: 923-6552). The reason? Michel's chefs, whose culinary artistry is every bit as magical as the view from your table, which can rival anything on the Riviera—you're practically next to the incredibly blue-green Pacific, and you can watch the boats and bathers of the Outrigger Canoe Club as you dine on the fruits of Michel's wizardry. For example, some chefs simply cook snails; at Michel's, they're sauteed in burgundy wine and topped with a tantalizing mixture of garlic (ever so slight), parsley, and butter. Some chefs just toss salads; at Michel's, island Bibb lettuce is graced with ripe tomatoes, green peppers, hard-cooked eggs, green onions, exotic herbs, and Michel's own French dressing, all gently tossed at your table. Little matter that the snails are $7 the half-dozen or the salad $4 per person. How can you put a price on ecstasy? I might as well tell you right now that Michel's is not the place to go if you are in a hurry. This is no steamtable operation, and one of the ingredients of the culinary art is time. Many discriminating diners who have been coming to Michel's over the years phone a day ahead for their favorite special dishes. You cannot rush such delights as canard roti à l'orange, or chateaubriand steak for two, or poulet sauté à l'estragon. For dessert, how about strawberries Romanoff, $4? The very best wines and liquors, *mais certainement.* Check, please.

Inside Information Department: If you can't afford to have dinner at Michel's more than once (or not even once), why, live like the rich at lunchtime. Lunch, served daily except Saturday from 11:30 a.m. to 2 p.m., is also à la carte, with the cheese soufflés and salads at $8 a person, omelets and other entrees averaging $4 to $9. Or try the Sunday champagne brunch, served from 11 a.m. to 2:30 p.m., and a lovely treat.

Right up there with the greats is a newer contender, **Bagwells 2424,** at the Hyatt Regency Waikiki, 2424 Kalakaua Ave. Sumptuous in decor, elegant in service, outstanding for its French and American gourmet specialties, Bagwells is for that special evening when price is no object. The room is done in warm earth tones, with cocoa velvet banquettes and big cocoa velvet armchairs to sink into, and lighting coming from the candles on the tables, wall sconces, and tiny white sparklers in the plantings. A modern light sculpture dominates the entrance, and there is original art and sculpture throughout the room. The Franciscan place settings (costing about $120 each) and crystal are works of art, too, and all this, along with background guitar music, sets the mood for the feasting to come.

Start your meal by a consultation with the wine steward (appropriate wines are suggested for each course on the menu), and then proceed to cold or hot appetizers like sashimi, smoked

Sacramento River salmon, or poached scallops; then on to, perhaps, a chilled, minted cream of avocado soup and salad. Appetizers are all á la carte, and not inexpensive (about $3.50 to $7). Now for the entrees, which average about $14 to $20. From the "New Continent," Bagwells serves a superb spit-roasted Long Island duckling glazed with almonds and honey; steaks, lamb, and a whole roasted chicken with tarragon; from the "Old Continent," it offers such items as veal and mushrooms simmered in old cognac and sweet cream, and Pacific salmon served in its own poacher. Vegetables accompany the entree, but a copper skillet of Maxim's potatoes is another $2.50. Should you possibly have room for dessert, fresh strawberries Romanoff would be perfect, as would a serving of cheese, port and grapes, or Turkish coffee, topped off by a cognac, of course—and you're ready for *l'addition, s'il vous plaît.*

Bagwells serves dinner only, nightly from 6:30 to 10:30 p.m. There's entertainment in the adjoining lounge—whose windows overlook the pool or the moonlit ocean—before and after dinner. Make advance reservations by phoning 922-9292 and you'll be given personalized placecards and matches. A relaxing note: While sandals and T-shirts are not permitted for men, aloha shirts, sans jackets and ties, are perfectly acceptable.

When **John Dominus** opened its doors in late 1979 it became an instant success. Reservations were being taken for weeks in advance. It's not hard to figure out why: a combination of location, decor, and food has made it one of the more enjoyable restaurants in Honolulu. Sitting astride the channel leading to Kewalo Basin, at 43 Ahui St., John Dominus is close enough to the water so that you can hear the laughter and music from the sailboats, charter fishing boats, and tour boats that pass by. Low-ceilinged open dining lanais extending some 30 feet over the water create the sensation of being on a cruise ship yourself. Inside, lava rock and koa continue the feeling of old Hawaii. And an interior waterway swarming with tropical fish, sting rays, and even sharks provides constant visual excitement.

The menu, too, is dominated by the sea. You could start your meal with fish bisque, thick with seafood, or with such appetizers as steamed clams, oysters Rockefeller, or escargots, from $3 to $5. You can select your entree from a large center table, where the catch of the day is displayed on a bed of ice. This is your chance to try Hawaii's game fish, caught in local waters. It could be ahi or tuna (our favorite), local marlin, rock cod, ulu, mahimahi, or opakapaka. Catch of the day is priced from $14 to $16, and your entree is accompanied by home-baked sour-dough bread.

John Dominus is open for dinner every day from 5:30 to 10:30 p.m., with the bar in action from noon, and a pupu menu available from 3 to 6 p.m. and again from 10 p.m. to midnight. Local people like to come by for Sunday brunch; at $20, it includes a number of meat and egg dishes, champagne, tax, and tip. There are two sittings: 10 a.m. to 12:30 p.m. and 1 to 3:30 p.m. To reach the restaurant by car, go west on Ala Moana Boulevard from Waikiki. After passing Kewalo Basin harbor, turn left on Ahui street and go to the end.

Reservations are advised: phone 523-0955.

Like everything else in the graceful new Prince Kuhio Hotel at 2500 Kuhio Ave., the **Protea Dining Room** is a study in understated, refined island elegance. The low-ceilinged room, with its skylight highlighting a central glass-and-brass wine cellar, bouquets of rare protea blossoms and greenery all about, is the setting for beautifully prepared and presented continental cuisine. No wonder that after its 1980 opening it became an immediate success with local gourmets, who rank it up with Honolulu's best.

Protea serves dinner only, all à la carte, from 6 to 10 p.m., with French and continental accents. The appetizers are indeed appetizing: we find it hard to choose among fresh fruit marinated in Cointreau, Puget Sound clams in a hot Mediterranean sauce, or the French hors d'oeuvres tray, studded with the likes of salmon mousse. Soups include a rich cream of avocado as well as the expected French onion. If you're ready for the main event, there are over 15 selections, beginning with catch of the day at $11.50, on up to $16 for roast duckling à l'orange and noisettes of beef tenderloin. Among the beef and fish choices, I recommend the best of both worlds: filet and shrimp princess is a small filet of beef and several jumbo shrimp topped with sauce bearnaise and served with croquette potato, mushrooms, and sauteed fiddle-head greens. If you can handle dessert after that, my hat is off to you. Awaiting your selection are splendid flambés, coupes, soufflés, and mousses; soufflé glacé Grand Marnier is memorable.

A good way to experience Protea is to try the Sunday Champagne Brunch, 10 a.m. to 2 p.m. Again, the food is gourmet all the way. The appetizers, for example, which you select from a table of ten dazzlers, include galantine of duckling, tartlettes with ham mousse and quail eggs, and tiny gaspacho clams in aspic. $10 includes the champagne; it's $4.25 for children.

Reservations are advised always: phone 922-0811.

Can't decide between dancing and dinner? Both are available at one of the town's most elegant restaurants, **Rex's** at 2310 Kuhio Avenue, corner Nahua Street, where the food is continental, the setting lavish, and the music disco. Dinner is served from 6:30 nightly and continues to 1 a.m. to accommodate the dancers.

Dim lights, booths, and a crowded dance floor are the setting for excellent cooking, with an emphasis on seafood specialties. Freshly caught fish get gourmet treatment—opakapaka meuniere, for example. Live Maine lobster, a rarity in Hawaii, is usually ready for the pot. Rack of lamb for one—another rarity —is featured here. Dinner entrees, which include salad, beverage, potato, and vegetables, begin at $13.50 with choices like chicken parmigiana, mahimahi, or scallops, and ascend to $24 for the lobster.

There is valet parking on the Nahua Street side. Dinner only. Reservations are a must: phone 923-7618.

The number of people that **The Bistro,** a cozy, dimly lit French restaurant at 1647 Kapiolani Blvd. (one block mauka of Ala Moana Shopping Center) must regretfully turn away each day is proof of its well-deserved popularity. It's as good (or better) than your favorite little place in Paris, and it's been "discovered" by the Honolulu advertising and broadcasting crowd as well as by knowledgeable visitors.

Both the lunch and dinner menus offer a wide variety of choices for lovers of French cuisine. Recommended at lunch, for example, are the chef's own pâté, followed by such entrees as coq au vin rouge, veal Milanaise, and hard-to-find salad Niçoise. And a special garnished cocktail plate of spiced shrimp and lobster is an unusual touch in a French restaurant.

Dinner is more elaborate, offering even more choices of hot and cold appetizers, soups, and salads (caviar, double consommé with port, and Caesar salad are all excellent). Main dishes, which range from about $14 to $20, are expertly prepared; we can recommend the tender roast squab stuffed with rice and fresh mushrooms, the frog legs Provençale, the sauteed prawns, and an incredible stuffed lobster tail. There are a number of steak entrees, as well. After a meal like this a plate of cheese and fruits—if anything—makes an ideal dessert.

Le Bistro is open seven days a week for dinner, but no lunch is served on Sunday. If hunger strikes late at night, this is the place for supper, served from 11 p.m. to 1:30 a.m., and featuring light dishes like onion soup, Caesar salad, filet steak sandwich, and some extravagent desserts: cherries jubilee and peach melba. Cappucino, too. Reservations are a must; phone: 955-3331.

The same management owns **L'Escargot** at 3058 Monsarrat Avenue, with a similar but slightly pricier menu, and, on the island of Maui, **Le Tournedos.**

Anyone who knows San Francisco's Fisherman's Wharf and the succulent Italian seafood that Alioto's has served there for over 50 years will be happy to find an **Alioto's** right in Honolulu. It's located at 1580 Makalao Street, corner Kaheka, just three blocks from the Liberty House end of the Ala Moana Shopping Center, and is fast becoming as famous as its parent. Alioto's is reached by riding a private glass elevator to the building's 12th-floor penthouse. Tropical plants adorn the interior, while outdoors spectacular vistas of city and sea vie for your attention.

There is a variety of Italian dishes and steak here, but best choices are the freshly caught local and mainland seafood specialties. You could have calamari sauté (squid sauteed with onion, lemon and garlic), shrimps scampi, or snapper Italian as entrees; crabmeat canneloni is among the appetizers. Price of entree, which ranges from about $13 to $16, includes soup or salad, freshly baked sourdough bread, and ice cream or cheesecake. More in the Italian mood are Sicilian pastry and cannoli for dessert; but all are fattening and fun.

Alioto's is a dinner-only place, 6 to 10 p.m. seven days. Valet and validated parking. Reservations: 955-5511.

If there were such a thing as a list of the Top Ten—or Top Five—restaurants favored by Honoluluans, then **Nick's Fishmarket,** tucked away behind a door in the Waikiki Gateway Hotel, 2070 Kalakaua Ave., would surely be near the top of that list. Owner Nick Nickolas has built up a tremendous following among the local people and celebrated visitors; pictures of personal friends like Audrey Meadows and husband Bob Six, Sammy Davis, Jr., Frank Sinatra, and Jonathan Winters line the walls. They appreciate the super service, the cheerful red-carpeted and black-leather ambience, and the scrupulously fresh and delicious seafood that Nick has flown in daily from Louisiana or Seattle or Maine to supplement the catch from local waters.

It's fun to begin with a few drinks at the animated bar and move on to your table for the main event. You can have a complete dinner for $18.75 that includes Fishmarket chowder or

Nick's special salad, vegetable, and beverage, with entrees such as stuffed baked trout, seafood au gratin, a combination seafood salad, roast chicken oregano (Greek style), even fresh catfish. Or you can go à la carte with great appetizers like feta cheese and Greek olives, sashimi, or smoked Nova Scotia salmon; the plate of assorted appetizers, $4.75 per person, is a particular treat. Main-course specialties, ranging from about $14 to $20, include a memorable bouillabaisse and New York steak Nick-the-Greek style. Lobster is flown in fresh from the cold waters of Maine, and at this writing the price was $30 per person for a two-pound live boiled lobster. After a meal at Nick's there's no room for dessert, so Nick doesn't offer any. Just great food, cooked and served by people who are very proud of this place. Dinner from 6 to 11:30, seven days a week; naturally, reservations are a must—phone 955-6333.

In a hotel with the unlikely name of Waikiki Park Heights is a famous steak house called **Hy's,** with the unlikely—for Honolulu—decor of the British Victorian era. Located at 2440 Kuhio, Canadian-based Hy's (you may recognize it from Toronto, Winnipeg, Calgary, or Vancouver) looks like somebody's elegant living room—bookshelves, family portraits, upholstered chairs, turn-of-the-century chandeliers, and mahogany-like walls. Here steak is king. Prime meat, charcoal-broiled and served on wooden planks with potatoes of your choice done to your specifications. New York strip steak and rib steak are $13 each, filet mignon is $14, and sirloin comes in three sizes, priced from $11 to $15—for all of 20 ounces. All entrees come with soup or salad and delicious hot, fresh garlic-cheese toast. Yes, you can also get baby back ribs or rack of lamb or several fish entrees (from $7.50 up), but I wouldn't miss Hy's masterful steaks.

Appetizers are wide ranging, including lox, linguini with a delicious clam sauce, and pâté maison, and for dessert there's a variety of gourmet cheesecakes as well as parfaits doused with liqueurs. There is, of course, a large wine list in the British tradition. Valet parking. Dinners only, seven days a week, 6 p.m. to midnight, closing a bit earlier on Sunday. For reservations, phone 922-5555.

At what Waikiki restaurant can you find Quilcene oysters flown in twice weekly from Washington or fresh Dungeness crab legs or San Francisco Bay shrimp? The answer is the famed **Canlis Charcoal Broiler Restaurant,** opposite Fort DeRussy at 2100 Kalakaua Ave. (phone: 923-2324). If you've ever dined at a Canlis in San Francisco or Seattle, you'll know that a meal here is expensive but worth every extravagantly tasty moment. Canlis has been a pacesetter for gracious dining in Honolulu for many years. It's an intimate, romantic place, and so handsome is the subdued modern decor that the restaurant has won several decorating awards. (I should tell you that men who do not wear jackets will be seated in a separate but equally attractive area.)

Now for the food, the delicious food. The appetizers mentioned above run from $3 to $5.75. Someday, someone will get the idea that they can have dinner at Canlis for all of $4.50 just by ordering the Canlis Special Salad. This tremendous salad, as delicious as it is filling, is made with romaine lettuce tossed with croutons, minced bacon, and fresh-grated Romano cheese, and blended with a dressing of lemon juice, imported olive oil, coddled eggs, freshly ground pepper, and herbs. But don't miss the rest of the menu. Canlis does great things with steak and seafood. Fried jumbo shrimp are of the whopping New Orleans variety; steak Pierre consists of thin slices of filet sauteed in a piquant sauce; Canlis shrimp is pan-fried just right; these and other entrees are priced from $9.50 to $18, à la carte. The desserts run to very good cheesecakes and ice creams, but try the unusual liqueur combinations for something special. Dinner only is served from 6 to 11:30; be sure to make reservations.

At 2168 Kalia Rd., opposite the Cinerama Reef and on the grounds of the Edgewater Hotel, is **Trattoria,** home of some of the finest Italian cuisine in the islands. This is a dinner-only establishment, serving from 5:30 to 11:30 p.m. seven days a week. Allow plenty of time to savor your dinner, because everything here is prepared to order by the skilled chefs. Full dinners begin at $10.50, and you may also order à la carte. You might start with one of my favorites, clams casino (fresh clams baked with chopped bacon and shallots) or the escargots. Pastas are well done here, and are modestly priced. Among the fish dishes, I recommend the scampi alla Sergio, giant prawns broiled and served with a zesty wine sauce; and from the meat choices, the bistecca pizzaiola—sirloin sauteed in olive oil—is unforgettable. The meat and fish entrees run from $7.50 to $14.25, à la carte. Phone: 923-8415. Piano entertainment is available at the adjoining La Dolce Vita from 10 p.m. to 2 a.m.

For one of the ultimate dining experiences in Honolulu, don't miss the **Maile Restaurant** at the Kahala Hilton Hotel. The Maile keeps on winning *Travel/Holiday* Awards and it's no wonder! From the moment you walk down the winding staircase to the restaurant, set against a lava wall covered with orchids, you'll know you're in a special, rarified atmosphere. Although the room is large, the feeling is an intimate one; you dine by candlelight, amid a background of sparkling fountains, beautiful flowers, and truly gracious island hospitality. But the true marvels come from Chef Martin Wyss's kitchen. He has taken classic dishes from around the world, given them his own island variations, and come up with a magnificent result. Dinner is $30, table d'hôte, not including tax and gratuity. You may have your appetizers either hot or cold, and it's not easy to decide between things like the Alaskan king crab legs in avocado with brandy sauce, or a chicken liver pâté on toast topped with creamed morel mushrooms. Salads are also quite special: I like the fresh spinach salad, prepared with egg whites and crisp bacon. Then on to the soups—essence of fresh opakapaka is a special treat. The entrees get even more elaborate: that old island standby, mahimahi, comes poached in a light white-wine sauce and wrapped in romaine leaves. Roast duckling is served on wild rice along with bananas, lichees, mandarin oranges, and a fabulous Grand Marnier sauce.

For a good sampling of the Kahala cuisine at a slightly lower price, you might try the **Hala Terrace** on a Sunday night for the $20 buffet. It's probably the most lavish buffet table in town, and here you'll get a chance to try such island delicacies as lomilomi, limu (seaweed), sashimi (raw fish), and octopus, as well as more familiar fare like prime ribs of beef, mahimahi, and beef Stroganoff. A Hawaiian trio plays for entertainment. Reservations are a must (phone: 734-2211).

Medium-Range Meals ($7 to $15)

We've got quite a selection here, divided into categories depending on type of cuisine.

AMERICAN—MOSTLY STEAK AND SEAFOOD: One of the famous old-timers of Honolulu is **The Willows**, 901 Hausten St. The Willows was converted from a private estate into a restaurant more than 36 years ago, and has since enjoyed an enormous following. It's such a beautiful spot, situated on a pond filled with Japanese carp and surrounded by gorgeous trees and flowers, that it's practically a must, especially if you're not going to visit the neighbor islands, where this kind of unspoiled atmosphere is much more prevalent. After being owned for many

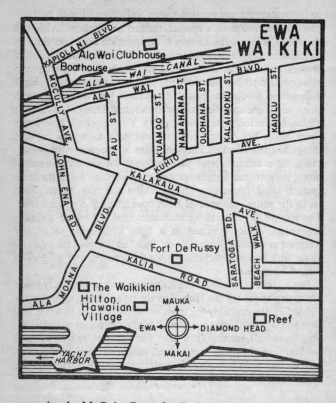

years by the McGuire-Perry family (whose good friend Arthur Godfrey made its name famous), the Willows was recently taken over by Randy Lee, formerly of the Halekulani Hotel; and the new menu is full of delightful island treats. Lunch is gracious and relaxed here, and the prices are moderate. In the evening, when à la carte entrees range from about $8.95 to $11, you can dine on a variety of seafood and meat entrees, including scallops royale sauteed in butter and sherry, their famous curry, twin lobster tails, and a lavish Hawaiian Poi Supper (the latter repeated on Saturday noon and Thursday noon for "Poi Thursday," a festive event with music and dancing). Whenever you dine, though, be sure to save room for dessert. Traditionalists should not miss the legendary mile-high coconut cream pie; but there are also a dreamy chocolate haupia cake and a guava glue sundae, which tastes better than it sounds. While you're enjoying the natural beauty and the good food (The Willows is one of *Travel/Holiday's* six recommended restaurants in Hawaii and the only one in a garden setting), strolling singers will serenade you with the old Hawaiian songs. At lunch, à la carte dishes are available from $4.50.

The Willows serves dinner daily from 5:30 to 9:30 p.m., lunch Monday through Saturday from 11:30 a.m. to 2:30 p.m., and on Sunday there's a splendid garden buffet brunch from 9:30 a.m. to 2:30 p.m.

Reservations are suggested, especially if you want to sit on the lanai. Phone: 946-4808.

Horatio's, in the Ward Warehouse shopping complex, is decorated in such a lavish and imaginative manner that it might easily be mistaken for a movie set. Its interior looks exactly like that of an old sailing ship—it is modeled after the *H.M.S. Victory,* commanded by Lord Horatio Nelson of Trafalgar fame, and the 19th-century nautical mood continues throughout. You can dine in the Ship's Quarter Deck or the Lieutenant's Wardroom, be served by attractive young people—the girls costumed as "wenches," the young men as British tars—and pay your bill Wharfside (the cashier's desk). There's even a lifeboat with seats in the bar. The food, too, is smashing, and visually appealing as well. The big hit at lunchtime are the salads (spinach or chicken and avocado), under $5, as well as quiches, omelets, and sandwiches, all served with a hearty clam chowder or salad, plus French fries or cole slaw. My favorite at dinner is the fantastic seafood sauté—prawns, crab legs, shrimp, fish, and mushrooms, sauteed in a buttery wine sauce. Chicken Florentine (breast of chicken with spinach, crab, and hollandaise sauce) is another winner, and steak and ribs are also good. Everything comes with salad or clam chowder, a basket of crusty bread, vegetable, and potato, and the tariff runs from about $7.50 to $11. California wines are available by glass or bottle. Do not, under any circumstances, miss the burnt cream for dessert; one serving of this super-rich, calorie-laden caramel custard, $1.50 at lunch or dinner, is enough for four or five weight-watchers to grow ecstatic about. Horatio's serves lunch from Monday to Saturday, from 11:15 a.m. to 2:30 p.m.; dinner from 5:30 to 10 p.m., Sunday to Thursday; from 5:30 to 11 Friday and Saturday. It's extremely popular, so be sure to call for a reservation: 521-5002.

Rudyard Kipling would have felt right at home at **The Colony,**

A Steak House, in the Hyatt Regency Waikiki, 2424 Kalakaua Ave. It's a bit of the British Colonial past in India come to life, with its rattan furniture, palm trees, revolving ceiling fans, and Indian accents in both food and decor. The plush India print carpet, the gazebo-like tables in the center of the room, and the brilliant use of live greenery all create a warm ambience. Select your own piece of meat—filet mignon, rib eye, New York cut, T-bone, or teriyaki steak, each individually priced, from $7.25 to $13.50. Then proceed to the glorious salad bar while your meat selection is being cooked to your order. House wine comes along with your steak. A few side dishes are available, like the luscious sourdough bread with melted cheese, jumbo mushroom caps broiled in herb butter, or crisp Maui onion rings. Pupus are great fun, and I heartily recommend a platter to serve two: baked crabmeat Madras, barbecued spareribs, and tempura fried shrimp suggest the exotic flavors. Desserts? I'll take the popular Colony ice cream cake with nuts, $3.95. The room is open nightly from 6 to 11 p.m., and the lovely adjoining cocktail lounge, in a harmonizing decor, serves from 6 to midnight. You'll catch a sophisticated performer, perhaps even ukelele virtuoso Ohta-San as I was lucky enough to do on my last visit. Reservations: 922-9292.

Finding a quiet, homelike dining room is no simple matter when you're traveling. Most restaurants look like just what they are. But things are different at a special place called **David J's,** 1050 Ala Moana, located upstairs at Ward Warehouse Shopping Center. The gracious owner herself will probably meet you as you enter and escort you to your table. She is the mother of David J., after whom the restaurant is named.

Your table is likely to be by a window overlooking Kewalo Basin and the sea. Its candlelit white tablecloth and sparkling crystal and servingware enhance the refined dining-room atmosphere. You could start, as I did, with soup of the day (it was Malaysian style), or with salad, which is included in the price of the entree, as are relish tray, vegetables, and very good home-made muffins. Prices range from $7.50 for mahimahi up to $14.50 for veal slices sauteed with escargots. The roast boneless duckling, served with bing cherries and brandy sauce, is typical of the French and continental flair of David J's. Dinner starts at 6 p.m. with closing hours variable, lunch at 11:30 p.m. It is open seven days a week.

Lunch is also a homey affair; prices range from $4.95 for chilled red salmon to $8.95 for strip loin of beef entrecôte. My braised lamb shank at $7.50 was exquisite. Reservations are preferred but not insisted upon. Phone: 521-9717.

Buffet Bonanza

$7.50 doesn't go very far these days when it comes to a meal, so it's a pleasant shock to find that the **Ilikai Canoe House's** grand buffet lunch, a breathtaking spread that tops just about anything in the islands (with the possible exception of the Kapalua Bay Hotel on Maui), comes in at that low figure.

You can pick a table inside or out on the lanai overlooking the Ala Wai boat harbor. Then proceed directly to the salad tables, take a plate, and load up. There are cold cuts, cold steamed chicken, sausage salad, shrimp salad, artichoke hearts, pickled herring, raw fish, cole slaw, marinated onions, and a dozen other choices, including one you must not miss: cold papaya soup. Leave your used plate on the table when you've finished and go back—for more salad, if you like; but remember, you still have hot entrees and dessert in your future. With a clean plate you can choose from curried chicken thighs, fried rice, roast duck, sliced pork, meat loaf, and roast beef, to mention a few. You can have them all, if you wish. Now you are ready for dessert: rum cake, chocolate mousse, strawberry mousse, fresh fruit, chocolate layer cake, and a dozen more. Again, have some of each and come back for your favorite. Your waitress will serve your beverage and remove the soiled plates as fast as you load up afresh. Many of your neighbors will be local people who like the island foods and local dishes offered here.

The Canoe House buffet is on every day from 11:30 a.m. to 1:30 p.m., but reservations are advised on Sunday, when it can get crowded. Phone: 949-3811. The Ilikai is at 1777 Ala Moana Boulevard.

Call a meal at **Bobby McGee's Conglomeration,** in the Colony Surf Hotel at 2885 Kalakaua Ave., an experience, a happening. The five dining rooms are illuminated just enough so you can barely make out the incredible conglomeration of antiques and oddities that fill up every inch of unused space. The costumed waiters (I was recently served by a magician named Michael the Magnificent and by Amelia Earheart, who finally returned home) keep up an amusing line of banter that can turn the meal into a comedy routine if you'll play along. But the food is also good, and so decently priced that the place is always packed with locals and visitors alike; you sometimes have to wait a day or so just to get a reservation.

Bobby McGee's specialties are an excellent prime rib of beef au jus for just $10.95 and a good choice of fish, seafood, and steaks, ranging from $7.95 for a mahimahi served with macadamia nuts and a skewer of fresh fruit and $8.95 for a "complete brochette" (teriyaki steak, shrimp, and chicken on rice) up to about $12.50 for a spicy pepper steak. Steak, seafood, and fowl combinations like steak and crêpe (top sirloin and a crab-filled crêpe) run from $9.95 to $14.75. Deep-fried zucchini is a tasty appetizer. Along with every entree come Bobby McGee's extras: all the salad you want served from a gigantic bathtub (salad bar alone is $5) and all the soup you can handle from a wooden stove, plus a great big baked potato or fries. After all that, and what with keeping up the repartee with the waiters, you probably won't have energy for dessert; if you do, English trifle is recommended. After dinner, they'll offer to seat you in the disco part of the operation.

The goofy goings-on go on from 6 to 11 p.m. Sunday through Thursday, from 5:30 to 11 p.m. Saturday and Sunday. Valet parking. Be sure to reserve: 922-1282.

Not far from the Ala Moana area, Eaton Square, 444 Hobron Lane, is a charming little community shopping center with walks and benches and trash baskets that say "Thank You" in humorous ways when you use them. At the top of Eaton Square is **Cork and Fork,** a lanai restaurant, open to the breezes and quite casual and comfy, with a view over the rooftops and palms of Waikiki; an escape from the madding throng.

Dinner only is served at Cork and Fork, 6 to 10 p.m. daily. You can make a meal at the generous salad bar, which has enough variety to please everyone, plus wonderful hot breads, for just $5.50. Most of the chicken, steak, chops, and island fish dinners range from $8.95 to $11.95. Salad bar is included. I heartily recommend their garlic kebobs, the house specialty, and also that you treat yourself to an order of sauteed mushrooms.

Tuesday through Saturday the well-known Arthur Lyman plays his tropical rhythms, complete with bird-calls and other equatorial sound effects. Phone: 946-8488.

A three-story glass enclosed aquarium alive with fish dominates the new **Oceanarium Restaurant** in the Pacific Beach Hotel at 2490 Kalakaua Ave., corner of Liliuokalani. The Oceanarium is on the ground floor, and there are more restaurants and a disco higher up; but this one affords the best view, and an almost-all-day menu (from 6:30 a.m. til 10:30 p.m.). It's fun to come at fish-feeding times: 9 a.m., 12:15, and 6:30 p.m.

Dinner here is an especially good bargain, since even á la carte items come with soup or salad, rice or potato, vegetable, rolls and butter. The complete dinner, priced slightly higher, merely adds ice cream and beverage. Prices for entrees range from the lemon mahimahi filet at $6.50 to the sirloin steak at $10.95. I sampled a tasty Gulf shrimp curry: large shrimps fried with bananas and onions, simmered in a curry sauce, and served with all the condiments; and my roast beef was the finest prime rib, served with yummy Yorkshire pudding and separate juice for dipping.

Lunch features hot plates on the order of fish 'n' fries and seafood combo from about $4.25 to $6.25, very good Reuben sandwiches, and lots of salads. Breakfast omeletes are good, and so is a unique Oceanarium specialty: black Alaskan cod served with homemade biscuits.

On Sundays, it's buffet for all three meals. The phone is 922-1233.

The master chef at **The Pottery Steak House,** 3574 Waialae Ave., is also a Master of Fine Arts whose specialty is ceramics. Although Sam Uyehara now confines his talents largely to the culinary arts, there are some friendly and energetic young potters employed at this pretty little restaurant in the Kaimuki part of town, and you are welcome to watch them at work in the anteroom. All the distinctive pottery they make is for sale, and that includes everything from the plates on your table to the works on display. My personal favorite item is a loaf of bread that is really a big covered dish for serving—you guessed it—bread! It's well priced at $15.90.

The food here is also good, with most of the selections from the steak kiln "fired to the desired cone." That means you can have your meat as rare or medium or well done as you choose, and the chef means what he says. Average price of entrees is about $13. The steak and prawns, served on a bed of fried rice, is a particular treat. Another of my favorites is the boned Cornish game hen, cooked in its own clay vessel and stuffed with wild rice. Maybe it's the cooking in clay that makes it so juicy and tender. And the pot is yours to take home. All entrees are served with salad, baked potato or rice, vegetable, and garlic bread presented in that cute ceramic loaf. Crab or shrimp cocktails served in a handthrown dish make excellent starters; ice cream, apple pie and cheese, or cheesecake make the perfect finish.

Alas, the Pottery is open for dinner only, but it is open seven days a week (reservations, 737-0633). And if you're planning to visit the Big Island, you can stop in at The Pottery in Kailua-Kona.

Should you find yourself in the Kahala neighborhood near the Kahala Hilton hotel some afternoon or evening (and it's a most agreeable place to find yourself at), you can have a very good meal in a plush, candlelit atmosphere at **The Spindrifter** at Kahala Mall. Folks who live in this lovely neighborhood swear by it for good steak and seafood dishes at night, juicy hamburgers and a Mexican touch at noontime. Both lunch and dinner come with nice extras: crisp green salad or iced vichyssoise or soup from the kettle and really tasty hot breads that soak up the butter. Most entrees are in the $8.95 to $12.95 range; some, like mahimahi or seafood salad, are a bit lower; others, like Australian lobster tail and rack of lamb, a few dollars higher. A few of my favorites here are the steak and enchilada plate at dinner, the tasty quesadillas (that's a flour tortilla stuffed with cheese, chili, tomato, and beef) and tostadas at lunch. Omelets are good, too, and so are those burgers. The pecan and cheese pies are winners for dessert.

Deep leather seats, red tablecloths, nautical paintings set the mood, and waitress service is deft and professional.

Spindrifter serves lunch from 11 to 3 (Sunday brunch at $6.25), dinner from 5 to 11 p.m. weeknights, 5 to midnight weekends. There's also a late menu (offered after 10 p.m. most nights) featuring a roast beef sandwich on sourdough bread and a glass of wine for under $5; plus onion soup or vichyssoise or escargots atop mushroom caps and hot French bread for under $4. And there's live entertainment in the lounge at night. Phone: 737-7944.

Check out the Spindrifters, too, at Coconut Plantation in Kauai, and right out on the waterfront in Kailua-Kona.

One of the most atmospheric (and long-established) seafood restaurants in Honolulu is **Fisherman's Wharf**, 1009 Ala Moana (at Fisherman's Wharf), where you can sit by a huge picture window and watch the sampan fishing boats moored just outside. The indoor decor is jauntily nautical, too, even down to the sailor-suit uniforms of its waitresses. You can eat well here in the Seafood Grotto, where there are some 20 to 30 items between $6.95 and $9.95, with my favorite, the lobster tail, at $14.95, and steak and lobster at $16.50. The complete dinner includes a choice of fruit or chowder (but we always opt for the Fisherman's Wharf soup with sherry at 30¢ more), vegetables, and coffee. Luncheon specials run from $4.25 to $6.25, and sandwiches like mahimahi burger on toasted bun run about $3.95. There are special *keiki* menus, drinks available from the bar, and a generally carefree mood. Upstairs is the Captain's Bridge, where fish is broiled to order and prices run $5.95 to $9.95. You won't go wrong at either dining room: Fisherman's Wharf rates high, with both visitors and *kamaainas.* Reservations: 538-3808.

One of the newer restaurants in town, the **Yacht Harbor** in the Yacht Harbor Towers, 259 Atkinson at Ala Moana, has more elegance than one would expect for the price. Spacious rooms handsomely appointed in turn-of-the century decor, white table-cloths, roses, candles in glass holders, seating far enough apart from other tables for privacy, careful service by dignified waiters, all add up to a class feeling, but prices are middle-of-the-road. Do try to reserve one of the tables overlooking the Yacht Harbor for a view of the boats bobbing at anchor. Dinner, which includes mixed greens or soup of the day, rice pilaf or potato, vegetables, roll and butter, coffee or tea, offers several entrees from $7.50 to $10, including broiled island chicken, veal canneloni, and beef Stroganoff; a bit higher are such specialties as roast duckling à l'orange, bouillabaisse, and individual rack of lamb. Steak tartare and smoked salmon are two not-to-usual appetizers. Catch of the day is $10.50 at dinner ($6.50 at lunch), and my ono, sauteed in a white wine sauce, was indeed *ono ono* (the best, as they say in the islands). Veal canneloni was fair. From my experience with a very ordinary chocolate cake, and a dish of four strawberries with sour cream and brown sugar absurdly priced at $2.25, I'd advise by-passing dessert. But coffee is hearty.

Lunch is pleasant here, too: crêpes, Stroganoff, eggs Benedict, crabmeat au gratin, crab and mushroom omelet, broiled sliced garlic steak, and shrimp soup are among the possibilities, priced from $3.50 to $6.50.

Lunch at the Yacht Harbor is served from 11:30 a.m. to 2 p.m., dinner from 6 to 10 p.m., until 11 p.m. Friday and Saturday. The piano bar is in tune after 8 or 9 most evenings. Validated parking in the apartment building downstairs. A neat place to dine in style. Reservations: phone 946-2177.

Can't choose between steak and lobster? You don't have to. **Buzz's Steak 'n Lobster House,** 225 Saratoga Rd. (phone: 923-6762) in the Reef Lanais Hotel, makes a specialty of both, and it does a terrific job. Enjoy your candlelight dinner surrounded by many antiques, nautical compasses, old maps of the islands, lamps, and plaques. A full glass outside wall lets you watch the flaming torches and street life as you enjoy drinks and dinner.

Beyond Town: P.C.T.

Twenty-six live monkeys cavort behind the bar, there's a roof garden of bonsai trees, four exotic saltwater fishtanks, and the local citizens have been swearing by it for over 30 years. This is the **Pearl City Tavern,** affectionately known as P.C.T., off the beaten tourist path, but well worth the half-hour-or-so drive to reach it. Take the Aiea exit off the H-1 Freeway and stay on Moanaloa Road until you see the restaurant on the left at Lehua Avenue, within a few blocks.

P.C.T. is known both for the excellence of its seafood (it imports lobsters from Maine, soft-shell crabs from Maryland, oysters and cherrystones from Boston, salmon from Washington state) and for its Japanese cuisine. As for the seafood, I can vouch for the seashore platter (mahimahi, shrimp, and crab leg) and the shrimp tempura, both served at lunch accompanied by Boston clam chowder, potato, and French bread. The same dishes from the dazzling selection on the dinner menu, priced from $8.50 to about $15, are served with either Boston clam chowder or sashimi, hot crispy wonton, baked potato or rice, tossed green salad, and beverage. The Maine lobsters are mammoth here, currently running $22.50 for a 1½-pounder. You can also get unseafoody meals like boned squab stuffed and baked with wild rice, thick, juicy prime ribs of beef, and excellent New York steaks. The Japanese dinners are daintily served on an *ozen* (tray) by kimono-clad waitresses; two main dishes are $8.25 at lunch, and three main dishes are $15 at dinner, accompanied by soup, pickled vegetables, rice, and Japanese green tea.

Pearl City Tavern is a great place to take the youngsters, and they have special children's menus at both lunch and dinner. It is open continuously from 10 a.m. to 10 p.m. every day. Reservations are advised: phone 455-1045. All major credit cards accepted.

The prices of the entrees include a choice of baked potato, French fries or rice, a grand tour of the salad bar, and generous helpings of French or rye bread. Dinners are hearty meals with prices ranging from $4.95 for fish 'n fries to $16.95 for a steak-and-lobster dinner. Fresh fish from Hawaiian waters (when available) is a very popular entree. Buzz's specialties include huli huli chicken, Alaskan king crab, sauteed shrimp, New York cut steak, and many other varieties of seafood. The bar opens at noon, so you can relax on your way back from beach or shopping with a specially priced Happy Hour drink. Dinner served from

5 to 11 p.m.

The **Waikiki Broiler** at 200 Lewers St. (phone: 923-8836), in the Waikiki Tower of the Reef Hotel, provides both indoor and outdoor tables for those who don't want to lose one moment of sunshine. Start soaking it up at breakfast time (from 7 a.m.), along with a pancake sandwich with bacon and egg, or French toast, from $2.20 to $4.25. Lunches run from $2.05 to $4.65; try the sliced turkey sandwich on sourdough with cranberry sauce. Come dinner, I vote for the scampi or the rich and juicy Captain's cut of prime ribs. Along with your entree, priced from $4.95 to $13.95, comes a tour of the salad bar, homemade soup from the kettle, bread, and steamed rice. Note that lunch is on from 11 to 2, dinner from 5:30 until 10 p.m., seven days a week. From 9:30 in the evening until about 1:30 in the morning there is usually a group playing Hawaiian and disco music—all of which adds to the fun in this neat nautical spot, a big hit with the visiting crowd.

If you love dining with a view of the ocean—and if you love buffet dining, too—make a note of the **Ocean Terrace,** poolside at the Sheraton Waikiki Hotel. The buffet table really shines at night: juicy prime ribs, mahimahi, fried chicken, plus a hot surprise or two. And there's always plenty of salads, vegetables, desserts, and beverage. Considering that it's priced at $8.95, it's not bad for Waikiki. There's a buffet lunch, too—roast beef, stews, chop suey, cold cuts, salads, desserts (I counted some 20 choices recently)—and that's $6.75. The breakfast buffet is $6.25, and it's recommended for the big morning eaters; all you want of fruits, cereals, eggs, breakfast meats, pastry, pancakes. At lunch, there are also salads and delicious special items priced from $4.25. Like all of the Sheraton Waikiki, this is a strikingly alive spot, with brilliant green and apricot colors from floor to ceiling, even on the uniforms of the helpful staff. Dinner is from 5:30 to 9:30 p.m.; lunch, from 11:30 to 3; breakfast, from 6 to 11.

For a good steak at a good price, it's nice to know about the **Reef Broiler,** just off the lobby of the Reef Hotel. You'll recognize it by its smart copper-and-brick facade where, hanging from a wrought-iron chain, is the menu. I always feel right at home in this room, with its wood paneling, candlelight, black-leather upholstered booths, and pinpoint lighting. It's a dinner-only place, and steak is the big thing here. The top sirloin is priced at $8.95, and beef kebab on skewers is $8.25. Every day there are low-priced specials, like chicken Hawaiian—chunks of boned chicken sauteed with celery, onions, bell peppers, mushrooms, and a whisper of sherry—at $7.25. A glass of wine goes well with it. Or you can have a half-liter of chablis, rosé, or burgundy for $2.50. Dinner is served every day from 5 on, and there's live entertainment nightly from 8 p.m. to 1 a.m., with no cover, no minimum.

The Flamingo Chuckwagon, 1015 Kapiolani Blvd., is one of the best places in town for lovers of a truly hearty buffet. The enormous chuckwagon is spread with prime ribs, fried chicken, salads, gelatin desserts, vegetables, rice, hot breads, and you can fill your plate as many times as you like. Beverage and dessert are included. The price of all this largesse is $8.50. It's a cheerful setting with paintings on the walls, comfortable booths and tables. Drinks are dispensed from the Silver Dollar Bar. Dinner is served every day from 5 to 10; at lunchtime there's no chuckwagon, but you can choose from at least six selections starting at $4, among them roast pork with applesauce, breaded veal cutlets, beef stew with fresh vegetable, all served with tossed green salad, potato or rice, and roll. The Flamingo people also own three other restaurants (**Cafe Flamingo,** 574 Ala Moana, **Flamingo Kapiolani,** 871 Kapiolani Boulevard and **Flamingo Royal Lanai,** 1529 Kapiolani Boulevard), and their reputation is tops for really good food at well-below-average prices.

CHINESE AND POLYNESIAN: A new incarnation of Honolulu's famed Chinese restaurant, **Lau Yee Chai,** has opened its ornate doors in the Waikiki Shopping Plaza, 2250 Kalakaua Ave. Originally housed in its own Chinese-style building at the entrance to Waikiki, it was embellished with fine teak furniture, rare screens, murals, moon gates, and two antique lifesize lacquer statues of the goddess Kuan Yin. After a decade in storage, they now grace what must surely be one of the most beautiful Chinese dining establishments anywhere.

Count on lunches (11 to 2) and dinners (5 to 11 p.m.) seven days a week, and count on dependably good Chinese dishes, most between $3.50 and $6. Lunch is a communal affair, with entrees served family style. Special favorites are lemon chicken, ginger-onion oysters, and stuffed duck. A variety of dim sum is also available, well priced at $1.10 to $1.20 per order.

At dinnertime, the menu expands to include more of the exotic favorites, like abalone with vegetables, shark-fin soup, crisp-skin chicken, almond duck, and a variety of seafood dishes (these run up to $19 and more for such items as lobster braised in the shell). Drinks are reasonable and your feeling of hiding away is complete in the Gung Ho Lounge, where you climb upstairs, then down, into anonymity. For reservations: 923-1112.

Just about the granddaddy of Polynesian restaurants in Honolulu, **Trader Vic's** in the International Market Place has a mood that is totally South Seas, from the authentic figurehead at the door to the Hawaiian artifacts and tikis on the wall, the romantic lighting, and the treehouse for sipping cocktails. The food, as you would expect from a Trader Vic's, blends harmoniously with the exotic tropical setting, and you can choose from Pake or Chinese dishes, Indian curries, a Hawaiian dinner, or meats from the Chinese oven, cooked by the old-world method of kiawe wood smoke and heat. A complete dinner costs from $8.25 to $9.50 (soup, rice, entrees like teriyaki steak or barbecued spareribs, sherbet, cookies, and tea), and good it is, but if you order à la carte, which is the most fun, the price can begin to add up. The exotic rum drinks are temptations, and so is the $5.95 pupu platter—practically a meal in itself. Soups are delicately flavored and unusual; perhaps egg flower or Tahitian French onion soup. Among the entrees, which go from $4.50 to $15, the lobster curry is excellent, and then there's the shrimp with almonds or the lobster black beans or the Javanese sate (meat-on-a-sword), to make choices difficult. And who could pass up desserts like banana fritters with whipped cream and hot buttered rum to finish it all off?

Lunch here is almost as atmospheric, and several dollars cheaper, from $2.50 to $6.95. But the real magic is at nightfall. Plan on this one when you're ready for a big evening. For reservations, phone: 923-1581.

Perhaps the biggest hit in the Cultural Plaza downtown is **Fat Siu Lau,** at 100 North Beretania St., a huge place with a huge following among the local people. The decor is traditional Chinese restaurant, but it's the food that counts most—dishes like lobster with black bean sauce, pressed almond duck, or diced chicken with bird nest soup. You can spend a little or a lot here, but the best thing to do is to follow the advice of a local friend who advises that you "make a deal" with the waitress. Tell her how much per person you are willing to spend and mention a few things you like—shrimp, chicken, beef, etc.—and she'll emerge from the kitchen with a huge variety of flavorful dishes. She may try to get you to come up 50¢ or so per person, but once you agree on a rate, she will keep her word. Don't miss trying at least a few of the tasty dim sum—stuffed dumplings—everything from crispy chicken rolls and turnip cakes to egg tarts and baked black sugar cake. They begin at $1. Phone: 538-7081.

Seafood is delicious. Chinese food is delicious. Add the two together and you have a unique specialty restaurant: **Won Kee Sea Food,** another standout among the restaurants in the Cultural Plaza. This is a gourmet seafood place. There are house dinners from $15.95 for five courses to $43.50 for eight courses, but I suggest you wander freely over the menu as I did. I ordered five courses for four people, and the cost of this banquet totaled $40 before the tip.

The menu abounds in dishes like prawn, lobster, oysters, abalone, shrimp, crab, and a number of fish stews, the price ranging from about $4.95 for the stews up to $15 for the lobsters. I especially enjoyed the steamed clams in black bean sauce, the shrimp with vegetables, the steamed fish, and the Maine lobster. Soup of the day (mine was turnip), rice, and tea are included in the entree prices. Won Kee is open daily for lunch and dinner. Don't expect an ornate place; here you have green tablecloths with Mandarin red plastic covers, simple wood-paneling, and Chinese-style wrought-iron fixtures. It's the food that's ornate. Lunch 11 a.m. to 2:30 p.m., dinner 5 to 9:30 p.m. Phone: 524-6877.

FRENCH: There's a bit of the Riviera in Waikiki. **Chez Michel,** long one of Waikiki's best French restaurants, has moved to a gardenlike setting in Eaton Square, and 444 Hobron Lane in the Ala Moana area. The new restaurant is roofed and walled in by lattices hung with tropical plants, furnished with highbacked and comfortably cushioned wicker chairs, and graced with splashing fountains that create a cool, romantic atmosphere. Michel himself may greet you, if he's not on his annual wine-buying trip to Paris. This is a popular lunch rendezvous (Monday to Friday, 11:30 a.m. to 2:15 p.m.), so join the members of the business community dining over the likes of crêpes of crab with Mornay sauce, fresh mountain trout, tournedos bearnaise, or a superb chicken sauteed with mushrooms and artichoke. Everything is à la carte, from $6 to $8, but the dishes are well endowed with Michel's gourmet potato and vegetable creations.

At dinner, the French onion soup is a must. Michel's sauces and gravies are exquisite, so that even chicken livers become a dining experience—not to mention the most exotic selections like carré d'agneau jardinière, fresh opakapaka sauté Grenobloise, or the memorable canard à l'orange flambé. Entrees range from $11 to $18, including fresh vegetables and potatoes. Desserts are quite special: you can choose from chilled orange soufflé, crêpes suzette, or Grand Marnier soufflé. Espresso and cappuccino are offered.

Dinner is served daily from 6 to 11 p.m., and the Sunday brunch (11 a.m. to 2 p.m.) features fresh fruits, omelet or strawberry crêpes, rolls, and beverage for $7.50. Reservations are always advised. Phone: 955-7866.

The promise of elegance—in the canopied entrance, the subdued sign reading **Le Bon**, and the polite valet for your car—is fulfilled in this intimate French restaurant at 1376 Kapiolani Blvd., opposite the Sears end of the Ala Moana Shopping Center. Because of the alcoved layout, you feel you are in a private paneled dining room with only a few other tables in view. Recessed lighting and chandeliers with pinpoint lights keep the atmosphere subdued.

The dinners on the right side of the menu are the best buy, as you get a tureen of soup (it was cream of broccoli the evening I was there, but it could be mushroom or cream of vegetable), a delicious salad with an oil-and-vinegar dressing that has to be the best in town, and beverage along with the entrees; this means a complete meal for $8.50 to $17.50. Recommended dishes include filet of sole Bretanne (covered with bay scallops, mushrooms, and shallots in a cream sauce); coq au Chamberlin; beef bourguignon, and a very elegant rack of lamb. Hot cheese toast is served as quickly as you can consume it. Portions are huge, from soup through entree, so you will be forgiven if you must skip a strawberry dessert or the lovely mousse au chocolat. The service is suprisingly fast.

Entertainment at the piano bar is in view of all, punctuated by singing performances by the waiters and waitresses. Dinner only, from 6 to 11 p.m., Tuesday through Saturday, closing an hour earlier Sunday and Monday. Phone: 941-5051.

If you're sightseeing or shopping in downtown Honolulu and the craving for fine French food strikes, repair immediately to the only French restaurant in the area: the **Palm Garden Restaurant** in the old Blaisdell Hotel, at the mauka end of the Fort Street Mall. It's a casual place, open to the breezes (with the assist of old-fashioned ceiling fans), its walls covered with murals of Diamond Head and other island views. A charming young couple, Jean and Denise Ducroix, are in charge here: Jean was

The Continental Touch

The sophistication of a fine meal in one of the great European cities is what awaits you at **Checkers,** at 667 Ala Moana Boulevard in downtown Honolulu. The restaurant, a "celebration" of Swiss proprietor Alfred and German chef Paul, serves the evening meal only, in a serene ambience: blue-velvet-like armchairs and dropped-parasol chandeliers, locally made ceramic mugs and matching hurricane lamps, cordial service, fine wines from a well-stocked cellar. As soon as you sit down, several bowls of salad ingredients and tangy dressings are placed on the table family style for you to mix your own. Then comes a big basket of luscious country-style breads with plenty of butter and a steaming kettle of soup, all preludes to the superbly prepared main dishes.

Dinner entrees, with soup, salad and vegetable begin around $10 for breast of chicken Riesling and go up to $16.50 for roast of baby lamb Provençale. The Rheinischer sauerbraten (beef marinated in red wine and served with red cabbage and "spatzle") is tasty, as are a variety of steak creations, from tournedos to entrecôte. Freshly caught fish of the day is done remarkably well. Desserts are too good to miss, so ignore the calories and find some room for, perhaps, the soufflé glace cappuccino (a frozen cappuccino parfait) or German cheesecake (chef Paul's own family recipe).

Weekday lunches (11 a.m. to 2 p.m.) offer delicious sandwiches on dark bread, quiches, escargots, and lunch specials like wiener schnitzel; these include vegetables, soup or salad, and rice or potatoes, and are priced from $4 to $7.

Now for the checkers. Yes, they're right there, up at the piano bar; you can have a game while your table is being prepared if you haven't thought to call for reservations. The phone is 523-1602. Dinner is served Tuesday through Sunday, 6 to 10 p.m. Closed Mondays. Both validated and valet parking are available.

formerly at Maxim's of Paris, and served as chef at one of the city's poshest dining spots in Honolulu before opening his own restaurant. Some of his luncheon specialties, which run from $3.25 to $7.95, include coq au vin, seafood coquille, fish soup Marseillaise, and salade Niçoise. Homemade soups and pastries are served both at lunch and dinner, when a good plan is to order the "Menu Gastronomique" at $12.50. You have a choice of onion or fish soup, pâté or salad, and an entree of rainbow trout, escalope de veau Viennoise, coq au vin, or sirloin steak à la

Bordelaise. With this come potato Dauphine and vegetable, and a choice of mousse au chocolat or crême caramel for dessert. Regular dinner entrees, priced from $6.50 to $14.50, are served with potatoes, vegetables, and house salad. If you call Jean 24 hours in advance, he'll whip up any French specialty you can dream of.

Reservations: phone 523-8511.

ITALIAN: Rudy's, a bright little bistro in the Outrigger Hotel, 2280 Kuhio Ave. (corner of Nohonani), is warm and pretty, with its plushy red carpet and deep-red tablecloths. You'll want to luxuriate in one of the comfy tufted booths, bask in the soft light from the red tulip-shaped art nouveau hanging lamps, and watch the swimmers in the pool through the big picture window. And if you tire of that, you can watch the chef do his thing (part of the spotless kitchen is in full view of the dining room).

The complete family-style Italian dinners are a bargain, priced from $5.75 to $9.75, and served with a hearty homemade minestrone soup, tossed green salad, spaghetti or ravioli, vegetable, and hot French bread. Owner-manager Rudy Biale recommends Rudolpho Suprême, his favorite dish, invented by his grandmother back in Genoa. It's shrimp in batter sauteed in wine and butter, served with spaghetti and butter sauce—very rich and filling. I also liked the Italian-style scampi and the tender filets of veal picante with lemon slices. Spaghetti and ravioli dinners are even more reasonable, starting at $2.95 for spaghetti with tomato sauce. There's also an excellent dish of green spinach noodles with pesto, that unusual sauce made with basil, at $4.75. Rudy's serves dinner only, from 5:30 to 10 daily. For reservations, phone 923-5949. A good place to take the kids.

A speakeasy to outclass any speakeasy that ever was, **Spats,** in the Hyatt Regency Waikiki at 2424 Kalakaua, is a marvelous bit of the Roaring '20s reborn. Part restaurant, part disco, it's got to be the kickiest place in town, with its knockout gaslight and Tiffany-lamp lighting, flowered carpeting, and a look right out of *The Godfather*. Honolulu's Italian consul Guido Salmaggi, of the New York operatic family, is "The Boss" who presides over this place all done up in spats and very foxy '20s attire, and the Boss's mama does the cooking, turning out steaming platters of fine Italian food. You can program your own gourmet Italian trip from such à la carte choices as fettucini Alfredo and scallopine con funghi, both prepared at table; or cannelloni or chicken

Tettrazini; prices run from about $7 for pastas to $15 for the meat dishes. Salad bar connoisseurs should not miss Spats' wonderful salad and antipasti bar, highlighted by imported Italian delicacies. If you're feeling particularly flush, you may rent "The Boss's Office," a private dining room for a party of eight, which has one-way mirrored walls—so that you can see out, but the people outside can't see in. A mere $399.99 includes use of the room, dinner for eight, bodyguard service (!), and "The Boss's Limousine" to pick you up at your home or hotel and escort you back again after dinner. Safely esconced in the private room, you can watch the dance floor action, or venture out yourself, sans bodyguard; the disco comes to life at 9 p.m. and swings until 4 a.m. Dinner is from 6 to 10 p.m. Reservations: 922-9292.

JAPANESE: For an authentic Japanese dining experience, try **Furusato Japanese Steak House,** in the Waikiki Grand Hotel, 134 Kapahulu Ave., just a few steps from Kalakaua Avenue (phone: 923-8878). Take your shoes off on entering. Meditate for a moment on the serenity of the miniature Japanese gardens. Pay your respects to the Japanese craftsmen who constructed the exquisite dining room with materials imported from Japan, in the old-world manner—without using a single nail. From the moment you enter the door and face the ohdaiko drum, traditionally sounded to signal the arrival of special visitors, you'll know you're in for a treat. You could sit at a regular, American-style table, but I think it's more fun to take one of the lower tables with the traditional Japanese stove in the center, over which you will cook part of your meal. (If you're a group of four, be sure to make reservations to sit in one of the screened-off tatami rooms and eat the way they do in the old country.) You can have a complete dinner from $8.75 to $14.50, or order à la carte, with appetizers like the tasty tempura (my favorite) or sashimi. Sukiyaki is nicely prepared. Dinner is served from 6 p.m. to 1 a.m. Lunch, served 11:30 a.m. to 2 p.m., priced from $4.75 to $10, features many good tempura dishes.

There is another Furusato in the lower level of the fabulous Hyatt Regency Hotel, specializing in teppanyaki preparation of steaks and seafoods. Live Maine lobster and, of course, sukiyaki are also on the menu. Complete dinners start at $8.75. Or just have some sushi at the Sushi Bar upstairs. Phone: 922-4991.

When you dine at **Benihana of Tokyo,** a charming Japanese inn "transplanted" to the Rainbow Bazaar at the Hilton Hawaiian Village, you'll know why a Benihana chef is referred to as "the fastest knife in the West." If you order one of the entrees cooked right at your table (part of which is a hibachi), the knife-wielding artistry of the polite gentleman who appears bearing meat and vegetables and proceeds to dissect and cook them will astound and delight you. You could order other entrees, of course, but to me it is madness to come here and not have one of the hibachi creations: perhaps hibachi chicken and vegetables, $7.95; sukiyaki steak with vegetables, $10.25; hibachi steak, $10.95; or filet mignon with vegetables, $11.95. Prices for the same dishes are about $3 less at lunch, and there is a special luncheon of hibachi steak with vegetables and a Benihana salad bowl priced at $6.50. All prices include rice and tea.

The decor is charming, from the rustic wooden bridge and waterwheel outside to the calligraphic drawings. Makata woodblock prints and beautiful ceramics adorn the purportedly 400-year-old farmhouse (transported from Japan) within. Benihana of Tokyo serves lunch Mondays to Saturdays from 11:30 to 2:30; dinner, from 5:30 to 10:30 p.m. every day; phone: 955-5955.

One of the loveliest Japanese restaurants in town is the sophisticated **Tanaka of Tokyo,** on the top level of the Waikiki Shopping Plaza, at the corner of Seaside and Kalakaua Avenues. Although dinners are on the expensive side, from $8 to $18, this is one Japanese restaurant that serves Western-size portions, and you walk out well satisfied. You'll be seated at a table for eight, centered around a table-range combo, watching the chef do amusing antics with paring knives and spatulas as he prepares your meal. Three main dinners to choose from are chicken teriyaki, salmon (fresh Pacific) teppanyaki, and Tanaka sirloin. But there is also lobster, mahimahi, and lobster and sirloin. All dinners include delicious soup, grilled shrimp appetizer, cold and crisp salad, teppanyaki vegetable, fruit and sherbet desserts, and green tea. You could easily believe you're in Tokyo, with the Japanese music in the background, the waitresses in kimonos (actually, they are all local girls of Japanese ancestry who speak perfect English and radiate island warmth rather than Japanese formality), the low lights, and the understated Japanese decor.

Dinner is served daily from 5:30 to 10:30 p.m., until 10 on Sunday; lunch, Monday through Friday, 11:30 to 2:30 p.m. The lunch menu, priced from $3.50 to $6.50, includes the same main entrees mentioned above, but without all the extra courses and trimmings. And a late-night menu (10:30 p.m. to 1 a.m.) is now served in the new Kokoro Lounge. Phone: 922-4702.

Informal and Inexpensive ($7 and Under)

In Hawaii, a coffeeshop can be a pretty glamorous affair. Take, for example, **Trellises** in the beautiful new Prince Kuhio Hotel, up Diamond Head way at 2500 Kuhio Ave. This lovely "casual dining" spot (they don't even like to use the term coffeeshop here, although that's what it is) is artfully decorated with greenery, has doors that open for outside serving, and overlooks a waterfall. All three meals are served here, at surprisingly economical prices. Dinner entrees, for example, which are accompanied by a cup of soup or salad plus vegetable and beverage, are mostly priced at $5.50 to $6.95, and that includes honey-dipped fried chicken, sauteed mahimahi, crêpes of shrimp and crab, and beef and shrimp brochettes. You can also order à la carte (fresh fish of the day is $8.75), add on some interesting appetizers and soups, and choose from a fanciful array of desserts that includes peach Melba and macadamia nut pie.

Similar entrees are even lower-priced at lunch, and that's when you can also get good sandwiches, burgers, chilled salads, and a tasty International Cold Buffet Plate ($4.75) laden with German-style sausage and deli meats, Swiss Gruyere cheese, Norwegian sardines on buttered rye bread, Russian vegetable salad, German potato salad, and more. Watching your diet? Go with one of the "Light Health Lunches," like turkey breast, sprouts and tomato on toasted branola bread; a bowl of Swiss Muesli with shredded apples, nuts, and fruits; or a Twiggy's Salad—that's shrimps on greens, tomato, and egg with yogurt dressing; all are priced from $2.25 to $3.50.

Trellises serves from 11:30 a.m. to 5 p.m. and from 5:30 to 9:30 p.m. daily.

Another coffeeshop that is way out of the ordinary is the **Waikiki Circle Coffeeshop** in the Waikiki Circle Hotel. Directly across from Kuhio Beach, this comfortable place with its red carpet on the floor offers a fine sunset view—through the traffic and exhaust fumes, of course! The food is very good and the prices even better: the $4.95 dinner special offers half a pound of U.S. Choice New York steak, and includes salad and rice or mashed potatoes. Priced from $4.35 to $4.95 are ground beefsteak, teriyaki steak, mahimahi filet, fried chicken, and lamb chops. Lunch is similarly inexpensive, and a special $1.89 breakfast offers two golden buttermilk hot cakes, an egg, and a choice of ham, bacon, or sausage. Banana hotcakes are $1.75.

Unless someone told you about the **Liliane Restaurant**, located in the new Inn on the Park at 1290 Ala Moana, opposite Fort

DeRussy (phone: 947-8440), you wouldn't suspect that this plainly decorated, unassuming restaurant harbors some of the best Chinese food in town. You might think the moderately priced American-continental food (lamb chops, chicken in the basket, veal cordon bleu, from $7 to $9) is all there is to this place; but forego this menu and choose the Chinese one instead and you're in for a rare treat. Recently moved from downtown Chinatown in Honolulu to Waikiki, family-run Liliane specializes in seafood and offers some extraordinary dishes from several Chinese provinces seldom seen elsewhere in town; like sauteed oysters with ginger and ground onion, Shanghai-style pine-nut fish in sweet-and-sour sauce, and fried clams with black bean sauce. Casseroles of stewed seafood and fish are excellent, and the Szechuan cabbage soup, laced with shredded pork, is a masterpiece. These delicacies are priced from $3 to $14.

Prawns and other fish used in the preparation of the food are kept in an open freshwater tank; a saltwater tank is home to Dungeness crab, king clams, and lobsters. Red booths give privacy to diners. There is parking one ramp above street level. Liliane is open seven days a week until 10 p.m. The luncheon menu is the same as the dinner menu. American breakfasts, too, from 7 a.m.

There's nothing very glamorous about the **Minute Chef** in the Princess Kaiulani Hotel, all vinyl and Formica at its counter and tables, but this place has one of the best reputations in town for good, inexpensive food, and how it packs the people in! At lunch or dinner (same menu, same prices), you can have dishes like chicken pot pie and Hungarian beef stew from $2.75; and, served with French fries or rice, roll and butter, and beverage, entrees like beef pot pie, mahimahi, and teriyaki steak, from $3.65 to $3.95 Fried chicken, chili, hamburgers, and a very popular breakfast special—Canadian bacon, scrambled eggs, toast, marmalade, fruit or juice, and coffee, at $3.50—round out the menu.

If you choose to dine at a **Jolly Roger** in Waikiki, you have your choice of two locations: one is in the heart of Waikiki, right on Kalakaua Ave. at No. 2244, and another, Jolly Roger East, at 150 Kaiulani Ave. Both seem to be packed most of the time, since the food is always tasty and reasonably priced. On Kalakaua there are a few sidewalk tables and a cooler and quieter mood inside. At Jolly Roger East, there are comfortable booths, a step-down bar, and entertainment nightly at 9. At both you can eat a good dinner for $6.95 or under: perhaps beef liver with sauteed onions or bacon, honey fried chicken, breaded veal cutlet. There are also changing daily specials like baked meat loaf with mushrooms, $3.95. Dinners are served with soup or salad, French fries, rice or potato, and a dinner roll. There are also plenty of salads, sandwiches, and burgers (from $2.45) to choose from. Doors open around 7 a.m., and breakfast, lunch, and dinner are served.

The **Original Pancake House** is for lovers of those breakfast delights who would like to eat them morning, noon, or afternoon (to 2 p.m.). A simply decorated restaurant overlooking and sharing an open garden in Suite 103 at the rear of 1221 Kapiolani Blvd. (corner Piikoi Street), it's an offspring of Portland's Original Pancake House, which later spread around the world and has been given a *McCall's* Citation and a James Beard Award. More than 20 varieties of pancake are at the ready, plus five types of waffle and sourdough French toast; the tab is from $1.75 to $5.65. A few possibilities might be Swedish pancakes, coconut pancakes, Kijafa cherry crêpes (a Danish treat), and Palestine pancakes (rolled with sour cream and Cointreau). Of course, eggs and omelets any style plus ham, bacon, and sausage side dishes are also available, but the star of this show is pancakes— clam pancakes, Mandarin pancakes, potato pancakes, pecan- and-apple pancakes. Open daily from 6 a.m. Phone: 533-3005.

Everybody's been to an American drive-in, but how about a Japanese drive-in? Something different for mainland tastes is always available at **Yokuzuna,** adjacent to the Times Super Market at 1290 South Beretania, just Diamond Head of Piikoi St. This place is open during the day and closes in early evening. You can try goodies like fish tempura (50¢ apiece) or vegetable tempura (35¢ apiece); sushi bento, a special rolled-up rice, is $1.30. Such local dishes as kalua pig, chicken curry, and beef stew are also available, all under $2.50. Midday only, they have teriyaki beef and pork at $1.25, served with rice. Tables are provided, outdoors but under a sheltering roof. And there is an electronic game room for the kids. This is a good way to sample Japanese food before you invest in a more expensive meal.

The **Rigger,** a smartly nautical coffeeshop at the Outrigger Hotel, 2335 Kalakaua Ave., is one of those places that always give me a problem: whether to go all out, calorically, on one of their wild fountain specials or to stick to the tried-and-true hamburgers and hot dishes. Whichever (or both) you choose, you'll be well satisfied. Fanciful hamburgers like the Islander Burger—one-quarter pound of steer, plus bacon, cheese, and a pineapple ring to boot—are really good. Or, try the simpler Surf

Burger at $2.45. There are daily specials like breaded veal cutlet and the very good chef's salad topped with strips of ham and cheese for under $3.95, and a secondary menu of meat and seafood combos that begin at $6.75 and $7.95. And the Early Bird Special served from 6 to 8 a.m. and 12 to 3 a.m. is just that: it consists of four pancakes, two eggs any style, and an endless cup of coffee. And now, ah—about those fountain specials. Let me confess that my favorite is the Buccaneer, a shake so thick you need a spoon.

The friendly young people at the **Red Lion Pizza Parlors**, at 2350 Kuhio Ave. and at 240 Lewers Rd., will be happy to pack your pizzas to go, but it's also fun to hang around these attractively decorated (wrought iron, stained glass) gourmet pizza parlors, both of which also offer full cocktail service. An individual cheese pizza is $3.35, a vegetarian combination $4.95. The Red Lion Special—a combination of pizza ingredients lightly baked on sourdough French bread—is a nice change ($2.75). In addition, the Red Lion at Lewers Street features live Country-Western bands nightly, with pizza and cocktail service at both parlors continuing until 2 a.m.

For something heartier, you might try the **Red Lion Rib and Spaghetti House** at 2330 Kuhio, next door to the pizzeria, which serves up gourmet pasta dinners from $3.95. Specialty of the house is a complete prime rib dinner for $5.95, including salad and baked sourdough. And there's rock-and-roll disco dancing from 10 p.m. until 2 a.m.

Could any roundup of budget restaurants in Waikiki possibly leave out **Perry's Smorgy Restaurants?** Hardly, since Perry's is practically a one-man answer to inflation on the Waikiki scene. Our favorite Perry's is the one at the Outrigger Hotel, which has tables facing the ocean; but the one at the Cinerama Reef Hotel is also oceanside, and the Perry's at the Coral Seas Hotel is pretty, too. The fare is the same at all three: an enormous buffet table stacked with heaps and heaps of good things to eat. The evening spread features a hand-carved round of beef au jus, and island pineapple and home-grown Kona coffee are served at every meal. The nicest thing about it all is the price, which, year, after year, manages to be the lowest in town for this kind of meal: breakfast (7 to 10:30 a.m.), $3.37; lunch (11 a.m. to 2:30 p.m.), $3.85; dinner (5 to 9 p.m.) $5.53.

Chapter V

ADVENTURES IN THE COSMOPOLITAN CITY

EVEN THOUGH there is more than enough to keep you busy in Waikiki, I do not think you should pass up the rest of Honolulu. For this is a city with more than the usual share of diversity and excitement, with a rich cultural past and a stimulating, cosmopolitan present. And how to see it need present no problem at all. If time is short or if you want to get an overall, bird's-eye view before you begin in-depth exploring, simply take one of the excellent commercial sightseeing tours that hit all the major points. Or you can rent a car and drive to all the things you want to see (details on car rentals can be found in Chapter II). But even without benefit of a car or guided tour, you can get around very well indeed. Honolulu is, after all, a major United States metropolis, and it has an excellent public transportation system: the Mass Transit Lines buses, popularly known as TheBUS. For 50¢ a ride, 25¢ for children, plus a little bit of ingenuity and determination, you can get almost anywhere in Honolulu you want to go.

IN DEFENSE OF BUSES: Besides saving you money, riding the buses gives you an added advantage; you go at your own pace, heading where your interests take you, lingering as long as you like in any given spot. On a guided tour, everybody has to see everything. While the ladies in front of you may just adore Iolani Palace, you might be much happier poking through the rickety little streets and alleys of Chinatown. Or you might want to skip all the historical sights and just come up for air once in a while as you peruse the splendors of the Honolulu Academy of Art or the Bishop Museum. On TheBUS, you're your own person; you decide when and where to go and how long to stay there. For

Honolulu is such a varied city, with such a diversity of things to see, that it should be seen at your own pace.

Renting a car, of course, is the easiest way to do the town. But cars and taxis can get to be expensive, and bus travel is quite congenial. The buses run all over the city, they maintain good schedules, and the drivers are friendly and genuinely helpful. If you need information about TheBUS, phone 531-1611. Visiting senior citizens are eligible for free passes after three to four weeks (phone: 524-4626). Remember that most major thoroughfares in Honolulu are one-way: most buses going in a Diamond Head direction should be boarded on Kalakaua Ave.; those going toward downtown Honolulu or Ala Moana, on Kuhio Avenue.

THE ORDER OF THINGS: In the pages ahead, I outline for you the major sights of Honolulu. The first section will trace, in more-or-less chronological order, the sights that will show you what Hawaiian life was and is like, from the Stone Age days of the Polynesian settlers, through the missionary period and the era of Hawaiian royalty, to the Space Age Hawaii of the '70s. At the end of this section, I'll show you how to take some walking, bus, and boat tours.

In the next section, I'll tell you a little about the ethnic life of the city, about the important ethnic festivals always going on in Honolulu. Should you be lucky enough to catch the yearly Japanese Bon Dances or the Chinese New Year, for example, these could be the highlights of your trip. I'll also take you on a tour of the Hong Kong of Honolulu, the city's engaging Chinese neighborhood.

The last section of this chapter gives you a look at the museums, galleries, concerts, theaters, experimental films, and educational centers that make Honolulu just about the most exciting combination of beach resort and urban metropolis anywhere. Put on a comfortable pair of walking shoes, arm yourself with some good maps, and off you go to savor the excitement of this cosmopolitan city.

Hawaii, from Stone Age to Space Age

Bishop Museum: One of the most important natural-history museums of the Pacific, the Bishop Museum makes the world of the early Polynesian settlers come alive, through such exhibits as outrigger canoes, a model *heiau,* feather cloaks of the *alii,* rare Hawaiian artifacts. There's an exciting collection of primitive art

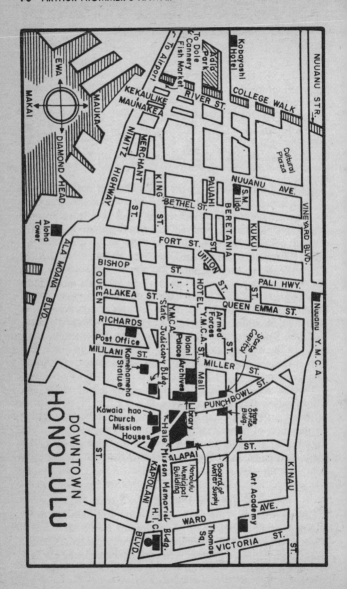

of Polynesia, Micronesia, and Melanesia. A visit here will give you a basis for understanding much of what you will see later throughout the islands. And the Vestibule Shop is laden with attractive items, everything from $2 kukui-nut pendants to a $60 chess set with carved Hawaiian figures. The Bishop Museum is located at 1355 Kalihi St. (phone: 847-3511); open daily from 9 to 5; admission $3 for those over 18.

Note: For one of the best sightseeing and education values in this or any other town, purchase a "Diplomat's Passport to Polynesia," ($10 for adults, $5 for children aged 6 through 17). This handsome passport, printed in Kalakaua Dynasty style, entitles you to admission to the Bishop Museum; the adjacent Atherton Halau, where live demonstrations of arts and crafts or Hawaiian entertainment are held; and the Science Center, where special exhibits, a planetarium show, and the observatory are housed. Included in the price of your Passport (or individual admission tickets) is free transportation between all these points in a real, red London double-decker bus. Board at King's Alley, Waikiki, from the Bishop Museum's Heritage Gift Shop location or other Waikiki locations (phone 847-3511 for information). En route to the Museum, your conductor will narrate a motor tour through historic Honolulu. At each of the three attractions you receive a guided tour. Afterward, you keep the Passport as a great souvenir of Polynesia in the days of old. "Diplomat's Passport to Polynesia" is sold at all Bishop Museum attractions and at most hotel tour desks.

Queen Emma Summer Palace: "Hanaiakamalama," the country estate of Kamehameha IV and his consort, Queen Emma, has been restored by the Daughters of Hawaii to its mid-19th-century Victorian splendor. The address is 2913 Pali Hwy.; open daily from 9 a.m. to 4 p.m., closed holidays. Guided tours. Admission: $3 adults, $1.50 ages 12-18, 50¢ under 12.

Royal Mausoleum: This is where the *alii* of the Kamehameha and Kalakaua dynasties are buried. The address is 2261 Nuuanu Ave.; open Monday to Friday, 8 a.m. to 4:30 p.m. Closed Saturday, Sunday, and most holidays (open March 26, Kuhio Day, and June 11, Kamehameha Day).

Pearl Harbor: It would be unthinkable to leave Hawaii without making a pilgrimage to the USS *Arizona* Memorial at Pearl Harbor. This tomb of more than 1000 American servicemen who died on December 7, 1941, the day bombs fell on Hawaii, is a silent, stark reminder of the continued folly of war. Although the easiest way to reach Pearl Harbor is by commercial tour boat from Waikiki, you can get there yourself by bus or car and then proceed to take the free National Park Service tour, which leaves continuously from Halawa Gate between 9 a.m. and 3 p.m., Tuesday through Sunday, accepting passengers on a strictly first-come, first-served basis (no reservations are accepted). You will be taken to the new Pearl Harbor Visitors Center, a splendid, $4.2-million complex that includes twin movie theaters showing films of the attack on Pearl Harbor, and an absorbing museum containing many personal mementos of the attack victims, plus photographs, paintings, and historical documents. If you have young children with you, leave them at home, as children under 6 are not permitted; those 6 to 10 must be accompanied by an adult. Bathing suits and bare feet are not acceptable.

You can drive directly to Halawa Gate or, if you don't have a car, take TheBUS. Several buses passing Ala Moana Center go to Halawa Gate—they will be named Barber's Point, Waipahu, Makaha, Ewa Beach, Wahiawa Heights, and Wahiawa-Kaneohe. The bus stop is located on the *makai* side of Ala Moana, by Ala Moana Beach Park, just across from the shopping center. For $2 each way, you can take an express bus from Waikiki hotels; phone 955-1466 for reservations.

Mission Houses Museum: These three 19th-century buildings are still the way they were when the New England missionaries lived in them, full of antique furniture, mementos, clothing of the missionary ladies, aging trinkets, and Daguerreotypes on the wall. A fascinating look into the past, it's at 553 South King St. Open daily, 9 a.m. to 4 p.m.; admission (including a guided tour) is $2.50 for adults, $1 for those under 16, free for children 6 years and under. A daily walking tour of historic downtown Honolulu leaves the museum every weekday at 9:30 a.m. The $5 fee includes admission. Special events here are of a high quality; check the local papers for information. There's a charming gift shop, full of Hawaiiana. Behind the Mission Houses is a library containing the collections of the Hawaiian Mission Children's Society and the Hawaiian Historical Society. Researchers are welcome. Phone: 531-0481.

Kawaiahao Church: The church the King, his subjects, and missionaries built has been, since its dedication in 1841, the "Westminster Abbey of Hawaii." Even if you don't get to Sunday services (10:30 a.m., conducted partially in Hawaiian; free guided tours afterward), take a look around any day from 9 a.m. to 4 p.m. Note the fine portraits of Hawaiian royalty recently hung in the church. 957 Punchbowl St. is the address, across Kawaiahao Street from the Mission Houses.

Iolani Palace: The only royal palace under the American flag, Iolani was designed in the European manner for King Kalakaua, "the Merry Monarch." Royalty ruled here for 11 years (1882 to 1893) until it was overthrown. Up until 1968 the building functioned as the state capitol and now it is a museum, reopened to the public after a nine-year, $6-million restoration-reconstruction. As of yet, there is no furniture in the building (less than one-third of the original furniture remains and much work must be done on it before it can be displayed), but a tour of the building is well worth your time to see the intricate woodwork, the highly polished fir floors, the shining bannisters and mirrors, and to be taken into the lovely rooms as guides fill you in on the furnishings that were there and the history that went on in each room. Tours are conducted by the Friends of Iolani Palace from 9 to 2, Wednesday through Saturday; they last 45 minutes and cost $3 for adults and $1 for children 5 through 12 (children under 5 not permitted on tours). Reservations are essential: phone 536-2474.

On the same grounds are the **Archives of Hawaii,** the largest collection of Hawaiiana extant. Location is at King and Richards Sts.; open Monday through Friday from 7:45 a.m. to 4:30 p.m.

Downtown Honolulu: The highlight of a little walk downtown will be the **Aloha Tower,** Hawaii's Empire State Building. Even though it's now dwarfed by the two 21-story Amfac towers and other modern buildings, it's still the symbol of the city, overlooks the harbor, affords spectacular views of the metropolis, and is open 8 a.m. to 9 p.m., seven days a week. You can come down to earth now and head for Hawaii's Wall Street, **Merchant Street,** where the major corporate empires of Hawaii, the "Big Five," still have their offices. The architecture of Alexander and Baldwin, Castle and Cook, Theo. H. Davies, among others, is 19th-century elegant. Then you can head toward **Fort Street** and a pleasant shopping mall closed to traffic where you can browse among some of the big downtown department stores.

State Capitol Building: The first unit and the crowning jewel of the growing Civic Center (completion date: 1985) is already finished and it undoubtedly is one of the grandest capitols in the world. Using Hawaiian materials and motifs, the colors of sand and sea, the building soars upward from expansive pools to an open-air crown suggesting the peak of a volcano. There is a

"Welcome, Enter" sign on both the governor's and lieutenant-governor's offices during regular working hours, and they are worth at least peeking into. Outside the building, a huge medallion bears the state seal and motto, *Ua Mau ke ea o ka aina I ka pono* ("The life of the land is perpetuated in righteousness"). Note Marisol's controversial statue of Father Damien out front. Opposite Iolani Palace; open every day.

Foster Botanic Garden: Fifteen acres of rare tropical plants from around the world plus orchid displays. A cool interlude. 180 North Vineyard Blvd., phone: 531-1939. Open daily from 9 to 4. Free.

Queen Kapiolani Rose Garden: This is a spectacular garden located on Paki Avenue just behind the Honolulu Zoo, and well worth a visit if you are strolling in the area. It has received a certificate of merit from the American Rose Society and has been accredited as an outstanding public rose garden. Daytime only. Free.

Paradise Park: Walk back into the Hawaiian jungle, emerge into a charming park where trained birds go through their antics in regular shows. This 15-acre stretch of tamed jungle is delightful for everyone, a must for the kids, who will get a kick out of walking through a giant aviary. New features include five multiethnic villages and gardens representing Hawaii's people; "Aquatic Carnival," an outdoor show featuring ducks and chickens; puppet shows, and educational films on the history of Hawaii. Tour guides are available at a nominal charge. With or without entering the park, you can lunch at the beautiful Polynesian Restaurant, with its view of gardens and waterfalls. The park is located at 3737 Mano Rd. in Manoa Valley (phone: 988-2141), open daily except Christmas from 9:30 a.m. to 5:30 p.m. Admission: $4.50, children 4 to 12, $2.50, under 4 free.

Lyon Arboretum: Just above Paradise Park, in lush upper Manoa Valley, this superb arboretum is open to the public on the first Friday of every month; a free, 1½-hour guided tour will tell you all you'll ever need to know about the flora of Hawaii. Reservations are a must; call 988-7378 between 9 a.m. and noon weekdays.

Hawaii Science Center: If you can't get to the moon yourself, you can at least observe it through a powerful telescope at this important center for the study of astronomy. Sky shows are held at frequent intervals throughout the day and evening. It's science for all ages, but children under 6 are not admitted. It's part of the Bishop Museum at 1355 Kalihi St. (see above). Admission is included with your ticket to the museum, and also as part of the "Passport to Polynesia" package (phone: 847-3511 for show times and information).

CASTLE PARK: Hawaii's first Disneyland-style amusement park —albeit on a much smaller, 16-acre scale—is fun for everyone in the family. There's a castle à la Sleeping Beauty's located on an island; a Grand Prix racing-car ride; "Water Country," with rafts for shooting the rapids, 400-foot slippery slides, and flume; Bumper Boat Lake for doing just that; three 18-hole miniature golf courses with such whimsical/weird obstacles as a giant candy house and a haunted mansion; and a batting range with nine authentic major-league pitching machines. Inside the castle are all manner of electronic games, as well as a restaurant and gift shop. Admission is free: you can pay for each attraction (Water Country, for example, is $5.75 for adults and $4.75 for kids) or have it all with a $13.75 book for adults or kids.

Castle Park is just eight minutes from downtown Honolulu on the H-I Freeway: follow the Aloha Stadium signs. Open Sunday through Thursday from 9:30 a.m. to 10:30 p.m., until 12:30 p.m. Friday and Saturday nights.

DOLE PINEAPPLE CANNERY: Watch those pineapples get into those cans in an absorbing $2 walking tour through the world's largest fruit cannery. Canning season is usually May through August. Other months there's a film tour, always a free drink from the pineapple-juice fountain. Combine this with a visit to Hilo Hattie's Fashion Center at 440 Kuwili St. and you get free bus pickup from Waikiki hotels (phone 537-2796). Or take bus 8 direct to the cannery (phone: 536-3411).

HISTORY AND ARCHITECTURE BUFF'S WALKING TOUR: Begin this morning or afternoon walking excursion at the **Mission Houses Museum,** described above. If you're driving downtown you may, depending on space available, be able to park your car here. After you've steeped yourself in the atmosphere of the past at the Mission Houses Museum and browsed through the gift shop, walk ewa on King Street. You will come to historic **Kawaiahao Church,** described above. Continuing in an ewa direction, you will pass the **War Memorial** in front of the Territorial Office Building. Beyond is the imposing **Statue of King Kamehameha I,** dressed in golden helmet and feathered cape. He stands at the entrance to the **State Judiciary Building, Aliiolani Hale,** built by Kamehameha V for the legislature, courts, and cabinet officers of the king's domain. It was formally opened by King Kalakaua for the legislative session of 1874. Just beyond is the **Post Office,** done in Spanish style with a large courtyard entrance garden.

Cross King Street now, and have a look at **Honolulu Hale— City Hall.** It's the off-white stucco Spanish-looking building on the corner. There is usually an art exhibit in the courtyard. Continuing in a Diamond Head direction (back the other way; we're strolling in an S-shaped route) on the mauka side of King, you will pass some very attractive white-trimmed brick buildings that house various city agencies. The thing just beyond them that appears to be numerous sections of castoff black stovepipe gone mad is really an "art object": **"Sky Gate,"** commissioned by the city and county at a six-figure fee, has caused a bit of artistic controversy in Honolulu. There are often free noontime concerts in its vicinity during the summer; check the newspapers for details.

The tall, gray concrete slab just beyond Sky Gate is the **Honolulu Municipal Building** (the rationale behind putting a gigantic structure in the midst of all the low-rises seems to have been making a choice between losing a lot of rolling green lawn or spoiling the view—and the latter won). Diagonally across from it, you will see a monarchy-style building with a terra-cotta roof; that's the **News Building,** home of the *Honolulu Advertiser and Star-Bulletin.* Now walk straight through—or around—the Municipal Building, and you'll be on Beretania Street, preparing to walk the third leg of our "S." The soft green building just mauka is the main **Board of Water Supply** office complex. Walk ewa (turn left) on Beretania Street and note the very lovely building across from City Hall. This is **Kalanimoku,** one of the new state office buildings. Have a look at the abundant tropical plantings that surround it. Just across Punchbowl from Kalanimoku is the **State Capitol** building, described above, where we end our walk.

GUIDED TOURS: Certainly the easiest way to see the sights of Honolulu and the island of Oahu is to take a guided tour— especially if your time is limited. Of the major tour operators, **Gray Line** (P.O. Box 8539, Honolulu, HI 96808, phone: 922-8222 is well recommended; basic city tours begin at around $9, while a round-the-island excursion is $14. If you don't mind spending a few dollars more, however, it's usually more fun to go on one of the smaller tours. **E Noa Tours,** 1110 University Ave., Room 306, Honolulu, HI 96826, phone 941-6608, for one, takes you out in an 11-passenger van and provides delightful, personalized looks at the island sights. You can't go wrong either way. Travel agents and hotel desks can arrange tours with both companies.

Sightseeing on the Sea

Although it's admittedly more costly than going by the bus, a cruise to Pearl Harbor is not something you're likely to forget. The *Adventure V* leaves Kewalo Basin daily at 9:30 a.m. and 1.30 p.m. for a narrated cruise to Pearl Harbor and the *Arizona* Memorial. *Adventure's* route takes you past the Aloha Tower and Hickam Air Force Base. There's a snackbar aboard. Tickets are $8, $4 for kids; call 923-4123 for reservations. Another popular Pearl Harbor cruise is on the 550-passenger ship *Hawaii State,* with similar departure times (9:30 a.m. and 1:30 p.m.) and a charge of $8.

Although your sightseeing is mostly limited to a vista of sunset over Waikiki, the daily Sunset Dinner Sail aboard Windjammer Cruises' catamaran *Aikane* is lovely. The two-hour journey gives you a chance to relax and watch the lights of Waikiki, while hostesses serve free, unlimited mai tais (and other drinks) and an excellent dinner. A Hawaiian group is there to serenade you, and $18 is the price for adults including hotel pickup. For information, phone: 521-0036.

HAWAII, THE MELTING POT: Perhaps the most intriguing thing about Hawaiian life is the fact that everybody here came from somewhere else. First the Polynesians, then, centuries later, the English, the Americans, the Chinese, the Japanese, the Filipinos, the Koreans, the Puerto Ricans, the French, the Irish, and so on, ad infinitum. Since so many of the races intermarried, the result is a colorful melange, a tapestry of hues and textures unmatched anywhere else. But, fortunately, many of the races have still maintained their own traditions and cultures, and these are particularly evident in their yearly festivals and celebrations. Visitors are warmly welcomed to these events, and we suggest that you take in as many as may be going on when you are in the islands. Some people even plan their vacations around the festival calendar; for them, the Chinese New Year or the celebration of Philippine Independence Day or the Japanese Bon Dances of the summer season are the highlights of their trip. Below is a seasonal calendar of events to watch for.

Chinese New Year's: Help the local people welcome in the Year of the Dragon or the Year of the Horse or the year of the whatever. Chinese New Year is usually at the beginning of February, and for three weeks before and five days after there's the Festival. There are cultural shows, banquets, the crowning of a Narcissus Queen, parades with lanterns and lions, and dancing in the streets.

Japanese Girls' Day: Look in the windows of the big Japanese department stores at Ala Moana Center and in downtown Honolulu for displays of regally costumed dolls, all in honor of this holiday—March 3—when all Japanese girls receive dolls as presents.

Prince Kuhio Day: March 26 is the day on which the native Hawaiians celebrate the birthday of the "People's Prince," Jonah Kuhio Kalanianaole. Catch the ceremonies at Iolani Palace, at the tomb in the Royal Mausoleum, and at the site of his home at Kuhio Beach.

Cherry Blossom Festival: Since the Japanese are now Hawaii's largest ethnic group, it seems as if everyone gets in on this spring event. In March or April, for about six weeks, you can see exhibitions of Japanese art at the Honolulu Academy of Art, displays of flower arranging, judo, the tea ceremony, parades in the streets, and an "International Revue" straight from Japan.

Wesak Day: April 8, the birthday of Gautama Buddha, is the signal for the islands' Buddhists (mostly Japanese) to gather in Queen Kapiolani Park for a sunrise ceremony. You can join the day-long celebration of music and dance.

Lei Day: May 1 is dear to the Hawaiians. Join the islanders in wearing a lei and be sure to see the free sunset festival and hula pageant in Queen Kapiolani Park. In the afternoon, there's a lei competition and exhibit.

Japanese Boys' Day: May 5 is the day ancient tradition specifies to decorate the family residence with colorful paper and fabric carp in honor of the eldest boy in the family. On the first Boys' Day after his birth, all of his grandparents and aunties and uncles, etc., would send a carp to be flown in his honor. These days carp are flown for all the family's male offspring, and you'd be surprised how many families of other nationalities also fly the bright fish for their boys.

Kamehameha Day: June 11 is one of the biggest celebrations of the year—a huge parade, luaus, fancy-dress balls, all in honor of the conqueror and uniter of the islands. The statue of Kamehameha in front of Iolani Palace is draped with hundreds of enormous flower leis, and the Mission Houses Museum runs a charming "Fancy Fair" on the grounds where local craftsmen show their work.

Filipino Festival: Philippine Indepence Day and Rizal Day fall in mid-June, and it's then the local Filipino population goes mad with a 17-day, Spanish-accented fiesta including dancing, singing, and a big-name show at the Waikiki Shell.

Bon Dances: Watch the papers for the dates of the Bon Odori Dances, which are given throughout the islands in July and August. These ancient religious dances, honoring the spirits of the ancestors who have reached paradise, are probably the most colorful affairs of the summer. The dances are performed outdoors, both by adults and the especially adorable Japanese keikis dressed in their native costumes. Visitors can observe or even take a few lessons in Bon dancing (classes are announced in the papers).

Aloha Week: Once a year, in late October, all the varied racial and ethnic groups get together for one big blow-out, and Aloha Week explodes. Kalakaua Avenue is blocked off, stages are set up along the entire stretch for almost nonstop entertainment, and the whole celebration begins with an enormous parade. The other islands also hold celebrations during different weeks in October. A good reason to come to Hawaii in October.

The rest of the big holidays—Thanksgiving, Christmas, New Year—are observed just as they are back on the mainland. Except that the faces around the Thanksgiving table gazing at the turkey may be Hawaiian-Chinese and people sing Christmas carols in the sand rather than the snow. That's the fun of Hawaii.

A WALK AROUND CHINATOWN: Whether or not there is anything special going on among the various ethnic groups when you are in Honolulu, you can always have an Oriental adventure of your own. An hour or two spent walking around Chinatown, either by yourself or on a guided tour, is a facinating experience. Mrs. Eunice Derby conducts an excellent shopping-and-temple tour sponsored by the Chinese Chamber of Commerce every Tuesday morning at 9:30 a.m. from 42 North King St. The tour costs $2.50, and there is an optional lunch at $3.50. Phone 533-3181 for reservations.

If, however, you don't have the time for an organized tour or just want to walk about on your own, it's easy enough (although you miss the engaging running commentary that the ladies provide). You should start at the **Cultural Plaza** (in the block bordered by Beretania, Maunakea, Kukui, and River Streets). Pause to look at some of the shops, if you like (**Lane East** has delicate porcelain snuff bottles from $6 and up; **Bin Ching Jade Center** and **Peninsula Jewelers** have beautiful jade and pearl jewelry from the Orient), then continue your walk along Maunakea Street. Here you could poke your head into a bakery and munch on those irresistible Chinese pastries, candies, and buns (don't miss the moon cookies if the Chinese Moon Festival happens to be going on; otherwise almond or wedding cake will do nicely). Then on to a food market across the street where you can pick up the bladder of an eel or sharks' fins. Or get some birds'-nest soup. It used to take the Chinese cooks days to prepare this, since they had to carefully extricate the feathers from the birds' saliva. Now it's all conveniently packaged, and no traditional nine-course Chinese banquet would be complete without it.

If you've got a cold or tummy-ache, you might stop in at the herbalist's shop next—there are several on Maunakea Street. Lots of *haoles* as well as the local people consult the herbalist (who studies for four years, then undergoes an internship and is licensed by the state to practice). He makes a diagnosis by examining your pulse in several different spots, to determine the condition of different organs, then prescribes a concoction to be brewed and sipped; his office is usually behind the pharmacy. The brew may be made out of sea horses and sea dragons, antelope horns, or snakes (they're good for arthritis) and whatnot. Don't say you weren't warned.

There are literally dozens of gift shops in the neighborhood, where you can buy anything from a $1 sandalwood fan (very useful in the hot Hawaiian sun) to a piece of rare jade or an antique Oriental screen. And don't miss **Cindy's Lei Shoppe** at 1034 Maunakea St. Somehow or other, Cindy manages to keep her prices lower than just about any other place in town, and her work is beautiful.

Probably the single most interesting place in Chinatown, and one you should visit whether or not you make the rest of the trip, is the **Kuan Yin Temple** at 170 North Vineyard St. near the

Foster Gardens. It's straight out of the Orient, complete to its huge gold-leafed statues of Kuan Yin, the goddess of mercy, and various other gods, burning incense and joss sticks, offerings of fruits and flowers on the altars, and the people rustling about lighting candles. It's an authentic bit of Oriental life that should be seen and experienced.

A Japanese Adventure

The Japanese neighborhood of downtown Honolulu is all but gone now, its rickety hotels and pool halls and saimin stands torn down for shiny new office buildings. You could visit the wholesale fish market auction early, early in the morning, at River and King Streets. But there's an easier way to catch the flavor of the old neighborhood-that-was, and that's to take a trip to **Tamashiro Market**, 802 North King St. (at the corner of Palama). This is the Kalihi neighborhood, near the Bishop Museum, and it's easiest to drive here. It's nominally just a fish store, but so unusual that people come from all over Honolulu, and school groups regularly make visits. The place is huge, crowded, pungent with the odors of the weirdest varieties of fresh seafood you can imagine. Like to try octopus? or Kona crab? raw aku? or sea cucumber? They're all here. There's also a huge table of fresh seaweed, barrels of snails, live clams, live crabs, live lobsters, and live Malaysian prawns in running water. So fresh is the fish and so excellent the quality that many of the leading restaurants buy here. Besides the fish, there are fascinating local dishes to buy and take out, like Filipino rice cakes made with coconut milk and mochi rice, Puerto Rican pasteles made with pork and bananas, Korean cucumber kim chee, and dozens of types of Japanese tsukemono. You may need a native to help you pick and choose the dishes, but even if you just look, it's lots of fun. Tamashiro Market is open every day of the week.

Hawaii, the Cultural Center

Too many tourists think there is no entertainment in Hawaii besides hula shows and slack-key music. That's all well and good, but what they don't realize is that there's plenty going on in the arts-entertainment-cultural scene and that they're missing a good bet if they don't join the local people in enjoying it. Most of the shows and events are inexpensive, compared to mainland prices, and the quality is high. For the imagination of the people of Hawaii, the result of the blending of great ideas from many divergent cultures, has produced some ingenious results. To wit:

THEATER: It's 5000 miles from Broadway, but it's pretty good and it's getting better all the time. The top local group is the **Honolulu Community Theater,** housed in the Ruger Theater at Fort Ruger, just behind Diamond Head. Major Broadway shows are the fare here, and you see them sooner than you'd expect, since the rights are easier to secure 2500 miles out in the Pacific than on the roadshow touring circuit. Sometimes name performers come out to join the local acting company. Check the local papers or phone 734-0274 for specific attractions and prices.

Up at the University of Hawaii at Manoa, serious theater endeavors continue all year long. The **John F. Kennedy Theater** here showcases University of Hawaii productions, as well as lectures and performances by students attending its East-West Center.

The **Windward Theatre Guild** brings contemporary theater to the windward side of Oahu. Performances by this talented group are held in the Kailua Elementary School Auditorium. Phone 261-4885 for information on current performances.

The **Hawaii Performing Arts Company** (known as **HPAC**) is another of the top-notch theater groups in town. This nonprofit resident theater company, sponsored by the State Foundation on Culture and the Arts and supported by the National Endowment for the Arts, was established in 1969, and has since earned a reputation for presenting exciting new playwrights as well as reviving the classics. You might catch *Knock, Knock, P.S., Your Cat Is Dead,* or *Damn Yankees.* Performances are held at the Manoa Valley Theater, 2833 East Manoa Rd., for information, call 988-6131 or check the entertainment section of the newspapers.

The nationally acclaimed **Honolulu Theater for Youth** puts on excellent productions for children, but adults enjoy them too. We recently saw *Maui the Trickster and Other Stories,* a brilliantly staged and very well-acted dramatization of Hawaiian folklore. Everything in the show was completely understandable even to classes of preschoolers. For information, call 533-3472.

ART: Hawaii's citizens, so attuned to the glories of nature, are also attuned to the glories of art. The islands are producing some talented young artists, and the local citizenry eagerly seeks out their works at a number of galleries. Art is constantly being commissioned for public buildings, and one of the great prides of the city is the **Honolulu Academy of Arts,** a must-see.

The Academy is a supremely graceful building, a model of what an art museum should look like. Small galleries look out on serene courtyards through which you can wander after getting your fill of the treasures within. While both island artists and the masters of Western art—Picasso, Braque, Van Gogh, etc.— are well represented, the real glory of the museum is in its collections of Oriental scrolls, paintings, tapestries, screens, and sculptures from Korea, China, Japan. Be sure to see the awe-inspiring statue of Kuan Yin, a 12th-century representation of the Chinese goddess of mercy, which is far more beautiful than the one in the Kuan Yin temple in Honolulu. Newly opened at the Academy is a gallery devoted to the traditional arts of the Pacific, the Americas, and Africa; a contemporary art collection in the Luce Wing; and a sculpture garden containing master-pieces from the Academy collection, including some Noguchis and Henry Moores. The Academy is located at 900 South Beretania St. (across Thomas Square from the Neal S. Blaisdell Center). It's open Tuesday, Wednesday, Friday, and Saturday from 10 a.m. to 4:30 p.m., Thursday from 11 a.m. to 4:30 p.m. and 7 to 9 p.m. A delightful lunch is served in the Garden Cafe from September to May. Phone 531-8865 for reservations. Outstanding primitive art of the Polynesian peoples can be viewed at the Bishop Museum, which we've discussed above.

There are a number of private galleries that deserve a look-see, like the beautiful **Following Sea** at Kapiolani Boulevard next door to Ala Moana Center, which represents outstanding work by craftsmen from all over the United States. . . Another bright star of the arts and crafts scene is **The Foundry,** 899 Waimanu St., which actually was once a working foundry. The central gallery area displays works by local artists and craftsmen; the surroundings include a ceramic studio, jewelry workshop, and studios for sculpturing and woodcarving. Visitors are invited to watch the craftsmen at work. . . **Gallery Hawaii** has a showcase in the Hyatt Regency Hotel, another right in the International Market Place, and both specialize in international art pieces. Graphics by Chagall, Picasso, and the like, as well as originals . . . **The Downtown Gallery, Ltd.,** 125 Merchant St., concentrates on island artists, with two floors devoted to their works: paintings, sculpture, batik paintings, drawings, etc. Downstairs is an international print gallery. . . Up at the Kahala Hilton Hotel is

Bernard Hurtig's **Oriental Treasures and Points West,** a collector's haven for fine antiques and contemporary works of art and jewelry... **Gima's** in Ala Moana Center specializes in paintings, prints, and sculpture by local artists. Note the large selection of original ceramic work and handcrafted jewelry... **The Hand and Eye** in Manoa Marketplace, just above the University of Hawaii, is the place to catch craft exhibits and to see some outstanding contemporary works in jewelry, macramé, pottery, and the like ... Well worth a stop as you travel around the island of Oahu is **Punaluu Gallery,** 53-352 Kamehameha Hwy. in Punaluu, which features only original works, by top island artists like Peter Hayward as well as lesser known fine artists, with prices beginning at very little and going way up.

MUSIC: There's more to Hawaiian music than the ukelele and the old island songs. Much more, for Hawaii is a music-minded community. The local people flock to the concerts of the great orchestras and soloists who play engagements here en route to the Orient (or vice versa), and take great pride in their own splendid **Honolulu Symphony Orchestra.** Since it plays over 100 concerts a year throughout the island chain, including summer concerts under the stars at the Waikiki Shell, you will probably get a chance to hear it.

If you're in Honolulu in the spring you may get to see the yearly **Opera Festival** at Neil S. Blaisdell Concert Hall. World-renowned opera stars sing with local choruses, under the auspices of the Honolulu Symphony Society.

DANCE: Hawaii's unique contribution to the art of the dance is, of course, the hula, and it is much more than just an entertainment for tourists. At one time it was a dance of spiritual significance. As you travel through the islands you will become aware of the importance the natives placed on the dance of Laka, the goddess of hula and the sister of the volcano goddess, Pele. You can still see the remains of a *heiau* on the Na Pali Cliffs of Kauai, to which devotees from all over Hawaii—men (who were the original hula dancers) as well as women—came to be trained in the *meles,* chants, and dances sacred to **Laka.**

Seeing the hula danced in Hawaii is always pleasant, if not always completely authentic. You should plan to see the **Kodak Hawaii Hula Show,** which is a good, solid presentation of Hawaiian dance and which, besides, is free. It is presented Tuesday and Friday mornings at 10 in Queen Kapiolani Park. Another free hula show is presented every Sunday morning at 9:30 at the Ala Moana Shopping Center. That's the **Young People's Hula Show,** and the adorable performers start at the age of about 5. When school's out, there are also shows on Tuesdays and Thursdays at 2 p.m. Check the tourist papers for exact times of dance shows at **King's Alley** and **Pearlridge Shopping Center,** both free. The free show in front of the **Reef Hotel** every Sunday night at 8 is always fun.

If you have a yen to learn the dance yourself, that can usually be arranged. Perhaps your own hotel will be giving hula classes, and there are often series of classes given by the city's Department of Parks and Recreation. Check the local papers for exact dates. There's usually a small admission charge.

But if you haven't got time for concentrated learning, at least observe the hula dancer carefully. You're supposed to keep your eyes on the hands, which tell the story, but you might be distracted by the wind-blown grass skirts (actually made of ti leaves), the flashing slit-bamboo rods used to beat out a tattoo, the feathered gourds *(uliuli)* that sound like maracas, the clatter of koa wood sticks against each other or the click of smooth stones *(iliili)*. And remember, if you see any really violent hula dancing, it's probably Tahitian, definitely not Hawaiian. For the Hawaiian hula is smooth as the trade winds, graceful as the swaying palms.

MOVIES: The latest Hollywood movies and the top films by international directors both draw big crowds in Honolulu. You can see them at various theaters in Waikiki and elsewhere in Honolulu, but you can also catch a Japanese movie, a Chinese, or maybe even a Filipino or Korean one—and you probably can't do *that* back home. Japanese films are shown at the **Nippon** and **Toyo** theaters; the **Liberty** theater, downtown, screens Chinese flicks; and there are quite a few small movie theaters in family neighborhoods that show Filipino and Korean films regularly. The entertainment pages of the Honolulu newspapers will provide the data. Experimental filmmaking is on the rise in Honolulu, especially at the University of Hawaii, and small, informal film screenings are announced periodically.

THE UNIVERSITY OF HAWAII: Pride of Hawaii's nine-campus public system of higher education, the University of Hawaii at Manoa is well worth your visit—not only for a theatrical presentation or a concert or an experimental film or a presentation of Asian folk dancing, but to see the campus itself.

Located in the lush, tropical Manoa Valley, with the mountains as a backdrop, the campus is just a short drive or bus ride from Waikiki, where a number of university students live. Originally a small, land-grant agricultural college, the university has grown the way everything in Hawaii has since statehood. It's now become an important center of higher learning for some 21,500 students, many from far beyond the islands. The campus itself is a flower garden, art is prevalent everywhere, and the buildings are beautiful.

There are no guided tours of the university, but visitors are welcome to explore the campus. Maps and directions for self-guided tours are available at the University Relations Office (Hawaii Hall, Room 2). If you're an art enthusiast, be sure to see Jean Charlot's two-story murals of the history of the island in Bachman Hall. There are other important murals by island artists at Bilger and Keller Halls and in the Music Building; good changing art exhibitions at the Campus Center, the gallery in the Art Building, as well as occasional exhibits at Jefferson Hall. For nature lovers, rare varieties of tropical plants and trees are everywhere. But for me, the most interesting sights of the university are the students, especially the ones in native costume who are studying at the **East-West Center.** This important institute accepts graduate students from both Asia and the mainland, trains them in each others' cultures, and then sends them on field work to the U.S. or Asia. Free tours are given Monday through Thursday at 1:30, starting at Thomas Jefferson Hall (phone 948-7702 for a reservation).

Iolani Palace

Chapter VI

HONOLULU AFTER DARK

WE HAVE HEARD IT rumored that there really are visitors to Honolulu who have dinner early, watch TV in their hotel rooms, and go to bed at 10 p.m. But we strongly suspect these are only rumors. For the streets of Waikiki are thronged at night, the bars and clubs are jammed to the gills, and there's so much to do once the lights go on over the city that it seems a shame to waste time resting (you can always do that during the daytime on the beach). On a night out in Honolulu you might catch anyone from Danny Kaleikini to Don Ho to Sammy Davis, Jr. You could see a hula show or a Tahitian revue, hear some "Hawaiian mod" sounds, drink beer with the kids at the university while the stereo rocks the tables, look in on the disco scene, or sit at a quiet oceanside garden and watch the sun set over the Pacific with someone you love. You may spend a few dollars, or you may have to go all out and blow the budget for the big-time shows. Happily, though, the cost of nightlife is much cheaper here than, say, in New York or Las Vegas. And there's plenty of it.

The Name Entertainers

Note: Because nightclub entertainers have a way of moving around a bit, it's always wise to check the local tourist papers and phone ahead to get details on prices before going to a show. Be sure to check the papers for coupons and discount deals. On a recent off-month, we found $25 shows being advertised for as low as $5.

The **Danny Kaleikini** show is practically an institution in Hawaii, as much a part of the scene as Diamond Head or Waikiki Beach. Danny is the star attraction up at the **Hala Terrace** of the Kahala Hilton Hotel. A one-man show in himself (he sings, dances, and plays drums, ukelele, and nose flute), Danny presides over a talented company of Hawaiian musicians and singers. He exudes charm, warmth, and genuine old-fashioned aloha. The Hala Terrace is set against a backdrop of particularly romantic sea and sky, and it's great for those hand-holding evenings. Cover charge is $6, dinner about $25 for the 9 p.m. dinner show. At the 11 p.m. show, $14 includes cover charge, two drinks, tax, and tip. Reservations: 734-2211.

After (or during) dinner, one of the best spots in town is the elegant **Monarch Room** of the Royal Hawaiian Hotel, where there is always a beautiful show headlined by a top entertainer. On my last visit the star was **Marlene Sai,** one of Hawaii's most renowned singers, assisted by an excellent hula troupe, the Ladies and Men of Na Kamalani. There was a $6 cover charge for the 9 p.m. dinner show, with dinners priced at $16; or you could see the show and have two cocktails for $13, and do the same at the 11 p.m. cocktail show. Reservations for the Monarch Room: 923-7311.

It will cost you about $25 to see **Don Ho,** Hawaii's best-known entertainer, in his lavish home at the **Polynesian Palace** at the Cinerama Reef Towers Hotel, 227 Lewers St. That price, for the 8 p.m. show, includes a prime-ribs buffet dinner and drink, tax, and gratuities. (At 11, the tab for the show, two drinks, tax, and tip is $15). But whether it's worth the tariff is strictly a matter of opinion. Lots of people have been disappointed in Don lately, since he sings very few numbers and spends most of the time making not-so-subtle innuendos to the adoring grandmothers in the audience. Still, he's very popular, and some people wouldn't consider their trip to Hawaii complete without seeing him. The phone for reservations is 923-3111.

One of the most "in" places in town, right off the entrance to the posh Hyatt Regency Waikiki, is **Trappers,** a gleaming, plush example of the decorator's art and the home of Waikiki's No. 1 jazz singer, **Jimmy Borges.** It is also a regular hangout for visiting celebrities who love to drop in and join Borges for a guest appearance. Trappers, which boasts the largest bar in town, is open from 4:30 p.m. to 2 a.m. and features Happy Hour prices and sophisticated piano sounds during the cocktail and early-evening hours.

Dick Jensen, one of the big names in Hawaiian popular music, holds forth every night but Sunday at the Hula Hut on Beach Walk. Four dancers and an orchestra provide the backup. Come for the 9 p.m. dinner show at $22.50 or the 11 o'clock cocktail show at $14. Reservations: 923-2988.

Nationally acclaimed TV and cabaret star **Jim Nabors** does a fast-paced Polynesian review nightly except Saturday at the Hilton Hawaiian Village Dome. Jim makes his home in Hawaii now and has become an instant kamaaina. Price for the 8 p.m. (food from 6:30 on) dinner show is $30, half-price for kids under 12. You can opt for just the show at $15, which is also the price of the 10:30 cocktail show. Reservations: 947-2607.

Talented local boys **Keola** and **Kapono Beamer** make beautiful music at the Cinerama Reef's Ocean Showroom at 9 and 11 p.m. Tuesday through Saturday. Wonderful standup comic **Andy Bumatai** shares the billing. The cover is $4.50; two-drink minimum.

The virtuoso of the ukelele—in his hands it truly sounds like a classical instrument—is **Herb Ohta**, who makes the rounds. Look for him.

Hawaiian and Polynesian Revues

Want to catch a great Polynesian show and a great buffet dinner at the same time? "Tavana's Polynesian Spectacular," one of the most professional in the islands, lets out all the stops. The sensational Tahitian shimmy, the gentle Maori stick dances, the heart-stopping Samoan fire dance, and of course the languid Hawaiian hulas are performed by top artists. They're on twice nightly in the lovely **Banyan Court** of the Moana Hotel, and while you're watching the fireworks on stage you can feast on a bountiful buffet for an all-inclusive tab of $24.95 per person, $15.90 for children under 12. Cocktails and show only runs $17.50 per person, $11.50 for children under 12. For reservations, phone 922-3111.

Another top Polynesian show can be found at the **Hawaiian Hut** of the Ala Moana Hotel. That's "Kalo's South Seas Revue," featuring, again, the dances of Tahiti, Samoa, and the Maori, all done with great style by highly skilled artists. Also featured is an elaborate prime-ribs buffet, which includes an exotic drink along with the prime ribs and Southern-fried chicken. Two shows a night, 6:30 and 9:30 p.m.; the all-inclusive tab is $23. Or just have a drink and watch the show for $13.50. Reservations: 941-5205.

Al Harrington, who used to play Ben Kokua of **Hawaii 5-0**, now has his own extravaganza, "The Al Harrington Polynesian Experience." A big show with a big cast, it plays Sunday through Friday at 8:30 p.m. (dinner) and 11 p.m. (cocktails only) at

House of Lono, 1270 Ala Moana Blvd. Have dinner, ($25), or cocktail and show ($12.50). Reservations: 524-6711.

Free Shows

If you'd like a free show for a change—and who wouldn't?—I can recommend several. Every Sunday, beginning about 8 p.m., there's an informal hula show on the beach in front of the **Reef Hotel**. The performers are all talented amateurs and the show never winds down until about 9:30 or 10. At the **Fountain Mall Stage** of the Ilikai, you can hear authentic songs and *meles* performed by the Lilikoi Sisters. Their music is preceded by a short torchlighting ceremony at 6:30 p.m., and the ladies continue to make lovely music until 8. You can frequently watch singers and dancers perform at the Lewers/Kalakaua corner of the Royal Hawaiian Center; most events take place from 6:30 to 8:30 p.m.

A Filipino Show

One of Hawaii's longtime favorite entertainments, "A Night in the Philippines," is still holding forth in the **Monarch Room** of the Royal Hawaiian Hotel on Monday night. A buffet of unusual Filipino dishes begins at 6:30, and at 8 the Pearl of the Orient group provides a colorful program of native songs and dances. Adults, $24.50; children under 12, $22.50. For reservations call 923-7311.

For Romance

It's hard to imagine a more romantic spot in Waikiki than the spectacular **Hanohano Room** in the Sheraton Waikiki Hotel. The view is nonstop from Diamond Head to Pearl Harbor, the sunset is unforgettable, and, from 9 on, you can listen and dance to the "hot and sweet" sounds of trombonist Trummy Young while you're having dinner. Fine for just a drink.

La Ronde, the revolving restaurant atop the Ala Moana Building, has glorious views of Honolulu, plus soft background music by which to dine and drink.

From the top of the world to the bottom of the sea you go, and right into **Davy Jones Locker II**, "Under the Pool" at the Outrigger Hotel. This one is really far-out. Imagine, if you can, being in a bubble at the bottom of the ocean. The grotto-like entrance has fish tanks lining the wall, but the biggest fish tank is over the bar; it's the underside of the hotel's swimming pool.

You may be so intrigued by the view that you won't even bother watching the entertainment, but for what it's worth, various local acts do perform here. The entrance, of course, is right under the pool.

And the cozy and rustic **Blue Dolphin Room,** overlooking the pool at the Outrigger Hotel, offers music with no cover or minimum every night of the week. It's known for old-style Hawaiian music, and there's a dinner show every night at 9. Breakfast, lunch, and snacks are also served right on the beach, poolside, every day.

Where the Discos Are

The disco craze has spread just about everywhere, and Honolulu has gotten right into the action. To join the local fanatics, you can make the scene at places like **Spats** at the Hyatt Regency Hotel (no cover, no minimum); D.B.G.'s Dance Menagerie in the Waikiki Beachcomber Hotel ($1 cover, including one drink); the **Infinity Room** of the Sheraton Waikiki Hotel ($1 cover, more for special engagements); live entertainment between 1 and 4 a.m.) You might be tempted to jump in for a swim at the **Atlantis Disco,** which overlooks the giant Oceanarium at the Pacific Beach Hotel ($3 cover charge), but keep dancing. Perhaps the prettiest spot is the semiprivate club **Anabelle's** at the Top of the Ilikai, 30 stories up, from which you can see the glittering kaleidoscope of the city lights below. You can dance from 5 p.m. to 4 the next morning; the $3 cover charge does not begin until 9 p.m. And **Hula's Bar and Lei Stand** on Kalimouku Street, just across from the Kuhio Theatre, may look like a bit of Old Hawaii, but is, instead, a "Megasexual Disco" where you never can tell who will meet who.

Surfer

Chapter VII

A HONOLULU SHOPPING BONANZA

ASK ANYONE WHO'S BEEN there: Honolulu is a great place to shop. In fact, if you walk along Kalakaua Avenue any afternoon or evening, it sometimes seems that the tourists are doing nothing else. For even though there's no favorable exchange rate here (as in Europe) or duty-free shopping (as in the Virgin Islands), and prices are just about what you'd expect to pay back home, there are so many good buys in so many interesting things that everybody gets caught up in the shopping fever. New shopping complexes are blossoming all over Honolulu, with scads of temptations right in or very near Waikiki. Indulge and enjoy yourself—it can't be helped.

Spend an hour or two in the shops that line Kalakaua Avenue, in the Ala Moana Shopping Center, in the International Market Place, and in the hotel gift shops, and you'll have a pretty good idea of the things that everybody wants to bring back from the islands. Clothing is undoubtedly the most popular item—island resort wear in bright, bold Hawaiian prints, the colors of the sun and the tropical landscape. And then there are fragrant, flowery island perfumes; the carved tikis, figures of the Hawaiian gods; calabashes; carved woods; tapas, bark cloth printed with primitive religious symbols; dolls with grass skirts; ukeleles; shell necklaces and other fanciful island jewelry. And the food— macadamia nuts, Hawaiian jams, coconut syrup, Kona coffee— not to mention the pineapple and coconuts that you'll want to have or send back home. All these are typical of the islands and they are on sale everywhere.

Souvenirs

You will, of course, have to buy dozens of souvenirs—small, inexpensive gifts for a dollar or two, to bring to all the relatives and neighbors back home. I've found the best prices for these items—key chains, letter-openers, money clips, and the like, all decorated with some Hawaiian symbol or figure, as well as Hawaiian perfumes—are at the **ABC** discount stores, which are found everywhere in Waikiki (there's a new one at the corner of Kuhio and Kanekapolei). Other good places where you can pick up scads of these items are the **Woolworth's** on Kalakaua Avenue and Ala Moana Shopping Center, **Stewart's Pharmacy** on Kalakaua, **Long's Drugstore** in Ala Moana, and the Hawaiian gift shop at **Sears** in Ala Moana.

Clothing

Could you possibly come back from Hawaii without at least *one* muumuu or aloha shirt or bathing suit? Unthinkable! Let me first, however, tell the ladies a little bit about the Hawaiian fashion scene. Although every kind of contemporary fashion idea has hit Hawaii, I still think the most beautiful Hawaiian dresses are the graceful full-length muumuus that Hawaiian women have been wearing for centuries. You'll find them perfect for evening, and for daytime there are many lovely "shorty muus" as well as versions of the Chinese cheongsam. Men, of course, will want aloha shirts—boldly printed and cut fuller than ordinary men's sport shirts, since they are designed to be worn outside the trousers. You can find Hawaiian clothing just about anywhere, but I'll give you a few hints on my own special favorites, where I feel the quality is the best for the money.

After a while, so many of the clothing shops on Kalakaua begin to look like repititions of each other. One place where you won't run into this mass-production syndrome is **Ludi's of Waikiki,** with shops in the International Market Place (at Strawberry Circus), and merchandise on sale in several other stores. The prints are brilliant, the designs both demure and daring at the same time. Many things in junior sizes and prices that range from about $25 to $50 for women's dresses. The **Calabash House,** 2358 Kalakaua Ave., is another shop with distinctive clothing, prices starting at about $21 for women's muumuus, $8.95 for men's aloha shirts. There's no beating the quality and brilliant styling, for men and women, at **Andrade's** in the Royal

Hawaiian Hotel, also at Ala Moana Shopping Center, Kahala Mall, and Hyatt Regency Hotel, among many other locations.

Mary Jane's Country Store in the International Market Place has scads of long dresses from South America in natural cotton, heavily embroidered, for $50—plus crocheted stretch bikinis and gauze bare-midriff tops from India, hand-embroidered with pansies.

Other names to remember for top resort fashions as you make your way around town: **Liberty House,** one of the city's biggest department stores, with branches on Kalakaua, at Ala Moana Center, and elsewhere around town and on the other islands; **Watumull's,** with attractive branches in the Ala Moana Shopping Center, the Sheraton Waikiki Hotel, the Holiday Inn, and the Princess Kaiulani Hotel, among others; **Aloha Fashions,** right on Kalakaua (2368), at 224 Lewers St., and in the Hilton Hawaiian Village Hotel; and **McInerny's,** in the Royal Hawaiian Center and Kahala Mall. **Sears** at Ala Moana has one of the best-priced Hawaiian-wear sections anywhere; and prices are also quite low at **Holiday Mart,** a discount department store near Ala Moana Center, at 801 Kaheka St.

The boutique craze has hit Honolulu, too, and although most of the shops in the tourist areas feature Hawaiian resort wear, a few are cropping up here and there that could be straight out of New York or London or even Paris. Take, for example, **Fabrications,** at Kilohana Square, where designer-artists Janet and Jeffrey Berman create custom-made clothes. Their fashions are timeless, with simple classic lines, and their fabrics, ranging from soft georgette crepes to Swiss cotton jerseys, are exquisite. I fell in love with a long, sleeveless fluid dress in a soft-pink Trevira, with a graceful cowl neckline; a short jacket in a harmonizing print bound in the dress fabric had its edges finished in a manner that made them "ripple." It could have come from a Paris collection but the price was $185. There's also silver and costume jewelry, mostly items designed to accessorize a particular outfit.

The very posh **Carol & Mary** shops (there are seven of them, the largest at Ala Moana Center) carry the better Polynesian lines and a large selection of beautiful sportswear from mainland designers. They also carry European and American couture designer fashions, accessories, children's clothing, and crystal and china giftware.

King's Alley

As much fun to browse through as to shop at, King's Alley, at the corner of Koa and Kaiulani Avenues, recaptures the flavor of Hawaii's 19th-century Monarchy period with its cobblestone streets and classic architecture. You'll sense the European feeling as soon as you pass through the gate and see the royal guard standing in his kiosk, often posing for pictures; there's a changing-of-the-guard ceremony nightly at 6:15. The tiny shops might suggest Victorian London at first glance, but their wares are definitely international, with a smattering of Polynesia. Shop and poke around as much as you like; I'll simply point out a few of my favorites en route. Stop in at **Erida's,** which specializes in music boxes, glorious both to look at and listen to. . . **Butik Copenhagen** is a neat Scandinavian shop full of imports from all the Scandinavian countries—Danish jewelry, Royal Copenhagen porcelain and Christmas plates, Swedish wooden toys and puzzles that none of your friends, children, nieces, or nephews could possibly have. . . . You can get plenty of seashell jewelry and loose shells at **The Sea Shell.** . . . For resortwear, the boutiques include **Jacqueline's Bikini Shop** (the owner is the wife of one of Hawaii's most popular entertainers, Danny Kaleikini) for bikinis plus beautiful clothing, **Liberty House,** and **Harriet's Custom Made Ready to Wear** (select your material and your style and they make up garments to your size in 24 to 48 hours.) . . . **Mark Christopher** is King's Alley's largest shop. Here you'll find Hawaiian-made coral jewelry in gold rings and accessories (hand-carved rings from $30); Hawaiian fabrics in tapa prints, island floral designs, and hand-screened panels; gifts from Hong Kong in gem trees of jade and lapis, and pewter vases decorated with brass; even scrimshaw whale's teeth, the folk art of Hawaii's past, in jewelry and collectors' items. . . . **The Captain's Cargo** specializes in costume and fine jewelry from all parts of the world and Polynesian souvenir gifts from Pacific

While you're here, you can see a full-leng.. novie or take free hula lessons and watch a show, Wednesday and Friday mornings at 10; or have a glass of ale and a snack at the English pub **Rose and Crown.**

Hemmeter Center

Undoubtedly one of Honolulu's most outstanding attractions, Hemmeter Center houses not only the exquisite Hyatt Regency-Waikiki, that skyscraper on Kalakaua Avenue between Kaiulani and Ulunui Avenues, but an incredibly beautiful shopping complex, glistening with fountains, waterfalls, superb metal sculptures, massive plantings—and all in an elegant Hawaiian Monarchy setting. Three tiers of shops are reached by staircase or escalator. You'll recognize some familiar names here: several Mark Christopher stores, including the very special **Christopher II,** as well as branches of **Liberty House, Andrade's, The Royal Peddler, Maggie's International,** and many others.

Art lovers and collectors must stop in to see **Gallery Hawaii** in the Great Hall. A collection of quality sculptures and paintings is highlighted by the splendid sculptural fountains of Jan de Bovenkamp. They begin at $2,000 and go up, but they are exclusives in Hawaii—and they can be shipped anywhere. . . . **Souleiado** specializes in accessories, including shoes, from France and Spain. . . . **Joan René,** a boutique featuring luxurious resort and loungewear, and **Bugatti Leather** are two elegant shops that are definitely not for the timid purse. . . . You'll find plenty of jade jewelry at **House of Jade,** and all three kinds of coral—pink, black, and gold—in exquisite gold settings at **The Coral Grotto.**

Hemmeter Center is ideal for after-dinner walking and browsing, and, obligingly, it stays open from 9 a.m. until 11 p.m.

Waikiki Shopping Plaza

One expects to find open-air, palm-tree-lined shopping plazas in Waikiki, with booths selling grass skirts and coconuts; what one does not expect is a completely enclosed, several-storied building sporting the finest in European and mainland clothing and accessories. Yet that is basically what you'll find at the new **Waikiki Shopping Plaza** at 2250 Kalakaua Ave., corner of Seaside. From the ethnic snackshops on the lowest level to the luxurious international restaurants on the top floor (Japanese, Chinese, Greek, etc.), this new complex is an international adventure.

Some of the outstanding shops here include European fashion favorites like **Courrèges, Roberta di Camerino, Bally of Switzerland, St. Tropez** (for French jeans), **Paris Shops,** and, for tobacco, **Jacques Tabac;** Oriental outposts like **Yokohama Okadaia** for Japanese folk crafts (with many handmade Japanese paper products), **Asia Arts and Treasures, Cathay Kai** for fine Chinese objects, and **Okada** for men's and women's clothing from Japan. For island-flavored clothing and souvenirs, check out **Polynesian Fair** and **Mele Hawaii.** I saw some handsome crocheted dresses for $65 at **Lucille of Waikiki,** created by a Bangkok boutique, and elegantly tailored women's clothes at **KA Designs** and **Paradox. Janice's Place** has lots of cute keiki togs. The most artistic entrees here are **Ling's Things, A Gallery Unique,** showing driftwood tables, metal plaques, charming glass sculptures; and **Conversation Piece,** a showcase and market for island craftspeople, with wonderful creations in glass, wood, ceramics, and soft sculpture.

You can use the elevators here, but it's more fun to ride the escalators all the way to the top, admiring Bruce Hopper's five-story fountain with its dancing waters and changing colors as you go up. There's a large electronic game room for those who like that sort of thing on the top level. And free evening shows by entertainers like Eddie Kekula are often presented on the ground level.

Royal Hawaiian Center

The first phase of the new, $40-million Royal Hawaiian Center, which covers three entire blocks of Kalakaua Avenue in front of the Royal Hawaiian and Sheraton Waikiki Hotels, had just opened at the time of my last visit. By the time the last hard-hats have left, the complex should be a stunner (despite its heavy emphasis on concrete), especially when the projected Roof Garden in the Diamond Head building is open. Promised are a multitude of gourmet food kiosks, a 250-seat cafe, a wine bar, a multimedia film by award-winning filmmaker Saul Bass, and holographic and laser sculptures as well as a dancing light show created by the outstanding holographic sculptor Peter Nicholson.

Meanwhile, I'll concentrate on the shops that are already there. **McInerny's** is a must; in business in Hawaii since 1850, it has opened its flagship store here, with particular excitement in the island fashion and gift departments on the first floor, the Hermès Boutique (for those famous French scarves and hand-made leather bags) on the second, and the special Sports Fashion Boutique. . . . I also like **Butik Copenhagen** (this is the largest of their several stores with, in this shop only, Norwegian and Icelandic wool jackets, nondyed, that start at about $98, in addition to Hummel figurines, fine china (Royal Copenhagen, Bing and Grondal), and the like. . . . You'll want all the buttery-soft leather items in **Raku Leather:** attaché cases, backgammon sets, and beautiful bags. . . . **Camelot East** has intriguing folk crafts from the People's Republic of China. . . . **The Hawaii Country Store,** first floor, corner of Lewers, is a neat place for gifts and knicknacks; it also has a small restaurant for sandwiches and plate lunches, and a tiny cafe corner, fine for sipping a cappuccino or espresso.

Every Monday, Wednesday, and Friday from 6:30 to 8:30 p.m. there's free Hawaiian-style entertainment in the courtyard at the corner of Lewers and Kalakaua.

Rainbow Promenade

A few blocks further along Kalakaua you come to Rainbow Promenade at 2115, a largely Japanese vertical shopping center that is mainly occupied by **Hawaii Mitsuokoshi,** a leading department store chain out of Tokyo. While many of the customers are Japanese, there's plenty for every taste. The first floor is given over to such elegant names as Christian Dior, Dunhill, and Tiffany; scattered throughout the other floors are serendipitous finds like **Ryowa** for Indian arts and crafts; **Peony Arts,** which calls itself "the only Chinese linen store in Hawaii" and has exquisite embroidery and lacework; **Boutique Il Mondo,** which features exquisite bags and umbrellas bearing the Roberta di Camerino label; and **Saitoh,** where you can pick up a fur wrap or two. If you are interested in collecting netsukes (from $37.50 on up to about $2500) or superior ivory carvings, have a look at the beautiful works at **Takenoya Arts,** a Tokyo company that is the oldest maker and supplier of ivory carvings in Japan.

The fifth floor has another of those electronic game rooms, including a Taito Little Western area, which seems totally out of place in this atmosphere. But the half-dozen Japanese restaurants on the sixth floor (I've told you about some in Chapter IV), help restore the Oriental equilibrium.

Rainbow Bazaar

Hop over to the Rainbow Bazaar at the Hilton Hawaiian Village Hotel now (take bus 8 from Kalakaua or Ala Moana Center) for another quick trip to the Orient. Can you picture cobblestone alleys in Hong Kong, or a Japanese pagoda with an arched bridge leading into a silk shop? And tinkly Oriental music playing in the background most of the day? These are some of the sights and sounds of this marketplace for artifacts and treasures of the Pacific cultures. The formal entrance to these intriguing shops, some gold-tinted and unmistakably Thai, others more generally South Pacific, is through a Chinese "moon gate" guarded by two imposing Foo dogs. There are branches of the well-known Honolulu stores here, like **Liberty House,** but let's look first at some of the more foreign ones.

Beautiful arts and crafts from mainland China are displayed at **Camelot East.** Carved cork pictures, embroideries, hand brush paintings, and other delicate Chinese arts are reasonably priced.

You enter a small world of imports at **Maggie's International:** wall hangings from Colombia, papier mâché from India, leathers from Italy and Spain, and distinctive llama and alpaca rugs from Peru vie for attention here; unusual and elegant clothing, too. . . . Exquisite embroidered blouses, capiz shell chandeliers, and Tiffany-type lampshades are all very well priced at **Philippine Treasures. . . .** The Thai princess rings at **AA Jewelry and Gifts** are lovely, made in the shape of the crown of the princess of Siam, in multicolored precious stones.

Most Rainbow Bazaar shops are open seven days a week and every night. Whenever you come, you can stop in for a snack or a special meal. For quickies, there's **Banyan Snack** (Chinese and Japanese lunches around $2.50), the **Sea Food Bar,** and the **Village Parlor** for ice cream. For a more elaborate meal, try the charming **Benihana of Tokyo;** see Chapter IV for details.

Woodcarvings and Jewels

Since the days of the Polynesians, woodcarving has been a highly respected art in Hawaii. You'll find monkeypod and koa carvings all over town, but some of the very best are to be had at **Blair's;** considering the quality of the work, the fact that each piece is shaped by hand and guaranteed, the prices are eminently fair. Gift items start under $5, and go to $50 and over. Branches of **Blair's** are at the Outrigger and Outrigger East hotels, and in Kona, Hawaii. Free tours are sometimes offered at the factory at 404 Ward St. (phone 536-4907), which also offers seconds at substantial savings, as well as discounts on their regular merchandise.

There are, of course, trinkets of "Hawaiian jewelry" to be found for a few dollars in every souvenir shop in the islands. But for the real thing—pink and black coral culled from Hawaiian seas, jade and ivory from the Orient, as well as other precious stones—see the elegant **Pex of Hawaii** jewelry shops. The designs are original and almost everything is handmade. At the Pex Bijou Royale, for example, in the lobby of the Sheraton Waikiki

Hotel, you'll find superb jade pendants and rings in Oriental motifs for men and women, and, for the collectors in the crowd, ivory and semiprecious stone figurines. Pex's outpost at the Royal Hawaiian is **La Galerie Originale,** with a magnificent collection of jewelry, antique jade, ivories, and objets d'art. You'll find other branches of Pex at the Moana, Princess Kaiulani, and Kahala Hilton hotels, and on the island of Hawaii at the Kona Hilton.

Ala Moana Shopping Center

Ala Moana is a shopping center for those who hate shopping centers. It's 50 acres of island architecture at its best, laced with pools and gardens, plantings and sculptures, fountains and wide shady malls. In between are the shops—and what shops! An international array from East and West, as dazzling a selection of goods as can be found anywhere, in as wide a price range as possible, and a fascinating barometer of how far the 50th state has come into the modern world of merchandising.

All the big Hawaiian names are here: **Sears** has an attractive store with very well-priced selections in souvenirs and resortwear, as does **J. C. Penney.** You'll find excellent clothing selections at **Watumull, McInerny,** and **Carol & Mary.** Join the throngs of local citizens who flock to the Japanese department stores like **Shirokiya** and **Hotei-Ya.** And while you're still in the mood for the exotic, look in at **India,** as well as **Imports International,** with vast quantities of silken saris, dresses, bedspreads, Indian jewelry. **The Swiss Colony** has a tempting selection of gourmet foods and liquors, as well as Danish strawberry wine, imported candies and cheeses, exotic teas, Hawaiian coffees, European salamis. **Musahiya** sells beautiful fabrics by the yard; **Fiddler's** has imaginative, decorative hardware accessories that would make intriguing gifts (note their Oriental hardware, especially); and **Hopaco Stationers** has all sorts of tasteful gifts, Hawaiian specialties, and stationery. At the **Hale Kukui Candle Shop** you'll find tiki gods and pineapples to burn.

As for food, the restaurants on Ala Moana's lower level offer a tasty variety of international goodies, yours to eat indoors or take out and munch on the mall as you watch the crowds go by. **Lyn's Delicatessen** is super for a corned beef on rye, old-fashioned pickles, garlicky hot dogs, and a terrific weeknight steak dinner, with all the trimmings, for around $3.50! **Patti's Chinese Kitchen,** large and comfy, serves its delicious hot plates (none higher than $2.95) cafeteria-style to hungry and happy throngs. Its manapua (dumplings) selection is irresistible. Next door is **Bella Italia,** fragrant with cheeses and salamis, and low-priced meals of spaghetti, meatballs, and the like. **La Cocina,** the only Mexican restaurant at Ala Moana, has a takeout counter for quick servings of tortillas, tostadas, et al., plus an attractive Mexican dining room where the food is fresh and tasty, portions huge, and the prices just right: around $5 for a complete dinner. Cheers for **The Haven,** which offers attractive seating, natural-type sandwiches on nine-grain bread, lots of good salads, meat sandwiches, and intriguing desserts. And health-food freaks will be well contented with the huge vegetable sandwiches, juices, and smoothies at **Vim and Vigor.** A favorite next door at 1441 Kapiolani, in the Ala Moana Building, is **Heidi's,** which adds a touch of the German gourmet with king-size sandwiches of sausages and wursts (most under $3), delicious homemade breads, and European-style desserts. There are just about five red-checkered tables to sit at, but you can take everything out, and buy some of the breads to take home, too.

To reach Ala Moana from Waikiki, take either bus 8 or bus 19 from Kalakaua Avenue; it's about a 10-minute ride. The Center is open until 9 Monday to Friday; it closes at 5:30 p.m. on Saturday; Sunday hours are 11 to 4. There are acres of parking.

It's difficult to know whether to call **Following Sea** a shop or a crafts gallery, but this striking place at 1441 Kapiolani Blvd., next door to Ala Moana Center, is such a beautiful visual experience that it should not be missed. You'll see no mass-produced tourist junk here; everything is one-of-a-kind, created by outstanding American craftsmen, and truly unusual. With such individualized items, the inventory changes constantly, but you might see, as we did, a group of handblown glass oil lamps in three sizes, priced at $15, $25, and $28. Unusual pillows, paperweights, stained-glass items, carvings, ceramics—all priced from a little to a lot. Following Sea is open the same hours as the shops at Ala Moana Center. A new Following Sea has recently opened at the Waikiki Trade Center, corner of Kuhio and Seaside Avenues.

Kilohana Square

While shopping centers become bigger and more comprehensive, smaller and more specialized centers—with charisma—are also developing. Such a one is Kilohana Square, where the accent is on arts and crafts, antiques, and boutiques. Located in the 1000 block on Kapahulu Avenue, just one block makai of the H-1 Freeway, Kilohana is a square built around a parking lot and looking very much the way buildings used to look in downtown Honolulu a century ago. Most of the shops spill out into the street, but do have a look inside; the best things are usually there. The **Carriage House** has antique furniture, porcelain, glass, and Orientalia. . . . **The Trunk** specializes in clothes for "big, beautiful women from size 16 up to size 52"—muumuus, blouses, dresses, pantsuits, and bathing suits (but no bikinis). . . . **Something Special,** decorated in keeping with the nostalgia craze, has beautiful plants, housewares like bamboo utensils and Oriental dishes, toys from all over the world, greeting cards, and the largest collection of baskets from mainland China in the islands. . . . **Fabrications** is a lovely specialty shop with yarns of all types for those who knit, crochet, macramé, or weave. In the adjoining boutique, described earlier in this chapter, you'll find a smashing line of clothing designed by owners Jan and Jeff Berman (made in their upstairs studio), plus accessories gathered from around the world to complement the clothes. . . . **Mazy Daze** has some very cute clothes and playthings for children.

Ward Warehouse

Another shopping center with loads of charisma is Ward Warehouse, at Ward Avenue between Auahi Street and Ala Moana, near Kewalo Boat Basin. The artistic level here is surprisingly high. Tucked away in the two-story wooden structures are a bevy of boutiques that are fun to browse through. **Lanai Things,** for example, has wooden swings, net chairs, delightful place settings and napkins, fabric wallhangings. . . . You can pick a bunch of beautiful silk flowers from Japan at **The Extra Dimension.** . . . Contemporary prints and posters are wellpriced at **The Art Board.** . . . Exquisite clothing for women, handcrafted by a lovely lady from Thailand, is available at **Kinnari.** . . . Local craftsmen are represented at both **Exhibit** and **The Artist's Guild**; original creations in pottery, glass, macramé, enamels, etc. would make fine gifts. And the ceramics, stained glass, soft sculptures, carvings, etc., at **Rare Discoveries** are superb examples of the craftsmen's art. A dazzler. . . . Buy some tea or coffee and a big coffee mug at **Coffee, Tea, Or.** . . . ? and have a cup of coffee to drink while you're about it.

Shopping hours at Ward Warehouse are 10 to 6, Mondays and Tuesdays; to 8 on Wednesdays, Thursdays, and Fridays; to 5 on Saturdays; and 11 to 4 on Sundays.

For a fun meal in a funky setting at Ward Warehouse, don't miss **The Old Spaghetti Factory**, laden with outrageous Victorian antiques, and serving meals at mini-prices. **Horatio's** (see Chapter IV) is a great choice for a more elaborate meal.

Kahala Mall

Islanders love to shop at **Kahala Mall**, and you very likely will too. It's an indoor, air-conditioned, fully carpeted suburban shopping center, with none of the frenetic pace of Ala Moana. Besides the big stores you're accustomed to—**J. C. Penney's, Liberty House, Long's Drugs, Carol & Mary, Woolworth's, McInerny**—there is a beautiful **Joseph Magnin** store here, complete with a Gucci boutique. . . . **Nancy Lang Couture Boutique** is a unique shop, with exclusive imports from Mexico, Greece, Malaysia, and accessories from the Philippines and the Marshall islands. They also carry the Malia and Princess Kaiulani muumuus, as well as high-fashion, ready-to-wear clothes from mainland designers. . . . For teens and young career girls, there's trendy **Wildflowers**. . . . And **Paul's Danish Interiors** is a two-level treasure trove of imports from all the Scandinavian countries—furniture, fabrics, tableware, decorative items, and toys might be fun to bring back home for presents. . . . One of my favorite natural food stores is here, too: **Vim and Vigor**, with a great line of healthful goodies. Try their great sandwiches and baked goods, made fresh every day. For beautiful decorative Asian antiques, yards and yards of exquisite Thai silks and Javanese handwaxed batiks, glamorous caftans, and other Asian treasures, see **Fabulous Things, Ltd.**

When it's time for a coffeebreak—or something more substantial—there's **Woolworth's Coffeeshop**, not to mention **Farrell's Ice Cream Parlour Restaurant**, the **Yum Yum Tree**, and **Spindrifter** for a gracious meal, and the **Winter Garden** for tasty Chinese food.

To reach Kahala Mall by car, take the Waialae exit from the Lunalillo Freeway East; it's about a 15-minute drive from Waikiki. Most of the shops are open from 9:30 a.m. until 9 p.m., Monday through Friday; until 5 on Saturday; from 11 a.m. until 4 p.m. on Sunday.

Special: Shopping for Surfers

If you're really serious about surfing, or learning to surf, I'd like to point you in the direction of **Lightning Bolt Unlimited Surf Company** at 1503 Kapiolani Blvd., near the Ala Moana Shopping Center (phone: 941-1502). Any surfer will tell you that in order to learn to surf safely and joyously you need good instruction and a well-constructed board. Many of those for rent at beach stands are warped to the point of being dangerous. Hence the need for a service like the one at Lightning Bolt, which will sell you a board and agree in writing to buy it back when you leave for $35 to $50 less for every week that you've used it. If you want to invest in a board to take home, this is also the place. All boards bear the Lightning Bolt name and are handcrafted to exacting standards. Owner-manager Jack Shipley will be happy to advise you, if he's not off somewhere judging an international surfing meet. All the friendly staff members, in fact, are surfers. Co-owner Gerry Lopez is a local boy who is one of the top-rated surfers in the world.

Store hours will most likely be from 10 to 7, Monday to Friday, until 5 on Saturday, and from 11 to 3 on Sunday.

Pearlridge Shopping Center

Shopping in Honolulu is not only a tourist sport, it looks as if it's getting to be the biggest islander pastime too. Witness the new Pearlridge Shopping Center in Aiea, a multimillion-dollar complex that's even bigger than Ala Moana. Both levels are enclosed, fully air-conditioned, and quiet. Although it's far from the usual tourist area, visitors do find their way up here. Take the H-1 Freeway to the Pearl City exit, about half-an-hour's drive from Waikiki. A devoted shopper could easily spend a whole day here. Pearlridge is that big. You may also be able to take in a free hula show or a cooking class or some other event; the weekend calendar is especially busy. This is a community-minded place where more goes on than just shopping.

You'll see lots of old familiars here, like **J. C. Penney's, Liberty House, India Imports, Joseph Magnin,** and **Thrifty Drug,** to mention a few. Not so familiar is a delightful Japanese department store called **Dai'ei,** which boasts the largest Oriental food department in Hawaii, and is very popular with visitors from Japan as well as with the locals. The second floor is a discount and-then-some store, with excellent values on jewelry and name-brand cameras, stereos, toys, binoculars, etc.

If you have any young shoppers with you, you'll have trouble keeping them out of **Playwell,** one of the two all-toy shops on Oahu, and the **Fernandez Fun Factory,** which abounds in electronic games for the amazement and amusement of young and not-so-young. Kids also love the special section at the **International Kitchens,** with low tables and stools and two TV sets tuned to their favorite kiddie shows.

Pearlridge is open until 9, Monday through Friday. On Saturday, the big stores stay open until 9, while the little ones close at 5:30. Sunday hours are from 11 to 4.

The House of Pearl Chinese restaurant offers hearty, low-priced meals, just fine for filling up hungry families. Hawaii's first (and only) monorail train shuttles back and forth between Phase One and Phase Two all day and evening; the fare is 25¢.

Statue of King Kamehameha I

Chapter VIII

CIRCLING OAHU

THE BEACH WAS BEAUTIFUL, the urban sights of Honolulu were exciting, but there's still more, much more, to see before you leave the island of Oahu. For on the other side of the mountains that border Waikiki is a verdant landscape almost as diverse as the city itself. Here are quiet country towns jostling bustling suburbs that feed commuters into the central city; ruins of old religious *heiaus* where sacrifices were made to the ancient gods near the modern meccas of the surfing set; cliffs thrusting skyward along the shores of velvety beaches where children play and campers set up their tents, not far from an enormous concentration of military muscle; acres of pineapple plantations using the most modern agricultural methods, and places where the taro is still cultivated the way it was in the old days. Hotels here are as peaceful as they should be, picnic spots are around every bend, and the restaurants are scenic attractions in themselves. And, of course, there are the sightseeing centers here, some of the most unique and interesting in the state. You'll have to see Windward **Oahu.**

Travel Choices

Should your time be short, you might want to pick out just one or two of the important sightseeing attractions windward and make a short, direct trip to them; you can take the tunnels carved through the mountains (the **Pali** or the **Wilson**) to get you to places like the **Polynesian Cultural Center** or **Kahuku Sugar Mill** or the **Byodo-In Temple** in less than an hour. But if you have the time, it is eminently rewarding to head out Diamond Head way and circle the island slowly, basking in the omnipresent natural beauty, stopping en route at the places that interest you the most. You must plan on a full day's trip, and it helps enormously if you have a car. Even without one, however, you can make this trip, thanks to Wahiawa-Kaneohe Bus 52, which departs from Ala Moana Center every 15 minutes during most of the day (from 6:15 a.m. to 6 p.m.). Regular bus fare of 50¢ can get you around the island, albeit quite slowly. You might also take a sightseeing limousine, which is easy and comfortable, but if you're on a group tour, you're not free to stay as long as you want in any one place or jump out of the car for a swim whenever you feel like it. Your own wheels promise the most fun; so get yourself a good road map, take the flat rate, and prepare for the memorable adventure that follows.

The Major Sights

We'll begin at Diamond Head Road. Circle around the beautiful residential area here and then get onto Route 72, which will lead you past Koko Head to **Hanauma Bay,** a turquoise beach at the bottom of a volcanic crater. Snorkelers rate this as one of the most beautiful spots on the island. Fish are so tame here that they will eat right out of your hand. Unless you stop here for a swim (or for the day) you'll soon be speeding along a stunningly dramatic coastline where ancient lava cliffs drop down to the surging sea below. But don't speed; slow down to enjoy the beauty. The colors are spectacular, and just ahead is a geyser in the lava called the **Blow Hole.** This is the place to stop the car and lose yourself in the wind and the spray, before you get back to the business of living in the 1980s. Just ahead of you, the island's daring—and expert—surfers are forgetting their problems in the giant waves of **Sandy Beach Makapuu.** You probably won't want to join them, but drive on and join, instead, what will seem like half the island's families at **Sea Life Park.**

Sea Life Park is a great place to take the keikis, and also yourself, for it's a thoroughly entertaining enterprise. Serious scientific research in oceanography goes on here, but what you come for is the fun: a lively show by gregarious porpoises and leaping whales in the Whaler's Cove; demonstrations by men and porpoises in the Ocean Science Theater; a chance to walk three fathoms down and around a glass-enclosed Hawaiian reef full of rare Pacific marine life. You can also have an inexpensive snack or cocktails here, and the Sea Chest has a collection of quality gift items at good prices. The park is open every day including holidays from 9:30 a.m., and the last complete show is held at 3:15 p.m. Admission, subject to change, is $4.50; children 7 to 12, $2.75; children under 7, free. *Note:* Several special excursion tours are available from Waikiki, including

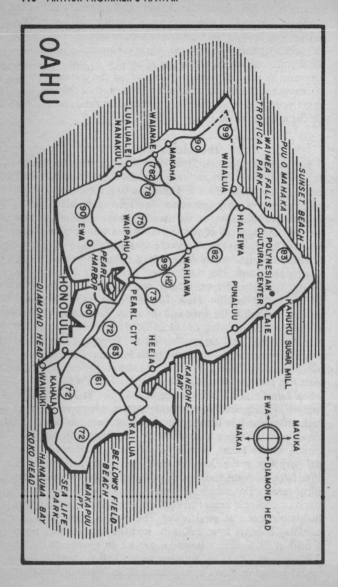

transportation and admission. Sunday evenings a luau is scheduled. Price: $23.50. The phone at the park is 259-7933; in Waikiki, 923-1531.

Back on the highway, the spectacular scenery continues, with beautiful **Bellows Field Beach** (open to the public only on weekends and holidays; other times it's just for the military) coming up on your right. There are lovely pine-tree groves for picnicking. Slow down now, if it's a weekend, for you'll soon be reaching **Pine Grove Village** out under the ironwood trees on Kalanianaole, just across from the entrance to Bellows Air Force Base. Here, local people sell crafts, food, jewelry, clothing, all manner of engaging items at prices considerably lower than those in the Waikiki shops. If you want to see Kailua, which has some good restaurants and a fairly windy beach, turn right on Route 61. If not, continue until the road meets Route 61, drive left to the intersection of Route 83, and turn right. If you're ready for lunch, a stop at **Haiku Gardens** is a peaceful—and scenic—interlude. Continue along 83 until you see Safeway on the right, and then go mauka (left) a short distance to the Gardens at 46-336 Haiku Rd. in Kaneohe.

Haiku Gardens, in fact, is worth a stop even if you're not going to have lunch, since it is situated in ten acres of tropical gardens, some of which the public is free to roam through. If you do have lunch or a drink, ask for a table out on the porch, where it's shady and cool and where you can look out over a lily pond and a grove of bamboo trees as you enjoy a buffet lunch ($5.95) or dinner ($7.50), or medium-priced sandwiches, salads, etc. With soft Hawaiian music (taped) playing in the background and the gorgeous scenery all around you, it's hard to leave. Haiku Gardens is closed Mondays; reservations: 247-6671. (To reach the restaurant directly from the city, take Likelike Highway through Wilson tunnel, turn left at Kahekili Highway, and turn left again at Haiku Road.)

ON TO BYODO-IN: Now drive back to Kahekili Highway (which runs parallel to Route 83 for a short distance), drive north for two miles, and prepare yourself for one of the most enthralling sights in the islands. No lover of Orientalia will want to miss a visit to **Byodo-In** in the Valley of the Temples, in the verdant Ahuimanu Valley. Byodo-In is a $2.6-million replica of the 900-year-old Byodo-In temple that has been proclaimed a National Treasure by the government of Japan. There is no doubt that this is one of the treasures of Hawaii. It was dedicated on June 7, 1968, almost 100 years to the day from the arrival of the first Japanese immigrants to the islands. The grounds are beautifully landscaped, with the temple sitting in the midst of a Japanese garden planted with plum and pine and bamboo. Before you enter the temple itself, ring the bell for good luck and the blessings of the Buddha. Inside the temple is an immense, imposing golden carving of Amida, the Buddha of the Western Paradise, an important work of sacred art, as are the filigree screens and panels. When you finish gazing at the treasures within, you can buy some fish food to feed the carp in the two-acre reflecting lake. You can also shop for Oriental souvenirs, walk through the tranquil gardens, and recharge yourself with the almost palpable serenity of the Orient. There is a small admission charge of $1 for adults, 50¢ for children under 12. (To reach the temple directly from Honolulu, take the Likelike Highway, turn left at Kahekili Highway until you see the signs for the Valley of the Temples.)

Get back on Highway 83 now, and backtrack a couple of miles until you come to Kaneohe Bay and the little village of **Heeia.** Here you may want to drive out to the Heeia Kea pier and board one of the glass-bottom boats to see the coral gardens under the sea. The charge is $5 for adults, $2.50 for children for an hour's trip. (For advance reservations, which are suggested, phone 247-0375 before you leave Honolulu.)

ON THE WAY TO LAIE: The next important destination on your trip is the Polynesian Cultural Center at Laie, but relax—you still have a way to go. And what a beautiful way it is, with gardens curving around to the green sea at every turn of the road. On the left are the remnants of the old **Waiahole Poi Factory,** which no longer is in operation. **Chinaman's Hat,** an island that looks just like its name, is the next point to notice on the right, and the ruins of an old sugar mill are on the left. Then, a few miles farther, you'll notice the rock formation called the **Crouching Lion,** which, with a little effort, you could imagine springing at you. But it's not at all menacing; it houses, in fact, a pleasant restaurant where you sit out on the lanai and have lunch. Go along a little farther now, and you'll find yourself at **Pat's at Punaluu,** a marvelously scenic beachside restaurant hidden behind a tall condominium building (which, incidentally, houses some of the neatest visitor's accommodations on this side of the island). Or have a picnic and a swim at **Kaaawa Beach Park** or **Swanzy Beach Park,** or stop off to admire the original art works at the **Punaluu Gallery,** 53-353 Kamehameha Hwy. (Don't spend too long swimming and picknicking, however, if you want to pack all of this trip into one day.)

THE POLYNESIAN CULTURAL CENTER: Laie is a Mormon town. Mormon missionaries have been in Hawaii for over a hundred years, and the island's largest Mormon population makes its home in Laie. Here you can see the beautiful Hawaiian Temple and explore its gardens (enter from Halelaa Boulevard), see the Hawaiian campus of Brigham Young University and, most interestingly, the **Polynesian Cultural Center.** Built about 16 years ago to provide work and scholarships for Polynesian students and to revitalize the ancient Polynesian cultures, the Polynesian Cultural Center is one of the top tourist attractions in the islands.

Seven authentic Polynesian villages have been created at the Center—Hawaiian, Tongan, Fijian, Samoan, Maori, Marquesan, and Tahitian—and they are staffed by Polynesians who have been brought here from their respective islands for just this purpose. They demonstrate their crafts, perform their ancient songs and dances, explain their cultures to you. Events are going on almost continuously at the Center: depending on when you arrive you might see the "Music Polynesia" show at noon and the Pageant of the Long Canoes at 3:30 p.m.; dine on a Komo Mai buffet luncheon (served 11:30 a.m. to 2 p.m.); catch the two-hour nightly music spectacular, "Invitation to Paradise," which many consider the most exciting dance show in the islands. The villages are open daily (except Sunday) from 10 a.m., and the evening show starts at 7:30 p.m. Admission packages begin at $9 for adults, $4.50 for children, which includes admission to the villages, cart and canoe tours, the "Music Polynesia" show, and the Pageant of the Long Canoes; a ticket for "Invitation to Paradise," however, is an additional $8.50 or so for adults, $4.25 for children. Reservations can be made at the Center's Laie office (phone: 293-8561) or at their Waikiki sales office (2222 Kalakaua Ave., phone: 923-1861). Again, if you're not making the circle trip, drive through the Pali or Wilson tunnels and proceed directly to **Laie.**

Coming up a few miles out of Laie is the **Kahuku Sugar Mill,** a former working mill that has been turned into an engaging visitor's attraction. You can tour the mill, see a multimedia presentation, meet "Wili Wili Mongoose," and learn a lot about what a laborer's life was like back in the old days by taking the one-hour tour, $3.95 for adults, $1.95 for children. Unfortunately, you have to pay the admission charge even if you just want to look around the grounds and shops—unless you are a Hawaii resident. Open daily from 10 a.m. to 6 p.m.

THE NORTH SHORE: Since you've now covered the major sight-seeing points on the Oahu trip, and since it may be getting late, you could drive back to Honolulu through the tunnels and be back at your hotel in about an hour. If, however, you're still game for more, and especially for some beautiful scenery, keep going. A few miles ahead, after the road dips inward and then comes back to the shore, you're in surfer's country. This is Oahu's North Shore, and here, along **Sunset Beach** and **Waimea Bay,** where, in winter, the waves can come thundering in as high as 30 feet, you may see some of the best surfing in the islands. In summer, the water is usually quite gentle here and good for swimming. **Waimea Falls Park,** which is just across the road from Waimea Bay Beach Park, could be a refreshing stop now; it offers an arboretum, a bird sanctuary, hiking trails, a Hawaiian games area, picnic spots, and the Proud Peacock Restaurant for a buffet luncheon and a gracious dinner. Open daily from 10 to 5:30. Admission, subject to change, is $3.50 for adults, $1.75 for children 7 to 12, free for kids 6 and under.

Should you like to indulge in a bit of *la dolce vita* now, stop at the **Kuilima Hyatt Resort Hotel,** just before you reach Sunset Beach. This luxury caravanserai, where the president of the United States and the premier of Japan once met for summit talks, is fun to walk around and explore. You can have a buffet lunch (around $7) in the attractive Garden Terrace overlooking the pool and ocean, or dinner plus entertainment in one of the two dining rooms. Or, plan your visit for the sunset hour and take yourself to the cocktail lounge overlooking the ocean at Turtle Cove in Kahuku, where you can watch the sun slip into the horizon and disappear behind that giant North Shore surf.

You may be interested in stopping off at Sunset Beach and Haleiwa and joining some of the young people who've found a relaxed, close-to-nature way to live here, far from the urban pace of Honolulu. Many of them work in or run attractive craft shops and galleries in the area.

Keep going now and turn left on Highway 835 for a climb that will give you a splendid view of Waimea Bay. This is the site of the **Puu O Mahika Heiau,** the temple and sacrificial altar of an old Hawaiian village.

You have two more chances for a swim now, at **Pupukea Beach Park** and **Haleiwa Beach Park** on Wailua Bay, before the road will turn inland. You cannot completely circle the island of Oahu since there is no paved road around rugged Kaena Point. You've got to go inland and start out from Honolulu again if you want to see the other coast. Now you pick up Route 82, Kamehameha Highway, make your left, and soon you're in the midst of the largest pineapple plantation in the world, **Leilehua Plateau.** At the top of the road is a stand where you can buy what will undoubtedly be the freshest Hawaiian pineapple you've ever tasted. Delicious.

The next town coming up on the map is **Wahiawa,** an area noted mainly as the home of the U.S. Army's **Schofield Barracks.** If you're hungry by now, this is a good time to stop in at **Kemoo Farm,** a favorite restaurant with the locals since 1927, with moderate prices. They have developed a map of this area that they'll be happy to give you. The address is 1718 Wilkina Dr., on Highway 99 (phone: 621-8481).

Also in Wahiawa are the **Wahiawa Botanical Gardens,** 1396 California Ave., where you can wander free of charge through four acres of lovely trees, flowers, and shrubs, including a garden of native Hawaiian plants.

Soon Kamehameha Highway becomes a four-lane freeway, and you can speed along home. Take Highway 99 to the left when it intersects with Kamehameha or Interstate Highway H-2 and proceed onto Route 90, which goes by Pearl Harbor. If it's dinnertime, **Pearl City Tavern** (at the intersection of Kam Highway and Pearl City) is a top choice for seafood and/or Japanese cuisine. At Middle Street, cross to the right side on Route 92 (Nimitz Highway) and it's nonstop past Honolulu Harbor and home to Waikiki.

Hawaiian Outrigger Canoe

Chapter IX

THE BIG ISLAND: HAWAII

WHEN YOU LIVE on an island, where do you go for a vacation? To another island, of course. The residents of Honolulu usually take their vacations on what they call the neighbor or outer islands—the Big Island of Hawaii, the Garden Island of Kauai, the Valley Island of Maui, the Friendly Island of Molokai. And so should you. Take a vacation-within-a-vacation to one or two or, better yet, all four of the neighbor islands. For while Oahu is the most important place to see in Hawaii, there is a great deal more beyond its shores. Although the outside world is fast catching up with the neighbor islands, they are still much more relaxed than Honolulu. And they offer a panorama of natural wonders unmatched just about anywhere. It's not expensive to visit the islands. Under what the airlines call "Common Fare" plans, you can visit each island for $32 when you hold a mainland ticket, and it is no longer necessary to enter or leave the islands from the gateway cities of Honolulu or Hilo—although it often works in very conveniently with travel plans to depart from Hilo. As for living expenses, expect about the same mileage from your travel dollar as you get in Honolulu.

No matter which way you choose to see the neighbor islands, see them you must. The lush mountains and glorious beaches of Kauai, the golden languors of Maui await you. But now, the Big Island of Hawaii beckons.

Hawaii: Hotels, Restaurants, and Nightlife

On Hawaii the earth is red, the sand is black, and a goddess named Pele still reigns. On Hawaii a jetport booms, the state's second-biggest city grows, and the beautiful people from the mainland arrive to lead *la dolce vita*. The island of Hawaii is a fascinating mix of legend and reality, of old beliefs and new ambitions. It probably contains more variety per square mile than any other part of the 50th state. It encompasses tropical

Seeing The Islands in Style

For a spectacular way to see the neighbor islands, and if money is not a major consideration, book yourself a berth on the *S.S. Oceanic Independence*, a 30,090-ton luxury liner that sails out of Honolulu each Saturday at midnight, making one-day stops at Hilo, Kona, Maui, and Kauai before returning home one week later. Sports facilities, entertainment, accommodations, and food are all first-rate on this ocean-going Hawaiian resort, which is your hotel each night. You'll see more of the ocean than of the islands this way, but it's a lovely trip. Rates start at $645 per person double occupancy ($695 in high season) and can go up to $1750. Information is available from American Hawaii Cruises, One Embarcadero Center, San Francisco, CA 94111.

beaches and snow-clad mountains; a very-much-alive volcano that spouts jet fountains of fire into the air quite often; lush, lush vegetation and rainfall, which make the orchids bloom as easily as weeds anywhere else; a cattle ranch as big as they make them in Texas; acres of coffee plantations; some of the best big-game fishing waters in the world; and a population fiercely devoted to their island and its legendary history. For it was from here that Kamehameha the Great went to conquer and unite the independent island kingdoms around him, and to the federation that resulted he gave the name of his homeland—Hawaii.

Although some people call it the Orchid Island and some call it the Volcano Island, there is just one name that the islanders really use to refer to Hawaii: the Big Island. And big it is—4038 square miles, almost twice as big as all the other Hawaiian islands combined, and about the same size as the state of Connecticut. To really see the Big Island, you should plan on a minimum of four days here, since you will want to spend at least two days at Hilo on the eastern coast and at least two in Kona on the western coast. As far as sightseeing goes, it makes no difference which town you hit first. Both Hilo and Kona are $30 stops under the common fare plans. And you can also arrive or depart from the islands via Hilo. So take your choice.

Note: The area code for all phones in the state of Hawaii is 808.

HILO HOTELS: When the jetport opened a few years ago, the resort business on the Big Island went into high gear, and the

giant new hotels are evidence of this. Happily, there is a variet
of accommodations, and the prices are not necessarily high-ris
whatever you choose, you can still enjoy the scenery, the breez
the views of ocean or lagoon at your feet, and the mountains i
the background. Although local kids do swim in Hilo Bay, it i
somewhat rocky and swimming is not really good; the hote
pools offer a better answer to the tropical heat.

Picture yourself in a South Seas village surrounded by a 1.°
acre tropical garden in which you have every modern comfor
and luxury, and you'll get some feeling of what it's like to sta
at the **Sheraton-Waiakea Village Hotel.** Instead of grass shack:
though, you live in an exquisite room done in Oriental wicke
and teakwood and brilliant Polynesian colors. There is evei
convenience—air conditioning, king-size or double beds, colc
television, and personal coffee service. Wide sliding doors ope
onto roomy private lanais, and in many rooms wooden fan
revolve lazily in the ceiling. The builders have artfully construc
ed little "villages" on a self-contained island overlooking Waia
kea Lagoon (a mirror for mighty Mauna Kea, which towers i
the distance); to supplement the lagoon, they created man-mad
canals. And, of course, there's a coconut-palm-tree-ringed poo
Other areas in the hotel are also extraordinary, and so is the ver
gracious spirit of aloha conveyed by a hotel staff ready to cate
to a guest's every whim.

There are numerous dining and entertainment facilities; th
chandeliered Kupuna Dining Room for Pacific-continental foo
served in an atmosphere of Hawaiian music and song; the E Kip
Mai Lounge for listening and dancing to contemporary Hawa
ian music over the torch-lit waterways; and the charming Planta
tion Kitchen coffeeshop for breakfast, lunch, and dinner. Also a
important part of the picture here is the Marketplace, an exoti
bazaar of some 20 shops, selling everything from Oriental ar
tiques to Polynesian fabrics to Chinese hats (details und
"Shopping in Hilo," ahead).

The prices are not as much as one would expect for all th
beauty: doubles run $48 to $66, singles are $3 less; $7 more fc
a third person in the room. V.I.P. split-level suites for up to fou
with kitchen, sauna, or Japanese furo, and a well-stocked win
cellar go for $165. Reservations: Central Reservations Offic
phone: 800/325-2525; or Sheraton-Waiakea Village Hotel, 40
Hualani St., Hilo, HI 96720.

The traditional site for luxury hotels in Hilo has long bee
along the shore of Hilo Bay, and it's here that you'll find th

fragrant, flowery **Naniloa Surf,** 93 Banyan Dr., its lobby blending into spacious tropical gardens and overlooking the oce~.. There's a gracious air about this place, despite its huge size, and we think you'll like the rooms, especially those from the fourth floor up—the wide-view rooms overlooking Hilo Bay. All of the rooms, from the standard at $49 double to the superior at $52, the deluxe at $57, and the surf deluxe at $68 ($3 less for a single, $8 more for a third person), are attractively decorated in Polynesian motifs, have full tub-shower combinations, air conditioning, TVs, radios, and coffee-makers; some have private lanais, and there's courtesy ice on every floor. The elegant suites, some of them with wrap-around lanais big enough to hold your own luau, range from $80 to $250. You can dine and dance nightly in the Sandalwood, which is well recommended by the local people for its delicious seafood menu, have moderately priced meals in the pretty Hutu Terrace coffeeshop overlooking the pool, and catch some entertainment in The Crown, a Las Vegas-type show room that can feature anything from mainland and Hawaiian entertainers to Polynesian shows. There is also the Hoomalimali Bar for light listening and dancing music, and the Polynesian Disco for the young and young-at-heart. You can write for reservations to InterIsland Resorts, P.O. Box 8539, Honolulu, HI 96815, or phone, toll-free, 800/367-5360.

A bit less luxurious than the first two, the **Hilo Hawaiian Hotel,** 71 Banyan Dr. (phone: 935-9361), is nevertheless a first-class choice. This beautifully landscaped, eight-story, 290-room hotel overlooks Hilo Bay, and its spacious open lobby with bamboo sofas is one of the most comfortable around. From its lanai terrace and pool you can walk right over to neighboring Coconut Island; in the distance is mighty Mauna Kea. Rooms are all of a piece, cheerfully furnished in a red, white, and blue color scheme, with twin beds, a table and two chairs, posters of seagulls and figureheads, air conditioning, color TV, separate dressing areas, full baths and showers. Lanais are on the smallish side. Standard rooms, $37 single and $40 double, are on the lower floors; superior rooms, $43 and $46, bring you up in the world somewhat; and deluxe rooms, which are more spacious and overlook Hilo Bay, are $52 and $55. Banyan Suites with kitchenettes go for $90, Ocean Suites, $110. The Queen's Court Dining Room serves up another marvelous view of Hilo Bay along with good food; and the Menhuneland Cocktail Lounge is a whimsical charmer. You can write to Hawaiian Pacific Resorts, 1150 So. King St., Honolulu, HI 96814; or, for toll-free reservations, phone 800/367-5004 in mainland U.S.A., 1-800/665-8818 in Canada.

There's not much in the way of a lobby or public lounges at the Hilo Pacific Isle, 121 Banyan Dr. (phone 935-7171); the emphasis here is all on the rooms. The five-story hotel, a member of the TraveLodge chain, overlooks Hilo Bay, which means that there are beautiful views—either of the swimming pool, the blue Pacific, or the palm-shaded grounds. The rooms are very large, Polynesian style, equipped with equalized pressure mattresses, individually controlled air conditioning, television, and direct-dial phones. Free parking is a welcome extra. Although the standard rooms, from $30 for a single or double studio, have no lanais, they are equal to the others in every other way. Superior rooms are $35 and up; deluxe ones $39 and up, and these have two very large double beds. Youngsters stay free unless they require a crib. We also like the large bathroom and the extra dressing and storage space here. And when you're hungry, try the attractive Voyager Restaurant downstairs for good food—plus entertainment every night.

Happily for the budget-minded among us, there's an outpost of the Hukilau Hotel chain here, the Hilo Hukilau Hotel, Banyan Drive and Kamehameha Highway (phone: 935-0821). It's a pretty place for comfort and relaxation. The various wings of this 135-unit complex are wrapped around a lush flower garden, a swimming pool, and an enormous fish pond. The rooms are nicely furnished and fully carpeted, many have lounge chairs, and the night winds whipping off Mauna Kea offer an alternative to air conditioning. The Hukilau is one of the older hotels on Banyan Drive, not as sleek and slick as some of its neighbors; but there's a low-pressure atmosphere here that is refreshing. There's often free Hawaiian entertainment poolside at 7:30. A standard room here costs just $21 single, $24 double, $31 triple; a superior room is $24, $29, $35; and a deluxe room will be $28, $31, $37. It's $5 more for an extra person.

Just a few blocks from the heart of town, in an area overlooking the bay, is one of the cutest little places to be found anywhere in the city, the Dolphin Bay Hotel, 333 Iliahi St. (phone: 935-1466). Full kitchens make this place ideal for the budget-conscious, and the hotel is as pretty as it is practical, since the grounds are resplendent with tropical vegetation (which you're welcome to pick and eat). The units are large, very nicely furnished, with big, modern tub-shower combinations; you couldn't ask for a cozier setting. A breeze from the bay provides natural air conditioning, and the price is certainly right—$23 for a double in the four studio units. The superior studios, a bit larger and fitted out with doubles, corner beds, or a double and a single, cost $29 for two. There are also one-bedroom units and a two-bedroom giant at $35 to $39; an extra person in any of the accommodations is charged $6.50. No pools or fancy restaurants here, just comfortable living in a place where you'll feel really at home. Write to John Alexander, the delightful manager, way ahead of time.

HILO RESTAURANTS: The **Sheraton-Waiakea Village Hotel** (phone: 961-3041) offers several possibilities for gracious and/or unusual dining. For the first, try its lovely Kupuna Dining Room, decorated in Hawaiian Monarchy style with portraits of the ancestors or old folks looking down from the walls. You can have a complete meal for $16, well prepared and nicely presented. Main courses include veal picatta, beef Stroganoff, fresh fish of the day, and top sirloin, preceded by soup or salad, and followed by chocolate mousse or caramel custard and beverage. Or go à la carte and have the house favorite, royal prime ribs au jus, $12.50, prepared in traditional Hawaiian style—i.e., encased by Hawaiian rock salt that seals in the natural juices. Dinner only, 6 to 10 p.m. nightly.

For Japanese dining, climb the steps one flight up to **O'Tome** at Sheraton, a pretty place overlooking the pond with Japanese lanterns and Japanese seating. Plan on spending about $8.25 for dishes like shrimp tempura and yakitori or yakitori and beef kebab; steak and shrimps is $10.25. Dinner is on nightly from 5:30 to 9:30 p.m.; there's a 4:30-to-7-p.m. Happy Hour with free pupus, and disco from 9 to midnight nightly.

Flickering torches out front, a curtain of gourds, and a carp pond nestled by a waterfall flowing out of lava rock set the scene for one of the prettiest—and best—restaurants in Hilo, the **Banyan Broiler,** next door to the Naniloa Surf Hotel at 111 Banyan Dr. (phone: 961-5802). Tapa-covered Hawaiian drums for lights, bamboo and leather chairs, ceiling fans overhead, and candlelight continue the romantic mood here, and the excellent food lives up to its setting. Specialties of the house are steak and seafood (opakapaka with lobster sauce, short ribs broiled Hawaiian style with rock salt, and shrimp scampi are all recommended); most entrees are in the $10.25 to $13 range, with a few choices around $9. Along with your main dish come long-branch potatoes or fried rice and a turn or two at the salad bar, one of the most generous and delicious I've seen in the islands. Several dishes are offered on the children's menu, $6.95 including salad bar. Daily specials, entrees like Hawaiian beef stew and broiled tenderloin ($4.95 to $5.95), as well as hot and cold sandwiches and good salads (try the spinach!), are offered at lunch, 11 a.m. to 2 p.m. Open every day but Monday, dinner from 6 to 9:30 p.m.

Henri's on Kapiolani, 139 Kapiolani St. (phone: 961-9272), is a beef-lover's dream. The small, choice menu focuses on cuts of roast beef (served au jus with creamed horseradish sauce), top sirloin, and porterhouse, from $8.95 to $11.95, and also offers sauteed scallops and chicken cordon bleu. With every meal comes a nice salad, baked potato or rice, dinner rolls, dessert, and coffee. The small dining rooms afford a lovely view of Hilo. Cozy. Lunch (meaty sandwiches from $2 to $2.75) is on from 11 a.m. to 2 p.m., dinner from 6 to 9:30, every day but Monday.

An elegant setting for a well-priced meal, the **Queens Court** of the Hilo Hawaiian Hotel, 71 Banyan Dr. (phone: 935-9361), affords a splendid view of Hilo Bay. Blue banquettes, beige caned seats, golden drapes, anthuriums on the tables, and portraits of Hawaiian royalty set the indoors scene. Service is friendly and professional, and the basically American menu is spiced with Japanese, Korean, Italian, and Hawaiian accents. Local people like to come here for lunch, so you're apt to find such dishes as bul-kogi (Korean broiled beef), shoyu pork, and braised oxtail among the daily specialties, from $2.95 to $5.45. Dinner features a few pastas, some good seafood dishes from $6.95 to $8.25 (seafood curry and red snapper seasoned Japanese style are tasty), charbroiled steaks and chops, plus a mini-luau, roast prime rib, and even a vegetarian platter, all from $5.75 to $9.95. And all dishes are served with rice or potato, vegetables, sourdough bread, and a trip around the salad bar, making this a very good value indeed. At both lunch and dinner the dessert cart offers such temptations as creme-de-menthe pie, strawberry cheesecake, and (my choice) a not-too-sweet, quite satisfying chocolate mousse pie. Open every day; dinner music Monday through Thursday.

K.K. is a highly respected name for Japanese food in Hilo, because the Kobata family has been feeding the local people and visitors deliciously for over 30 years now. The old restaurant on Kilauea Avenue is no more, but they still hold forth at two Hilo locations; at **K.K.'s Place,** 413 Kilauea Ave. (phone 935-5216), where they have a spanking-clean cafeteria and takeout operation, and at the **K.K. Tei Restaurant,** 1500 Kamehameha Ave. between Hilo and the airport (phone: 961-3791), where they operate one of the prettiest restaurants in town. There's a pleasant main dining room plus the newer Yakinuki House, where you can cook your own barbecue on tabletop broilers. Among the special dishes available in the Yakinuki House, I particularly like the shabu shabu, a meal of assorted meats and vegetables, named for the sound the meat makes while cooking; it's $9.25. Less expensive dinners, which are also available in the main dining room and average $6.50, include sukiyaki, yosenabe (a succulent soup of chicken, seafood, vegetables, and fish), and shrimp tempura (**K.K. Tei's** specialty). Each dinner comes Japanese style, with all the extras—miso soup, pickled cold vegetables, sashimi, rice, and hot Japanese tea. No matter what you choose, it's a bargain, and lunch is even more inexpensive, with complete Japanese lunches served in lacquer trays starting at $4.25. You can also get American-style food, and luncheon sandwiches from $3.20, including a choice of salad.

Note: If there are at least eight of you, reserve ahead for one of the tea-house rooms in the rear of the restaurant; they afford an all-dinner-long view of a beautiful Japanese garden, complete with graveled walkways and a spouting pool teeming with lilies and orchids, beautifully lit up at night.

Some of the best budget-priced food in town can be found at the **Hukilau Hotel** on Banyan Drive. Luncheon offers a dozen entrees priced under $2.75, and the selections include calf-liver steak, fresh crab omelet, and pastrami sandwiches. Dinner prices settle around the $4.75 to $6.75 mark, with such entrees as fried chicken and teriyaki steak. The prices include a complete dinner, and your dessert could be one of the always tempting fresh-baked pies. The complete steak-and-lobster dinner at $8.95 is a bargain I haven't seen matched anywhere.

Want some more budget ideas? That's easy. **Smitty's Deli** in the Kaiko O'Hilo Mall Shopping Center is clean and attractive, and serves up many luncheon and dinner specials for $3.50 and under. . . . **Hilo Natural Foods Kitchen,** in Hilo Natural Foods store at 306 Kilauea, offers vegetarian lunch specials from $1 to $2.25—eggplant parmiagiana, lasagna, Mexican dishes, etc. Eat at the counter or take out. . . . **Dick's Coffeeshop** in the Hilo Shopping Center is a big favorite with the local people. Many hot meals at lunch for under $4 (there's a daily special at $3.25), and at night most complete dinners are from $2.50 to $4.95. Cozy booths, a cocktail lounge, and fine food for the money.

HILO AFTER DARK: You probably won't have to leave the comfort of your own hotel for a drink in the evening, but you may want to go out to see a show. In that case, try the **Crown Room** of the **Naniloa Surf,** a Las Vegas-type supper club with top shows from the mainland as well as Polynesian revues. There, $24 will cover dinner, cocktails, tax, tip, and cover charge. The same hotel provides disco from 9:30 p.m. on in the Polynesian Room, and complimentary pupus during the 5-to-7 Happy Hour at the Hoomalimali Bar. Then it's listening and dancing the rest of the night, no cover, no minimum. There are also free pupus between 4 and 6 at **E Kipa Mai,** the classy lounge of the **Sheraton-Waiakea Village Hotel,** and entertainment and dancing nightly except Sunday. . . . A good family show is the one put on each night at **Kimo's** in **Uncle Billy's Hilo Bay Hotel,** at 6:30 and 7:30 p.m. The entertainment is casual island style, and dinners go from about $5.95 to $8.95, including a bountiful salad bar. . . . Most of the hotels have attractive bars and cocktail lounges, but if you're a Happy Hour devotee, note that the **Voyager Restaurant** in the **Hilo Pacific Isle Travelodge Hotel** has one of the most generous ones in town: from 4 to 6, free hot pupus are served with the drinks. Talented young musicians provide Hawaiian music from 6 p.m. until closing nightly. . . . The **Menehuneland Lounge** at the **Hilo Hawaiian Hotel** offers dancing from 8:30 to closing, free pupus from 4 to 6, and a clever mural of Menehune antics all the time. . . . **Rosey's Boathouse,** 760 Piilani St. is known for good food and good music by such artists as slack-key guitarist Moses Kahumoku, from 8 nightly. . . . Disco? Of course! Try **Club O'Tomo** at the **Sheraton Waiakea Hotel** Tuesday through Friday, no cover or minimum, and the **Tiki Garden Restaurant** of the **Hilo Lagoon Hotel,** 9:30 p.m. to 3:30 a.m., cover charge.

GETTING TO KONA: You'll want to rent a U-Drive to get from Hilo to Kona or vice versa, so you might keep the following car-rental agencies in mind. Besides the big companies like **Hertz, Avis, National,** and **Budget** in Hilo, you'll find smaller outfits like **Phillip's U-Drive** (phone: 935-1936), **Marquez U-Drive** (phone: 935-2115), and **Liberato's U-Drive** (phone: 935-8089). At most companies standard-shift Datsuns and Toyotas may rent as low as $13.95 a day, flat rate. Automatic shift and larger cars will of course cost more. **Tropical Rent-a-Car** (phone: 935-3385) does well with all flat rates, from $13.95 a day for compacts, no mileage charge.

If you're flying into Kona first and will rent your car there, you can choose from **Hertz** (phone: 329-3566), **Avis** (phone:329-1745), American International Rent-A-Car (329-2926), **Phillips** (phone: 329-1730), **Budget** (phone: 329-1649), and others at Keahole Airport. In town, you'll find **Tropical Rent-a-Car** (phone: 329-2437), among others. Note that at most companies there may be a ferrying charge (about $8) to return the car to its home base.

A HOTEL BETWEEN HILO AND KONA: Among certain members of the jet set the words "Mauna Kea" and "Hawaii" have become practically synonymous, ever since Laurance Rockefeller created the fabulous **Mauna Kea Beach Hotel** on the Kohala coast some years ago (it is now a Western International hotel). Presiding over a domain of some thousands of acres of cool ranchlands and gentle beachside, the hotel offers vacationers the best of many worlds: the bountiful slopes of Mauna Kea for hunting; deep-sea fishing in nearby Kona where the world records are set; golf on an 18-hole championship course designed by Robert Trent Jones; water sports, swimming, and the sun-worshipper's life on a glorious crescent of beach (where friends report the snorkeling is out of this world). The grounds and buildings are models of landscaping and architecture, with priceless treasures of art from the Orient and the South Pacific vying with the natural splendors of trees and flowers. The rooms are spacious. with every modern convenience, Hawaiian and Polynesian decor, and graceful lanais open to the view everywhere. The food in the Batik Room ranges from American to continental to Mandarin Chinese, and, of course, there is plenty of island-style entertainment. Harmonious and serene are probably the best words for Mauna Kea; it offers the ultimate in elegant resort living.

And now, oh yes, the price. All rates are on the modified American plan, and during the height of the season (from December 20 to April 1) double rooms go for $185, double occupancy, mountain views; $220, double occupancy, beachfront; $230, double occupancy, ocean views; single rooms, $15 less; third person, $60 more. Package plans are available between

Easter and December 20 each year. And, whether or not you're staying here, it's fun to stop by for the famous buffet lunch priced at $12.50. The address is Mauna Kea Beach Hotel, P.O. Box 218, Kamuela, HI 96743. The local phone is 882-7222, and the number in Honolulu is 923-8383.

CLOSE TO KONA: There's a lot of talk about Old Hawaii in the 50th state, but few ever get to really experience it—except those lucky enough to stay at **Kona Village Resort,** an enchanting old Hawaiian village that has been reborn a century and a half after a lava flow destroyed almost everything around it. The small area that was spared is the village of Kaupulehu, an idyllic 65-acre oasis in a 12,000-acre lava desert, the most purely get-away-from-it-all resort/retreat in the islands. At Kona Village, which is only 15 miles from the bright tourist world of Kailua Kona and five miles from Keahole Airport, there are no lobbies, no elevators, no sidewalks, no cars, clocks, radios, or television—nothing to remind you that you are living in the world of the 80's. Instead, there are 100 *hales*—thatched huts—built in the styles of Polynesia, Micronesia, and Melanesia; these luxuriously "primitive" cottages, with beautiful interior accoutrements (king-size or extra-long twin beds, dressing rooms, refrigerators, baths), stand on stilts facing ocean, beach, lagoon, or garden. They are not inexpensive: rates range from $190 moderate to $225 superior to $245 deluxe to $285 royal for two people. But they do include three meals; breakfast and dinner are served in the impressive Hale Moana, a New Hebrides longhouse, and lunch is buffet-style in a garden setting. Weekly luaus, international cuisine nights, and paniolo steak fries provide variety. And there is entertainment every night.

Also included is a wealth of activities: tennis, Sunfish sailboats, snorkeling, fishing, catamaran rides to secluded beaches (there are six on the property, with vari-colored sands), guided historical walks to nearby petroglyph fields. You can also swim in a lava-lined freshwater (from an underground ocean spring) pool. If you own a private plane, you can use their private airstrip (until recently the only means of access).

But the best thing about Kona Village is the feeling of seclusion, of retreat. Walking beside the almost mystically peaceful fishponds (designated long ago by King Kamehameha I), listening to the song of birds, swimming on a secluded beach, one begins to feel what Hawaii must have been like long before the modern age.

Kona Village also offers a number of intriguing package plans: scuba diving, deep-sea fishing, tennis, honeymoons—even a Hawaiian Wedding arrangement. Write Kona Village Resort, Kaupulehu-Kona, HI 96740, or phone, toll-free, 800/367-5290.

HOTELS IN KONA: Built high up on lava beds that meet the sea at Keahou Bay, a few miles out of the town of Kailua-Kona, the **Kona Surf** is one of the most purely spectacular hotels in the islands. This $24-million, 550-unit hotel is one of those places where it's hard to tell where the indoors ends and the outdoors begins, spread out as it is on some 14½ acres bursting with tropical vegetation (there are 30,000 plants on the property alone). There are lava cliffs and waterfalls (man-made but beautiful) wherever you look, and magnificent art works from the Pacific Basin casually interspersed among the public areas and walkways. The loveliness extends to the rooms, even down to the striped sheets, decorator towels, and sunken bathtubs, plus the more usual amenities like air conditioning, color television, private lanais with fine views. (Practical types will appreciate the coin-operated washers and dryers on each floor.) Rooms run $52 to $79 for a double, $3 less for a single, $10 more for a third person in the room. Suites go from $175 to $600, and are particularly elegant.

I can't imagine, however, spending too much time in one's room, since the facilities are exceptional, and the hotel is dedicated to providing many kinds of services. There are two pools. The Nalu pool has a fabulous slide down that the kids—and lots of adults, too—spend hours a-whooshing. It's a saltwater pool, and it's huge, which makes up for the lack of good swimming beach. Keahou Bay is fine for snorkelers, but not for casual swimmers. Then there's the freshwater swimming pool, where you can get free swimming lessons. Snorkels and fins are provided gratis, and so are bamboo poles for those who want to fish off the rocks. You can sign up for a lesson in scuba diving or, if you're lazy, for a sauna and massage. There are both tennis and golf pros on hand, several championship tennis courts, and a golf course that literally hangs over the water. Add to all this frequent shuttles into Kailua for shopping and to White Sands Beach for ocean swimming; shell-collecting trips; lessons in lei-making, hula dancing, coconut-palm weaving, you name it. And when you need to relax from all this activity, there's the Puku Bar for cozy drinks (and Happy Hour prices and pupus from 4 to 6 p.m.) and the Nalu Pool Bar; Pele's Court with its handsome mural for buffet breakfast and lunch. and à la carte dinner, and the handsome S.S. *James Makee* for great seafood and steaks at dinner. The Kona Surf is a fantastic place, so if you're not staying there, come by anyway Monday, Wednesday, and Friday at 9 a.m. for free tours of the grounds and buildings—it's a sightseeing stop in itself. For reservations, write, InterIsland Resorts, 2222 Kalakaua Ave., Honolulu, HI 96815. For toll-free reservations nationwide, phone 800/421-0811; in California, 800/252-0381; or call locally, in Los Angeles 213/937-5800; in Chicago, 312/782-9081.

Another winner in the Keahou Bay area is the gracious **Keahou Beach Hotel,** a 318-room, calmly beautiful resort only six miles away from the busy center of town, yet relaxing enough to be a world apart. And that it is, sprawling out on grounds that are rich in both natural beauty and Hawaiian history. The Island Holidays people who run this place have turned it into almost a living Hawaiian museum, with two restored heiaus, a reconstructed grass shack, an ancient fish pond or "sacred pool," and petroglyphs carved on a flat lava reef that runs straight out from the hotel, reminding guests of the olden days when this area, from which Kamehameha the Great launched his armies, was a favorite retreat of Hawaiian royalty. An exact replica of King Kalakaua's summer home, Ka Hale Kahakai o' Kakalakaua, has been reconstructed on its original site, complete with koa floors and exact reproductions of his furniture. Tours of the historic area are given daily at 10 a.m., and visitors as well as hotel guests are invited to attend.

Nature has been generous, here, too; the hotel has its own private swimming beach (rare for Kona) adjoining Kahuluu Beach Park, and even a volcanic tidal pool facing the sunning beach where one can watch the creatures of the deep swim in. There's an 18-hole championship golf course three minutes away, six tennis courts and a pro shop (lessons are available using the most modern facilities), and a beautiful freshwater swimming pool overlooking the ocean. And when you're hungry, you can choose from three dining rooms: Don the Beachcomber for continental, Cantonese and Polynesian specialties; the Sunset Rib Lanai for its famous prime ribs or mahimahi dinner plus salad bar, and the inexpensive and cheery Kona Koffee Mill for all three meals.

But let's not forget the rooms here. They are spacious and

handsome, decorated in subtle tones of beige, with every facility for comfort, including a small refrigerator, a spacious bath and dressing area, a radio alarm clock as well as color TV, air conditioning, of course, and even full-length mirrors on the closets. All rooms are the same; only the locations and views are different. Without much of a view, the standard double is $54; with a better view, the superior room is $64; with an excellent view, the deluxe room is $68; and with the best oceanfront location, $76. From April 1 to Dec. 20, it's $6 less per category. It's $2 less for a single person, $6 more for a third person in the room. And there are one-bedroom, two-bathroom suites for $105 double. For reservations, write Island Holiday Resorts, Central Reservations Office, P.O. Box 8519, 2222 Kalakaua Ave., Honolulu, HI 96815.

One of the nicest ways we know to live the lazy Kona life is at self-contained the **Kona Hilton Beach and Tennis Resort,** nestled on 12 acres of oceanfront just a half-mile from the center of Kailua-Kona Village. The three buildings containing some 450 guest rooms make the most of the natural setting here, and wherever you look there are stunning vistas of mountains and sea. You can dine or have a drink or watch nightly entertainment in the surfside restaurant and cocktail lounge; you can swim in a split-level circular pool close enough to the beach to hear the breakers crashing on a lava cliff below. And you can also swim at a sandy lagoon beach, unusual for Kona, where the waves can be rough. Children can swim at the half-moon-shaped shallow area of the pool reserved for them. And tennis players have four championship courts and a pro shop at their disposal.

The rooms are as handsome and spacious as you would expect, with dark wood paneling and tropical colors setting the mood. Under-the-counter refrigerators, separate dressing areas for him and her, air conditioning, coffee-maker, and color TV are standard. A sliding panel leads to your landscaped lanai from which you can view either the garden, mountain, or sea; the view pretty much determines the price tab. Rooms rent for $48 to $74 for double occupancy, $6 less for singles; add $10 for a third person, but your child—of any age—is free. The Hele Mai, Kona Rib Hale, Pasta Corner, and Lanai Coffeeshop are fun for meals, and there's a constant program of dining and entertainment events. Reservations at any Hilton Reservations Office; the local phone is 329-3111. Write to Reservations Manager, Hilton Hotels, 2005 Kalia Rd., Honolulu, HI 96815.

Right in the village of Kailua-Kona, the new **Hotel King**

Kamehameha (phone: 329-2911) has been rebuilt on the site of the old landmark hotel, combining the best of Hawaii past and Hawaii present. Adjacent to the hotel is the royal Kama Kahonu ground, where King Kamehameha ruled until his death in 1819; out on the peninsula is the restored Ahuena Heiau, or sacred temple. Two six-story twin towers with 230 air-conditioned guest rooms in each—all of which have color TV, free movies, radio, refrigerator, and their own lanai—are separated by the Banyan Tree Marketplace, a shopping mall laced with museum displays. Some of the rooms are fairly small, but all are richly decorated, as is the spacious lobby in its handsome sienna and orange hues, accented by three-dimensional koa-wood walls, Polynesian murals, and Hawaiian artifacts. Modern conveniences include four tennis courts (two of them championship), two saunas, good dining rooms like Moby Dick's for seafood; The Green Chili, a Mexican fast-food operation, and the Kona Veranda Coffeeshop. Not the least of the charms of the Hotel King Kamehameha is the fact that, in addition to its pool and engaging poolside bar, it has its own sandy beach, the only one right in the heart of town. And every evening at 7:15 as the sun goes down, the torches are lit along the waterfront; and later there's Hawaiian song and dance.

Double rooms at the Hotel King Kamehameha go from $51 for a standard to $71 for deluxe oceanfront, singles $2 less. A third person is charged $6 extra. One-, two-, and three-bedroom suites run from $110 to $245. From April 1 to December 20, all units are $5 less. The King Kam is one of those ubiquitous Island Holidays Resorts, which means that reservations are available from P.O. Box 8519, 2222 Kalakaua Ave., Honolulu, HI 96815.

Inquire at the hotel for information on their free guided tours of the *heiau* and the ancient artifacts.

There's a special feeling at a family-run hotel, and that's what you get when you stay at **Uncle Billy's Kona Bay Hotel** on Alii Drive. Right in the center of town, within walking distance of all the shopping-dining-fishing excitement, this is a crescent-shaped, 132-room low-rise, overlooking pools, restaurants, and gardens, with the emphasis on comfortable living at a reasonable price. Rooms are of good size, nicely decorated, with full bathrooms, ample lanais, air conditioning, refrigerators, TVs, and some have small kitchenettes as well. Owner-managers Kimo and Jeanne Kimi are family people, and families are made to feel right at home here. And the price is definitely right: standard rooms are $24 single, $27 double; superior rooms, $30 single, $33 double; and deluxe rooms, $35 single, $38 double. An extra person is charged $5; a kitchenette adds $5 to the daily bill. Reservations are handled at the central office in Hilo: 87 Banyan Dr., Hilo, HI 96720. The Kona phone is 329-1393. For toll-free reservations, you can dial direct to Hawaii: 800/367-5102.

Condominium Vacations

If you'd like to stay in your own apartment in Kona, complete with all the comforts of home, a condominium vacation is the perfect answer. The Kona Coast is liberally sprinkled with these vacation complexes, and all offer apartments with spacious living, sleeping, and eating quarters, full kitchens, and all the amenities. Minimum stays of three days are required; daily maid service is usually not included but is available on request.

To stay right in the heart of town, choose **Kona Plaza**, a 77-unit complex tucked behind the Kona Plaza Shopping Arcade (you can see the nightly "Dancing Waters" show from their pool) on Alii Drive. Apartments are fully carpeted, have lanais, full electric kitchens (washer-dryer, dishwasher, etc.), pleasant furniture; there are ocean views from the third- and fourth-floor rooms. A beautiful sundeck overlooks Alii Drive and the ocean. Below it is an outdoor dining area where guests gather for potluck dinners and picnic meals. There are also two recreation areas and a pool. One-bedroom apartments are $50 for two; two-bedroom, two-bath apartments are $75 for up to six; weekly rates are $300 and $450.

If you prefer a location a bit out of town, overlooking the waterfront, then choose **Kona Makai**. This sprawling, 102-unit complex has an oceanside swimming pool and Jacuzzi, two tennis courts, and handsomely decorated and spacious modern apartments. Kitchens have everything, including washer-dryers, eat-in bars, and instant coffee-makers. One-bedroom apartments are $55 and $60 for two; two-bedroom apartments with two baths go from $90 to $110 for four. Weekly rates run $330 to $660.

To make reservations for both of these places (or for several other condominium properties), write to Kona Vacation Resorts, P.O. Box 1071, Kailua-Kona, HI 96740, or call, toll-free, Condo Resorts International, 800/854-2823 excluding California, 800/432-7059 in California.

Down the coast, just outside of town and past the Kona Hilton, is a neat little budget find. The **Kona Tiki Hotel** seems sleepy enough when you pull off the highway into the parking lot, but once you're up in your room the action begins. This place intrudes upon King Neptune's territory, and he lets you know about it with a nonstop display of rainbow water that crashes against the (thank goodness) sturdy seawall surrounding the hotel. Free breakfast (coffee with doughnuts) is available in the lobby every morning. A freshwater pool competes with the ocean for attention. The rooms are modest but comfortable, with carpeted floors and double or twin beds, small but adequate bathrooms, and sliding doors that lead to a private lanai from which the sunset is spectacular. Standard rooms are $27 for a single or double, and rooms with minikitchenette are $30, with additional persons $4 more. The managers are on duty, it seems, just about always, generous with tips regarding excursions and car trips, restaurants, and island history. There are only 15 units here and they fill up fast, so write for reservations (three-day minimum) in advance to P.O. Box 1567, Kailua-Kona, HI, 96740 (phone: 329-1425).

RESTAURANTS IN KONA: For gourmet dining in the Kona area, most people would agree that **Dorian's,** in the Magic Sands Hotel, is the top choice. The room is a study in quiet elegance, with high-backed chairs, white napery, stem crystal on the tables, graceful touches everywhere. Service is impeccable—the waiters are all ruffle-shirted, good-looking, and charming—and the food of a high continental order. Everything is à la carte. Among the appetizers, the stuffed mushrooms with crab are highly recommended, and so is the thick and crusty French onion soup (the vichyssoise is also expertly done). My main course was the Chef's Silver Seafood Platter, served for two at $15.25 each, a truly magnificent presentation on a silver tray of ono, crab thermidor, shrimps in sauce, baked potato, cauliflower topped with onion rings, and fresh chunks of drawn butter. I was not as successful, however, with the chicken in champagne sauce, which was limp and tasteless. But the house salad, laden with shrimp, crabmeat, feta cheese, hard-boiled eggs, and topped with Roquefort dressing, was a wonder, a meal in itself. Entrees are mostly in the $7.50 to $14.75 range, and are accompanied by tossed lettuce salad and warm white bread, very fresh and moist, with lots of butter. Desserts are something special; save room for the guava cheesecake.

Lunch, which can be taken on the umbrellaed lanai, is lighter, featuring entrees, most under $4, such as crab or shrimp salad, eggs Benedict, and London broil. For reservations, phone 329-3195.

Another experience in gracious, relaxed di ...g awaits you at the **Hele Mai** dining room of the Kona Hilton Hotel (phone: 329-3111). Don't go in before you stroll around this beautiful hotel to put yourself in the mood for elegance. Look at the series of wall murals of Captain Cook's ships, and enjoy the fish ponds, the paintings, and the waterfall. Inside the dining room, a huge domed ceiling appears to be supported by a tiki-like sculpture. That red, candle-like object standing in front of you is really your napkin, unusually folded and placed in a wine glass. Complete dinners include appetizer or soup (like the delicious Portuguese bean soup), dessert, and coffee. You can feast on the likes of the regal mahimahi, sauteed with tropical fruits and macadamia nuts: or the catch of the day, fresh from Kona waters and gently broiled; or try, as I did, the Oscar of Japan teriyaki steak. Along with your entree, which ranges in price from about $12 to $16, comes a turn or two at the sumptuous salad bar, with an assortment of more than 20 selections.

For prime-rib lovers, the **Kona Rib House** of the Hilton, has a complete, succulent dinner, with shrimp cocktail, salad, potato or popover, and dessert, served along with the prime ribs for around $14. The atmosphere is Hawaiian *paniolo*—cowboy— and there's piano music for background.

If you're in the mood for something Italian, then just walk over to the other side of the Hilton's main dining room where you'll find the bright and cheery **Pasta Korner.** You have your choice of various pastas served with minestrone soup, spumoni, and coffee, for a tab of $6.95 complete.

Just about my favorite restaurant in town at the moment is the **Kona Inn** on Alii Drive (phone: 329-4425), newly reopened as a restaurant when the historic Kona Inn Hotel was converted into a shopping center. The setting of this lanai restaurant can only be described as idyllic: tall wicker chairs and beautifully inlaid koa tables overlook the Pacific, palm trees sway in the ocean breezes. In this storybook setting you dine on superbly fresh and beautifully prepared seafood and steak. Most dishes run $7.95 to $10.95 (although Great Barrier Reef lobster goes up to $16.95), and include a tangy chicken cordon bleu, a vegetable-cheese casserole that my vegetarian friends raved about, and a marvelous broiled seafood combination of shrimps, jumbo scallops, and fish. The local fish of the day is outstanding; it should be, what with all the big-game fishing off the Kona Coast. Along with your entree comes a good mixed salad with choice of dressing or hearty New England-style clam chowder, baked potatoes or rice pilaf, vegetables, and warm bread. On no account should you miss their Mud Pie for dessert; the taste of chocolate-cookie crust, coffee ice cream, and chocolate syrup will live in my memory. Children's menus are reasonably priced at $4.25 and $4.95.

Lunch is nice here, too, with good sandwiches, fish entrees from about $3.95 to $5.95, and a chowder-and-salad meal at $3.95. And Sunday brunch is another winner: entrees, $3.75 to $5.95, are served with fresh fruit and homemade blueberry muffin. Try the eggs Blackstone or the French toast with Canadian bacon. Yes, they have the Mud Pie then, too. Service is professional and not cloying, as it can often be in the Islands.

There's an informal, relaxed feeling about dining at **Quinn's,** 75-5655A Palani Road (phone: 329-3822), next door to the King Kamehameha Hotel. A lively young crowd hangs out in the garden dining lanai whose two open walls and one of lava rock give an outdoor feeling. Blue canvas director's chairs and glass-topped wooden tables continue the same mood. Dinner entrees average $10, and best bets are such seafood dishes as shrimp Niçoise (in tomato sauce over rice pilaf with papaya) and the grand combination plate of seafood, fish, pilaf, and zucchini at $12.50. Their "vegetarian delights" were not quite delightful enough for my taste, but seafood, burger, and roast beef sandwiches are fine at lunch, from about $3.25 to $4.75. Lots of cheer inside at the bar.

For more seafood in a sunset setting the **Kona Galley,** right on the bay on Alii Drive (phone: 329-3777), will do nicely, thanks. The sides of this one-flight-up restaurant, nautically decorated with wooden tables, leather and wicker chairs, are all open to catch the ocean breezes, very welcome on a tropical night. The menu leans heavily to seafood, with such specialties as coquilles St.-Jacques, shrimp Bombay, and crab Newburg en casserole, from about $8.75 to $12.75. Mahimahi, the most popular native fish, is always available, as are other native fish when the Galley can get them. Steak entrees, too. The generous portions are served along with salad, rice or French fries, and beverage. Potent, exotic drinks are at the ready. Lunch consists mostly of hot sandwiches and some very good seafood salads, with a daily special and fish 'n' chips at $3.25.

If you've eaten at **The Pottery Steak House** in Honolulu you know how good it is, so I'm happy to tell you that there's another

Pottery in Kona, on Kuakini Highway, just up Wailua Road from the Kona Hilton (phone: 329-2277). As in Honolulu, it's part working pottery and part restaurant, and you can purchase anything made on the premises, from your coffee mug to the attractive teapots, bread containers, and other works on display. Entrees come served with salad ("glazed with your choice of dressing"), rice or baked potato, fresh vegetables, and garlic bread in a handmade ceramic loaf. You can have a variety of steaks, from $10 to $17; or mahimahi; or the boned Cornish game hen stuffed with wild rice and fired in its own clay pot, which is yours to take home with you. Finish up with the very special Potter's coffee, served in a mug you'll probably want to purchase, $2. Dinner only is served from 6 to 10.

There are two areas to hit when the traveler's checks are running low. The first is **World Square** on Alii Drive, which has a number of tasty fast-food operations; the other is the **Kona Coast Shopping Center,** near the intersection of Highways 11 and 19, which boasts **Betty's Chinese Kitchen** for some of the freshest and best manapua (dim sum) in these parts; **Paniolo Pizza** for good Mexican food, salads, and subs as well as pies; and the amazingly low-priced **Sizzler Steak House,** a steak cafeteria, where you can get a top sirloin platter for about $4.

KONA AFTER DARK: There's plenty of excitement in the Kona night, and much of the action is centered around the big hotels. At the **Kona Hilton,** for example, the luaus are exceptional, starting with the imu ceremony and the one-hour open bar overlooking a spectacular sunset. The buffet dinner features both Polynesian and American food; there's Hawaiian music during cocktails and dinner, and one of the most "islandish" Polynesian shows around is held Tuesday, Friday, and Sunday at 6 ($22). Or you can dance and listen to music in the Windjammer Room or sing along at the piano bar at the Hilton's Promenade. . . . There's a terrific $20.50 luau at the **Keauhou Beach Hotel** Sunday, Tuesday, Wednesday, and Friday at 6:30. . . . They pop the pig into the imu every Sunday, Tuesday, Wednesday, and Friday at the **Hotel King Kamehameha,** the scene of Tihati's Kona Beach Luau. The tab for this in-town luau is $20.50, all inclusive. . . . It's worth a 15- to 20-minute drive out to Kaupulehua for the festive $29 luau given every Friday night at the **Kona Village Resort**. . . . Check the local papers when you arrive, since schedules may change. Children are usually admitted to luaus for half the adult price.

BETWEEN KONA AND HILO—ROOM AND BOARD: If you're driving the southern route (11) between Hilo and Kona, or vice versa, you'll certainly stop off at Volcanoes National Park, and you may become so enchanted with the area that you'll want to stay there for a few days. Great idea! The place to stay is **Volcano House,** which is situated in an incredibly exciting spot on top of Kilauea Crater. If Pele happens to be acting up, you'll have a ringside seat for the fireworks, and even if not, you'll have an attractive room from $28 to $38 single, $31 to $41 double, a chance to take a sauna bath in live volcanic steam, and a tingling-fresh mountain atmosphere to enjoy. The phone is 967-7321.

The famous buffet lunch at Volcano House is good, but it attracts hordes of tourist groups. If you'd like to avoid the mobs and have a refreshing treat, stop in at the **Naalehu Coffeeshop** in the little town of **Naalehu,** the southernmost community in the U.S.A., where Roy and Arda Toguchi cook delicious fresh food (try their fish sandwiches) at very modest prices. But don't just eat and run; take a look at the garden in back, Roy's collection of bonsais, and the informal "gift shop," filled with paintings and handicrafts. A delightful interlude.

The Sights and Sounds of the Big Island

If you really want to see the Big Island, you should plan on at least four days. The ideal way would be to spend the first day in the city of Hilo; the second, driving to Volcanoes National Park; the third, taking the Hamakua coast trip across the island, driving through the cowboy country of the Parker Ranch; and the fourth, exploring the Kona coast and luxuriating in the sun and water. You could also start your trip at Kona and work backward. We'll suppose, though, for the purposes of this discussion, that you're starting out—in your own rented car—from Hilo Airport.

THE FIRST DAY—SEEING HILO: I hope you'll start your trip early, since the first sight to see is at its most beautiful when the sun is new and the world is not yet too warm. From the airport, take H-12 (Kamehameha Avenue) all the way around the curve in the bay until you reach Waianuenue Avenue, which you'll follow until you get to Rainbow Drive. Here you'll find the glorious **Rainbow Falls,** so named for the transparent rainbows that appear in the mist from the falls when the morning sun glances through it. Drive on a little farther, up to Peepee Street, and you'll see the **Boiling Pots,** another scenic vista. Such beauty so close to the city is no surprise, since the city itself is a spot blessed by nature. It curves around a crescent-shaped bay, and always in sight are the two homes of Pele: the larger, extinct volcano, **Mauna Kea,** and the sporadically active smaller one, Mauna Loa.

Turn around now, and make a right on Puu Hina and another right on Kaumana. Follow this a few miles to the site of the **Kaumana Cave,** a lava tube similar to those you will be seeing later along the circular drive in Volcanoes National Park. This one was formed in 1881, when Pele came close to destroying the city of Hilo. The cave extends about a mile in the direction of the city, and a hardy spelunker could traverse the entire length with the help of a flashlight. The less adventurous can admire the lovely fern grotto at the entrance to the tube on the right (the one on the left is dangerous), and continue on.

Swing back the way you came, but make a right at Laimana Street, then left onto Haili Street. Follow it almost until Kapiolani Street, and in the middle of the block you'll find an impressive New England-type white building with green shutters. This old missionary home, built in 1839, is part of the **Lyman House Museum** and has been restored to look as it did in the mid-19th century. The ground floor contains the parlor and dining room furnished with authentic antiques. Upstairs are four quaint bedrooms, complete with four-posters, marble-top dressers, and washstands. Adjoining is the modern museum building built to house the many artifacts of the national groups living in Hawaii; you'll see a full-size grass hut of the early Hawaiians, artifacts from the missionary era, a 300-year-old Taoist shrine of gold leaf on intricate woodcarvings, plus exhibits reflecting the culture of the Japanese, Portuguese, Korean, and Filipino settlers. The top-floor galleries contain exhibits of volcanic displays, crystals, ores, glass, carved stone, ancient Chinese furniture, and marine objects. Admission to both buildings is $2. Hours are from 10 to 4, Monday through Saturday.

After you've finished here, turn left on Kapiolani and make a right back to Waianuenue Street. On your left you'll notice the Hilo Branch of the Library of Hawaii. Right out in front is the legendary **Naha Stone,** believed to be a gift of the gods to mortals. It was believed that any man strong enough to lift the stone would be able to unite the islands of the Hawaiian chain. Kamehameha, the island's favorite son, was able to do so, or thus goes the legend. At any rate, he went on to become first a chief, then king, and the rest is history.

Make a right now when you get to the corner of Kinoole and Waianuenue. Before you turn, though, notice the shaded, somber building in front of you. This is one of the buildings of the Hilo campus of the **University of Hawaii,** the second-biggest center of higher education in the islands. You can complete that turn now, take the next available left, get back onto Kamehameha Avenue, and swing out around Hilo Bay.

Continue on past Pauhi Street until you can make a left onto Lihiwai. Just before you reach the intersection of Lihiwai and Banyan Drive, you'll see an HVB marker on the right side of the road pointing to the fish-auction area. If you can manage to get up with the birds tomorrow morning, you can join the local dealers in a colorful 8 a.m. auction. Now, however, continue on Lihiwai as you swing in a circle around beautiful **Liliuokalani Park,** where a Japanese Yedo garden has been completely reconstructed. Stone lanterns and bridges accent the lovely setting here on the shore of Hilo Bay. A Japanese Tea Ceremony House has been dedicated on this site. Off to your left is **Coconut Island,** which used to be a popular recreation spot for the people of Hilo until the 1960 tidal wave carried a good portion of island soil into the ocean.

Now you can continue around the lip of Lihiwai and turn left onto **Banyan Drive,** so named for the small banyan trees (as banyans go) planted along the middle of the highway by famous people in the past half-century. Most of the elegant hotels in the city are ranged along here, and the setting is cool and easy. Follow Banyan Drive to its intersection with Kamehameha Avenue and drive left out of town, taking a left fork shortly to get onto Kalanianaole Avenue.

Drive along Kalanianaole Avenue to the Matson pier, turn right on Silva Road to just past the tanks on the right-hand side, and you're at one of Hilo's newer attractions, **Hilo Bird Village.** This all-indoor exhibit shows some 200 amazing members of the parrot family, including the Lesser Sulphur Cockatoo and the Blue-Fronted Amazon, to name just two. Open 10 a.m. to 5 p.m. every day except Monday; admission is $2.50, $1.25 children. Unusual.

Now you're approaching one of the best spots for swimming

and picnicking in the Hilo area (Hilo is not known for good beaches), an easy drive along Kalanianaole Avenue; it's **Onekahakaha Beach Park.** Here you either swim in the bay or wade in several wading pools—natural, of course—that the ocean constantly refills. Fishing is permitted from the rocks on shore. There are several pavilion areas, restroom accommodations, firepits for barbecuing, and a tiny but growing children's zoo that exhibits small samples of wildlife. All in all, there's quite a lot to do here. After you've done it, drive back out onto Kalanianaole and turn right to return to the center of Hilo.

Off the Beaten Path: Nani Mau Gardens

In a city famed for orchid nurseries, it might seem that one more garden was hardly necessary. But **Nani Mau Gardens** offers something uniquely different from any of the other gardens in Hilo. Here are 20 acres of the fruits and flowers of many lands, with a special emphasis on those that have figured in the life of the islands. Orchids are only a small part of the show. You'll get a chance to see macadamia nut trees, flowers that look like tiny cigars with an ash on the end, mysterious poisonous plants, many varieties of orchid (one, the vanilla orchid, smells like a vanilla bean), rare Hawaiian medicinal herbs, and acres and acres of hibiscus, torch ginger, bird of paradise —rich flora of the islands fragrant in the Hawaiian sun. A waterfall and pool with stone "Hawaiian Islands" makes a refreshing place to stop and rest, perhaps to have a picnic lunch. When your tour (which takes about an hour) is over, you're invited to spend as much time as you want relaxing in the Gardens. On your return to the main building you'll be given samples of ripe fruit from the fruit garden.

Nani Mau Gardens are open every day, from 8 to 5 in winter, from 8 to 6 in summer. Admission is $2.50 for adults, $1.25 for children, and well worth it. To reach the Gardens, drive about 3½ miles south on Highway 11 (the road to the volcano) from Hilo Airport. Take the left fork where Highway 11 divides onto Makalika Street, and the Gardens are right ahead.

More treats for lovers of gardens and flowers include a visit to **The Orchidarium,** 524 Manoa St., the only "orchid showplace" in Hilo (50¢ contribution requested); and two attractive nurseries, **Orchids of Hawaii,** 575 Hinano St., and **Hirose Nurseries,** 2212 Kaneolehua Ave.

Shopping in Hilo

You won't want to leave Hilo without a visit to the romantic **Sheraton Waiakea Village Hotel** and **The Marketplace,** surely one of the prettiest shopping bazaars in the Pacific. Laced by a network of streams and tropical gardens, the 18 little shops (in peaked-roof wooden buildings) offer treasures and pretty trivia from the South Pacific and the Orient, with plenty of ideas for gifting your friends back home—and yourself. At **Tonga South Pacific Company,** for one, you can find typical crafts of Oceania, all handmade by village people as they have been for centuries. Note the tapa cloth, the turtle-shell bracelets, beautiful basketwear, small models of outrigger canoes, under $20. . . . You'll probably want to take home lots of things from **House of Bamboo,** since they have just about everything that could conceivably be made of bamboo, from $1.25 pendants on up. I hope they have some of the uniquely designed Sarawak baskets and purses (from $6 to $15), tightly woven and comparable with the best of Southwest Indian and Alaskan baskets, on hand when you visit.

You can pick up some fascinating original works by local artists and craftsmen at the **Gift Gallery;** perhaps Hawaiian koa wood frames, Hawaiian quilt patterns and pillow kits, pottery, metal sculptures on lava, porcelain windchimes, scrimshaw, peacock feather wallets, petrolgpyh reproductions—and some Chinese handpainted boxes and cloisonné as well. There are a number of other shops here, so take time to explore and see where your fancy leads you.

For sherbets and ice creams made of island fruits and berries —guava, lilikoi, and the like—topped by such natural island sweets as crushed pineapple, freshly roasted macadamia nuts, and toasted coconut, stop in at **Fruit of the Land.** They also have sandwiches and drinks. Have lunch at the **Plantation Coffeehouse** or dinner and a drink at any of the Village's other dining rooms and cocktail lounges. Have a look at the gardeny hotel lobby, too, filled with the song of birds.

The Marketplace is open every day from 9 a.m. until 7 p.m. To drive, take Kilauea Avenue south to Kekuanaoa Street, turn left, and park in the C. Brewer lot.

Not far from the Marketplace is the less rarified **Kaiko'o Mall Shopping Center,** across from the Hilo Lagoon Hotel. It's a big, handsome place where the locals buy everything from clothes to crafts to papayas and soapsuds. Have a look at the absorbing **Book Gallery II,** with books of all kinds, many books for kids, and lots of books on Hawaiiana, including some fascinating ones published in Hilo by the Petroglyph Press. You can sometimes catch free Hawaiian revues here, and there are several inexpensive restaurants should hunger strike.

If this foray into less tourist-oriented Hilo shopping appeals to you, head downtown, along Kilauea, Kinoole, and Kamehameha Avenues, where you'll find many appealing local shops. Don't miss **The Most Irresistible Shop in Hilo,** at 98 Keawe St., laden with high-quality crafts—beautiful hand-turned pottery, featherwork, soft sculpture, patchwork, cards, and watercolors. Kids will be enchanted by the toys and doll-house furniture. The local natural-living set hangs out at two places: **Hilo Natural Foods,** 308 Kilauea St., which also has a small counter restaurant, and **Abundant Life, Herbs and Natural Living Store,** at 90 Kamehameha Ave., whose selection of herbs and spices is extraordinary. The original **Book Gallery,** with the Petroglyph Press a few doors away, is at Haili and Kinoole.

THE SECOND DAY—IN THE WAKE OF PELE: Although volcanology is now an exact physical science, you could never prove it to some of the residents of the Big Island. As far as they are concerned, Pele, the flaming goddess of the volcanoes, is still alive and well, and she lives in Halemaumau Crater on Kilauea. You'll have to see Pele before you leave the Big Island; you may observe her in action, or you may just see what she's been up to. Either way, the sights are unforgettable. You can follow in her trail all along the road up to **Volcanoes National Park** and even right up to the shoreline—an exciting territory that's well worth exploring.

To begin your drive to the Puna region, take the southern route, H-11, out of Hilo. Six miles out of town, and across the divided highway, you'll see the **Mauna Loa Macadamia Nut Corporation,** where, if you can get Pele out of your mind for a few minutes, you can take yourself on a quick tour of the grounds, Monday to Friday, from 8 a.m. to 3 p.m. Macadamia nut-raising is one of the fastest-growing industries in the state, and once you taste them you'll understand why.

But back to volcanoland. Several miles farther on you'll come to the small town of **Keaau** where, if you're still in a shopping mood, you might want to browse through the craft and antique shops of the **Sugar Mill,** where a potter, a photographer, a jeweler, and others are producing beautiful works. You can have an inexpensive photo-portrait that looks like a charcoal drawing done in three minutes at Charco-Classic. Continuing on your journey, you take H-12 on its rain-forested drive along the sea. At the fork in the road coming up later, take H-132 and head makai. You'll pass **Lava Tree Park,** where you could have a hike or a picnic while you observe the work of the molten lava all around. The casts of tree trunks in solidified lava still stand here; the lava burned out the trees inside and went hurtling on. There are also a few tremendous earth faults, which are fenced off. You can look into mini canyons for a glimpse of the rock layers under the surface. Continue on, passing fertile papaya fields and orchid farms. Just before your intersection with H-137, you'll pass the village of **Kapoho,** buried under tons of lava in a 1960 eruption that added several square miles to the island's geography. You might even notice the lighthouse, standing isolated and strangely inland. A few signs of village life remain, sticking out from under the smothering lava rock.

Now you turn right onto an unearthly stretch of highway that careens wildly along the seashore, giving you an unforgettable picture of what volcanic fury does to the land. Mound upon mound of rolling lava rock spills down to the ocean on your left, and on the right a few cinder cones, some wisping meaningless smoke, play hide and seek with the foliage that has managed to take root in the rich volcanic soil. The plant life reworks the volcanic earth, producing red dirt, which blows across and colors the highway on which you are riding. The road will dip into shady grottoes and emerge into the brilliant sunlight where nothing but black, frozen rock stares back at you from every side.

Note the intersection of the road now with H-13, but continue on just past it to see a beach unique unto the islands: **Kaimu Beach,** known popularly as the **Black Sand Beach,** at Kalapana. Here volcanic rock has been beaten into fine sand, as brilliant in its ebony texture as other beaches are in their golden hues. With swaying palm trees in the background, it's picture-postcard Hawaii, but the tides are too tricky for safe swimming. Instead, continue down the road a bit for a picnic at **Harry K. Brown Beach Park,** where lava rock has been used in the creation of the picturesque picnic tables and stools. Across the street is a man-made pool constructed completely of lava stones and fed with ocean water. A bit down the road, you'll pass the **Star of the Sea Painted Church,** one of two "painted churches" on the island. Since the ancient Hawaiians were accustomed to outdoor worship of their pagan gods, the murals on the walls of these little churches are designed to create an outdoorsy feeling. (This little church, however, is rather recent; you'll see a much older one just off the road to Hoonaunau, when you explore the Kona coast on the other side of the island.) About five miles from this spot is the **Queen's Bath,** a pond where those enormous and matronly monarchs of old Hawaii allegedly came to bathe. According to the old legend, any citizen found watching was immediately put to death—no questions asked. Don't worry, democracy reigns, and anybody can swim here, especially the local kids who have turned it into a favorite swimming hole.

On to the Volcano

Every visitor to the Big Island has one important question: "Will I see the volcano erupt?" Since Kilauea erupts only sporadically, the answer will have to be "maybe." But if Pele answers your prayers—as she once did mine—you're in for a fantastic experience. Several years ago, one of the fire pits along the Chain of Craters Road went into sudden action for only one night. I, along with several hundred others, queued up in park headquarters to see the raging fountains several miles away. The sky was painted red with the glow of lava, and sometimes the fiery geysers shot up over 1000 feet in the air. It was quite a show. I hope you'll catch a similar performance somewhere in the Volcano area, and there's a good chance that you will, as there has been a great deal of activity in some of the craters in recent years. You can call the park before you start out (967-7311) for news of latest eruptions and viewing conditions, and check with the rangers as soon as you arrive for directions to the site. For recorded information on eruptions, you can phone 967-7977 at any hour.

But even if there are no eruptions at the moment, you will, of course, visit the home of Pele, which the United States government has thoughtfully and handsomely turned into a national park. To reach **Hawaii Volcanoes National Park,** your best route is to continue a few miles to the Wahaula Visitor Center, which takes you to the Chain of Craters Road, which leads right into the park. If time is short, and you decide to skip the shoreline trip completely, simply take Highway 11 out of Hilo and stay on the road all the way to Kilauea. Park headquarters should be your first stop. The rangers on duty there will give you driving maps and information on nature walks, and tell you when the next movie on volcanology will be shown. It is well worth seeing.

To really see and experience the volcano, you should take one of the hikes that start out from behind Volcano House, across the street; the air is deliciously crisp (I hope you've brought a sweater with you), the views eye-filling, and the mountain flowers and trees different from what you've seen on the tropical beaches below. But if time and energy are lacking, you can get the impact of the place simply by taking the circular drive that surrounds the park and leads you alongside every major point of interest. First you'll come to the **Sulfur Banks** just out of park headquarters territory, and farther on are the steam vents where clouds of evaporating rainwater hiss off hot stones underground.

Farther ahead, you can swing to the right on Mauna Loa Road and come upon the **Tree Molds,** similar to the ones you saw earlier at Puna, and **Kipuka Pualu Bird Park,** perfect for a nature walk or a picnic. Head back to Crater Rim Drive now, and continue on around the rim of **Halemaumau Crater,** which stretches below you for half a mile. You can completely circle it by car and then walk to the observation platform and inspect the 300-foot-deep crater, spilling forth sulfur fumes at what is sometimes a pretty impressive rate. Continue on to the **Devastation Trail,** a man-made walkway stretching with spooky certainty through a forest of dead trees and winding around inert cinder cones. This walk takes about 15 minutes, so, to conserve energy, you might send one member of your party back to the parking lot to bring the car around to the lookout area at the end of the walk.

Back to the beauty of the forest you go now, and in the midst of an indescribably lush tropical setting you'll find the **Thurston Lava Tube.** Like the Kaumana Cave in Hilo, the tube was formed by cooled lava forming around a molten core that kept moving and eventually emptied the circular shell. The short path through the tube is clear enough, and you'll emerge into more forest at its end. Kilauea Iki and Waldron Ledge Overlooks comprise the last two stops on the loop.

Since this is a circular drive, you're now back where you started from, and you've seen the major sights of the volcano. Where you go from here depends on you. If you haven't seen the Puna shore area on the way up, you can take the Chain of Craters Road to the Wahaula Visitors Center, then head back to Pahoa, Keaau, and ultimately Hilo. Or you can return directly to Hilo via Highway 11. A third alternative is to continue from the volcano for another 96 miles to the Kona coast. The highway is good, but not especially interesting. You can stop at another black-sand beach—at **Punaluu** —and in **Kau** you can still see in the cooled lava the footprints of Hawaiian warriors routed from a battle by a sudden outburst of Pele. My personal preference is to go back to Hilo for the night, starting out the next morning for Kona by way of the varied and beautiful Hamakua coast.

THE THIRD DAY—FROM HILO TO KONA: The intriguing thing about driving the **Hamakua Coast** route is that, in a mere 96 miles, you pass scenery so unusual and so varied that it's difficult to believe it's all part of the same island—from lush sugar-plantation fields curving around the base of Mauna Kea on the Hilo coast, through the grassy pastures of the Parker Ranch, into remote mountain regions, posh seaside watering holes, and across barren lava landscapes until you reach the green and gold of the Kona coast. Plan on a full day and savor it all.

Begin your travels on H-19 in Hilo, which continues straight out of the city. You'll hug the northern shore of the island now, with Mauna Kea on one side, the surging sea on the other. The rich earth yields a bumper crop of sugar cane here. Your first stop should be in the little village of **Honomu,** ten miles out, where an HVB marker will point the way up a country road to **Akaka Falls,** a glorious waterfall surrounded by an incredibly rich bit of jungle, tamed enough to turn it into an idyllic little park where you might want to spend all day. But get back to the highway and continue on; there's another pretty park at **Laupahoehoe,** down on the shore. Back in 1946 this village bore the brunt of a tidal wave that swept a school and its occupants into the sea. Swimming, as you will notice, is terribly dangerous in the pounding surf near the jutting rocks. A picnic or a look is enough.

In Honokaa, 20 miles ahead, you'll find the **Hotel Honokaa Club,** which is the place to make arrangements for tours by jeep of dreamy **Waipio Valley.** If you don't have the time for that kind of lengthy excursion, you can stop here for lunch or to see **Hawaiian Holiday's** macadamia-nut-processing plant (open daily 9 a.m. to 6 p.m.; macadamia-nut gifts mailed anywhere; free sample), relax, and continue on your way.

A Stop at Parker Ranch

Now Highway 19 heads inland, and soon you're in cowboy country (they call them *paniolos* here), careening along the highway that borders grasslands reminiscent of Texas. This is **Kamuela** (also called **Waimea**), home of the enormous **Parker**

Ranch, one of the largest cattle ranches in the United States under single ownership. Although most of us don't associate Hawaii with ranching, it is a major industry on the Big Island. Parker Ranch was begun in 1847 when King Kamehameha III deeded a two-acre parcel of land to John Palmer Parker, a sailor from Newton, Massachusetts, who had managed to tame some wild cattle for the king. Today, the ranch covers more than 300,000 acres, and Parker's great-great-great-grandson, Richard Smart, is its owner. It's here in Kamuela that you may want to stop to see the **Parker Ranch Vistor Center Theater/Museum.**

Plan on about 45 minutes to see the complex. First, browse through the John Palmer Parker Museum with its Hawaiiana and Parker Ranch artifacts (there's a tapa bedcover from the old Parker homestead, a gown worn by Queen Kamamalu), and stop also to see a special section filled with mementoes and trophies of Duke Kahanamoku, Hawaii's greatest swimming star and Olympic champion. Then, in the Thelma Parker Theater, you'll see a 15-minute narrated color-slide presentation depicting the history and workings of the Parker Ranch; it's very well done. Located in the Parker Ranch Shopping Center, the Visitor Center is open Monday to Saturday from 9:30 a.m. to 3:30 p.m. Admission is $1.95 for adults, $1.25 for those under 18, free for children under 12.

Of course, you'll want to stop next door and visit **The Paddock,** whose tiny shops display arts and crafts that reflect Hawaii's ranching tradition. I found many unusual things here, many of them made right in the community, like the strawflower leis that paniolos wear at rodeos, coconut-wood belts, owl-feather pins, and Parker Ranch print shirts and T-shirts. Then finish your visit with a meal at the **Parker Ranch Broiler,** a plushly decorated gourmet dining room where you can feast on steaks and continental specialties like escargots bourguignonne and scampi à la Romano. A lavish buffet lunch is $7.95, sandwiches from $3.50, dinner entrees in the $9 to $15 price range. (If you like this area well enough to stay a bit, try the **Parker Ranch Lodge,** a ten-unit motel offering spacious rooms, kitchenettes, and rates of $30 single, $38 double, $43 for two queen-size beds.)

More About Waimea

Waimea is such a pleasant little mountain town that you may want to spend an hour or so wandering about. For an inexpensive meal, you can join the local folks at diners and drive-ins like the **Kamuela Drive-In Deli,** very close to the Parker Ranch Center, or stop in at **Homer's** (at the rear of the New Fukushima Store, on Route 19), a clean-as-a-whistle little place for hearty homemade soups, salads, and sandwiches, plus luscious desserts. Drive up the road a bit to **The General Store,** which is just what its name implies but with many sophisticated craft and gift items along with dungarees and work shirts. **Cost Less Imports** has vast quantities of foreign wares plus some nice local crafts, and the **Parker Ranch Center** shopping complex is where the local people buy their goods.

There's one more stop you might want to make in Waimea, and that's at the **Kamuela Museum.** John Parker's great-great-granddaughter and her husband, Harriet and Albert K. Solomon, Sr., are the founders, owners, and curators of this largest private museum in Hawaii. It's located at the junction of Routes 19 and 25, open daily including all holidays from 8 to 5, and boasts a collection of ancient and royal Hawaiian artifacts (many of which were originally at Iolani Palace in Honolulu), as well as European and Oriental objets d'art. Among the treasures: an ancient Hawaiian 61-pound, hammer-type stone canoe-buster, the only one in existence, used by warriors to smash enemy canoes; many ancient temple idols; a royal Hawaiian marble-top teak table once owned by Kamehameha III; and a traveling clock given to Queen Liliuokalani by Queen Victoria of England. Admission is $1; children under 12, 50¢; phone: 885-4724.

Now some of you might want to take a little sidetrip up into the **Kohala** region of the Big Island. It's an uphill drive along Route 25, and it's 22 miles in each direction before you can get back to Kamuela and continue your cross-island jaunt to Kona. But the scenery is among the most spectacular I've found in the island. The Pacific drops off into a faraway, misty horizon, and the snow-topped cliffs of Mauna Loa and Mauna Kea provide an alpine-like background to the drive up the slopes of the Kohala Mountains. At the end of the road, and the end of the island, is the little village of **Kapaau,** the birthplace of Kamehameha and the site of the original statue of the warrior chief (you've probably seen its copy in front of Iolani Palace).

Still game for another sidetrip? This one is a simple 12-mile jaunt to the deepwater port of **Kawaihae,** where you can either have a swim with the local people at **Samuel Spencer Park** or **Hapuna Beach,** considered the best beaches on the island, or watch the jet set at play at the **Mauna Kea Beach Hotel.** This $12.50 buffet lunch is sumptuous, but unfortunately only hotel guests can now tour the art collection and gardens. To reach the hotel, take Route H-26 from Kamuela, which will go past the Puukohala Heiau, and then, on the road to Samuel Spencer Park, to the hotel.

Now, whether or not you've made either or both of these sidetrips, get back to Kamuela on Highway 19 or 190 (the latter trip is a bit shorter) and follow the road south to Kona. Along the side of the road you will see stone walls all the way. These are the remains of border fences, constructed when Hawaii was not yet united and various chieftains would lay claims to territories stretching from the slopes of Mauna Kea (the austere mountain peak on your left) down to the ocean in almost pie-shaped wedges. The fences were such a tremendous engineering achievement, however, that they were never torn down, even after the coming of the white man. The landscape turns into a volcanic wasteland now, with HVB markers dating the lava flows before you, and finally you escape the path of Pele into the golden, glowing welcome of the Kona coast.

THE FOURTH DAY—EXPLORING KONA: Let's face it. Getting up enough energy to go sightseeing in Kona is difficult. The sea is so beautiful, the colors of the tropical blossoms so brilliant, and the mood so deliciously lazy, that you may want to spend all your time fishing or golfing or swimming or just plain doing nothing. But I think you'll find it more than worth the effort to spend a few hours sightseeing, since the culmination of your efforts—a visit to the **City of Refuge** at Honaunau—is certainly one of the highlights of a trip to the Big Island.

Preliminary sightseeing in Kailua-Kona is simple. The main street, Alii Drive, covers the entire length of the village in less than a mile. Situated in the middle of town is the **Mokuaikaua Church,** dating from 1823, and built by the Hawaiians at the request of the missionaries from lava stones and koa wood from the uplands. It is one of the oldest churches in the islands. Across the street is **Hulihee Palace,** the summer home of Hawaiian royalty, now converted into a museum showing furniture and accessories of Hawaiian royalty plus ancient artifacts. It's open weekdays from 9 to 5, until 4 Saturday and Sunday. Admission is $3 for adults and $1 for children. Just down the street, in World Square, Ami Gay sits and dispenses tourist information for the **Hawaii Visitors Bureau.** She is truly one of Kona's wonders and deserves a place on any map. Walk around Kona to get the feel of the place and relax in its atmosphere. There's a public beach area in front of the Hotel King Kamehameha, boats and guides for rent at every turn, bicycle rentals in the heart of town, and you can even take skin-diving lessons if you feel like it. For a great adventure, try **Pacific Sail & Snorkel's** snorkeling cruise that includes everything from transportation, equipment, and the inner tube in which you enter the water to a glass of passion-fruit juice for your $15. Phone: 329-2021. The lazier ones can see the wonders of the underwater world via **Captain Bean's Glass Bottom Boat Cruise:** $6 for adults, $3 for children. The Sunset Cocktail and Dinner Cruise ($22 for adults, no minors under 18 allowed) provides two hours on a Polynesian canoe, plus a beef tenderloin dinner, live entertainment, and all the cocktails you can consume. For reservations, phone: 329-2955.

Now, to start your serious sightseeing, get into your car and follow Alii Drive until it becomes a two-way street; take the mountain road and get onto Kuakini Highway, H-11. Now you're in Kona "up mauka," an area of small coffee plantations (this is where they grow that rich, wonderful Kona coffee), and if it's fall harvest time you'll see little red beans glistening against the green leaves of the coffee bushes lining the road. There are also small cattle ranches here. Follow the road past the Hongwanji Mission down the slopes of the mountains until you reach the sea at **Kealekekua Bay.** Across the bay, you can see a white monument that was erected to mark the spot where Captain James Cook was killed by Hawaiian natives in a scuffle in 1799. At the very spot where you park your car, however, you'll see two shrines: one that commemorates the first Christian funeral in the islands (performed by Captain Cook for one of his sailors) and another in honor of Opukahaia, a sailor who became the first Christian convert in the islands (he was instrumental in bringing those New England missionaries here in the first place).

Continue along the shore road now for your major destination —Pu'uhonua O Honaunau National Historical Park, formerly known as the **City of Refuge.** This ancient, partially restored *puuhonua* still has about it the air of sanctuary for which it was built over 400 years ago. In the days when many chieftains ruled in the islands, each district had a spot designed as a refuge to which tabu-breakers, war refugees, and defeated warriors could escape; here tabu-breakers could be cleansed of their offenses and returned, purified, to their tribes. (There is another such city of refuge on the island of Kauai, near Lydgate Park, but this one is far better preserved.) The *heiau* has been reconstructed, and tall wooden images (known as *ki'is* in Hawaiian) guard its entrance. A great wall surrounds the purification site, and next to it is a little cove, shaded by coconut palms, where the chieftain could land his canoe. Although you can wander about this place on your own, swimming and picnicking and enjoying the peace, you should attend one of the orientation talks given at 10, 10:30, 11, 2:30, 3, and 3:30 in the amphitheater staffed by the National Park Service. Several "cultural demonstrators" are also on hand; they carve wood and demonstrate poi-pounding and other ancient Hawaiian crafts.

On your return to Kealakekua and on up the hill to H-11, take the turn off to the **Painted Church,** about one mile in, on a bumpy side road. This tiny church was the first of all the similar churches on the island.

For one more possible stop on your way home, turn left on Kuakini Highway in the Keauhou area and descend to sea level; opposite the Keahou Beach Hotel you'll find **Kona Gardens,** a multimillion-dollar botanical and cultural park. Flowering plants from all of Polynesia grow amid the lava flows, highlighting historical sites: heiaus, the ruins of a temple, petroglyphs. The 12-acre park offers an audio-visual show about Hawaii, arts and crafts demonstrations, gift shops, and snack shop. Admission is $5.25 for adults, $3.25 for children 7 to 12, free under 7.

Shopping in Kailua Village

Return now to the sun and fun of Kailua-Kona. It's a great place to shop, so poke in and out of the little arcades along Alii Drive. The **Kona Inn Arcade,** for one, has many tasteful shops: **The Shellery** with its beautiful shell mobiles and lovely jewelry is a favorite of mine, as is **High as a Kite Toys and Kites.** The **South Seas Trading Post** in the **Banyan Market Place** of the Hotel King Kamehameha shows quality folk items from the South Seas; and the **Bamboo Shack,** near Hulihee Palace on Alii Drive, has clothing, jewelry, and art that is both inexpensive and original. The **World Square** shopping arcade is great fun; get your portrait taken by computer and put, perhaps, on a T-shirt at **Portrait Stop;** have inexpensive snacks and eat them at picnic tables in back; and catch "Dancing Waters," a free computer-programmed sound-and-water show that the kids will love, any evening.

Chapter X

THE VALLEY ISLAND: MAUI

THERE IS A LEGEND in the Valley Island that the great god Maui was powerful enough to stop the sun in its tracks. He lassoed the sun as it was making its way across Haleakala Crater one morning, and held it captive until it promised to slow up its route across the heavens, making the days longer and the skies brighter. The primitive Hawaiians never doubted the truth of this legend, and I am beginning to half-believe it, too. For any force that could have created the island of Maui must have been doing something right. Oahu is 20th-century brilliant; Kauai is green and lush, Hawaii is immense and exciting—but Maui is pure gold. By all means, make a point of seeing it.

Fortunately, the treasures of Maui—its glorious beaches, its swinging little boating-shopping town of Lahaina, its remote jungle valleys, and its mighty giant of a sleeping volcano—are all just 88 miles from Honolulu. It's a short hop by jet to either Kahului Airport ($32 on the common fare plan) or the landing strip at Kaanapali, site of a resort-hotel building boom that, some claim, will make it another Waikiki in ten years. Don't wait. Get there now.

Plan to spend a minimum of three days, four or five if you have them, to sample the island's various charms. The best places to stay are either in the island's central section, the **Kahului-Wailuku** area (on the bay, but no beach), a good starting point for your various sightseeing jaunts; in **Kihei,** about a 15-minute drive from Wailuku and on the beach; or my personal favorite, **Lahaina-Kaanapali-Napili.** Accommodations ranging from expensive to budget can be found in all. Although the last-mentioned is a 45-minute drive from Kahului, you'll be living at an exciting beach area, and the coastline is so gorgeous that coming home in the afternoon becomes just as much fun as starting out in the morning for a day of sightseeing.

WELCOME TO MAUI: The natives say that *Maui no ka oi* (there's no place better than Maui), and you'll begin to see why as soon as you arrive at Kuhului Airport. The large reception lounge, with its contemporary architecture, is open at one end, so the outdoors beckons immediately. A car is a must, since there is very little public transportation. At the airport, **Budget and American International,** among others, offer bargain rates. A phone call brings **Tropical Rent-A-Car** (877-0002) or **Atlas U-Drive** (244-7408) with excellent flat-rate deals. Best to reserve in advance. (Note to smart shoppers: While he's busy getting the car, she can check out the bargains at the airport shop; the usual souvenir items—shell necklaces, key chains, carvings—are about 10% less here.) If you need to check in with the **Hawaii Visitors Bureau,** drive right over to the County Building at 200 High St. in Wailuku, where, on the fourth floor, helpful Norman Honda and his staff have plenty of useful information about the island.

Note: the local airlines and car rental companies often offer special package deals with hotels on Maui; you might get a room and a car for $30 a day. Ask your travel agent to check out current offers.

The area code for all phones in the state of Hawaii is 808.

Hotels of Maui

HOTELS IN KAHULUI: One of the sleekest places to stay in Kahului is the **Maui Beach Hotel,** right on Kahului Bay. It's a low-slung, two story, Polynesian-style hotel whose units are air-conditioned, smartly furnished, some with private lanais, some with dressing rooms off the bathroom. Rates are reasonable: a standard twin-bedded room is $35 for a single; $38 for a double; a superior room, slightly larger than the standard, runs $38 for a single, $41 for a twin; deluxe rooms are $41 and $44; those deluxe rooms with an ocean view are $47 and $50. No matter what room you choose, though, you have the pleasure of the large swimming pool located on a concrete deck one story above street level, and the convenience of a good seaview dining room right at hand. There's an excellent $5 Rainbow Buffet lunch, featuring many local foods. The Red Dragon Room, which serves Chinese buffet dinners, turns into a disco after dinner on

Friday and Saturday. Downstairs is the wildly swinging bar that manager John Abe humbly admits is "the" place in Kahului for nightlife. Advance reservations, certainly, from Hawaiian Pacific Resorts, 1150 South King St., Honolulu, HI 96814; phone: 531-5235. Toll-free reservations: 800/367-5004. The local phone is 877-0051.

Right next door to the Maui Beach Hotel, on the main drag in Kahukui town, is the rambling **Maui Palms** resort, its long, two-story building spread out over five acres of land otherwise covered with vines, palms, and trees of an impressive variety. You'll get the feeling of a beach house as you enter your room from the bamboo-railed walkways. Standard singles start at $27, doubles at $30, and a third person in the room is $7. Although you could go whole-hog here and get a deluxe room, secluded and steeped in the mood of the ocean, at $35 for a single, $38 for a double, you can also play the budget game. Set back farther from the ocean, but still with all pool privileges, are a set of standard rooms, constantly full and very popular with business people in the know and on the go. For a small but perfectly adequate air-conditioned bedroom and a tub-shower combination, you can get by for $24 for a single, $28 for a double. A third person wouldn't fit. For reservations, write to Maui Palms, Kahului, Maui, HI 96732 (phone: 538-6817).

The **Maui Hukilau** is a cute little place right on Kahului Bay. The sandy beach that it fronts was once the site of an old *hukilau* fishing beach, and it's okay for swimming even though the currents are strong; but most of the hotel guests prefer to use the pool. The rooms are all attractively furnished and the rates are good: $25, $28, $31, and $35 for singles; $29, $32, $37, and $39 for doubles. An extra person in the room is charged $5. Hotel, car, and breakfast plans for two are $39 standard, $45 superior, $51 deluxe. The hotel has a pleasant dining room and bar, and many nights you'll get a good Hawaiian show along with your meal. For reservations, write to Maui Hukilau, Kahului, Maui, HI 96732 (phone: 877-3311).

Also on the white-sand beach at Kahului is the pleasant **Maui Seaside Hotel,** all of whose rooms are air-conditioned, have color TV, double beds, and a refrigerator. It's next door to the Maui Hukilau and uses the same swimming pool and dining facilities. Rates start at $27 for a single, $32 for a twin, going up to $32 and $37 for superior rooms, $37 and $41 for deluxe. A third person in the room is charged $5. Hotel, car, and breakfast plans for two are $41 standard, $44 superior, $48 deluxe. For reservations, write to Maui Seaside Hotel, Kahului, Maui, HI 96732. Or you may phone toll-free to Hawaii for both the Hukilau and the Seaside: 800/367-7000. The local phone is 877-3311.

HOTELS IN KIHEI AND WAILEA: For centuries, the calm beaches and windswept sands of the Kihei area of Maui were left relatively untouched. Even as tourist development boomed in the rest of Maui, this dry, sunny area just a 15- to 20-minute drive from Kahului was practically undiscovered—one hotel, a few cottages, that was it. But in the last ten years or so, Kihei has been discovered in a big way, and now, as the islanders say, it's wall-to-wall condominiums. In the neighboring Wailea area, more condominiums as well as two luxury resorts, Hotel Inter-Continental Maui and the Wailea Beach Hotel, have sprung up. While Kihei lacks the heady excitement of the Lahaina-Kaanapali-Napili area (less in the way of restaurants, nightlife, and shops), it is growing more interesting all the time. And it does offer excellent, safe swimming beaches, acres of peace and quiet, and plenty of apartment hotels that offer space and comfort enough for a long stay. Many guests do, in fact, winter in Kihei. The tourist who wishes to stay in Kihei has literally dozens and dozens of choices that would require a book in themselves to detail. The few mentioned below are among the most attractive, and are typical of the many in the area. Note that daily maid service is not the rule in the Kihei condominiums (although it is usually available at an extra price), so be sure to check if this factor is important to you.

Each of the two-bedroom apartments at **Kihei Sands** is actually a tiny little house; one of the bedrooms is on a balcony right above the living room, the other is to the side. These cute, compact little units also have two baths, a fully equipped kitchen, and a private lanai, and they rent for $50 for up to four, with each extra person charged $6, from April 16 to December 14. They can comfortably sleep up to six people. There are also pretty one-bedroom apartments (without the upstairs) and these, capable of housing up to four, go for $35 double, with each extra person charged $6. From December 15 to April 15, prices go up $15 a day. Although the white-sand beach with its oh-so-calm waters is perfect for swimming, Kihei Sands also boasts a freshwater pool. The shake roofs give this place a modern Polynesian feeling that is quite charming. Three-day minimum stay. For reservations, write Kihei Sands, 115 North Kihei Rd., Kihei, Maui, HI 96753 (phone: 879-2624).

High-rise rather than low-slung, **Kihei Beach Resort** is a handsome modern place each of whose apartments faces directly on the white-sand beach. The apartments are spacious and comfortable, the living-dining area is carpeted wall-to-wall, and the electric kitchen is complete with every convenience. From May 1 to November 30, the one-bedroom apartments, big enough to sleep four (sofa bed in the living room, queen or twin beds in the bedroom), go for $46 for a double; $10 per extra person. The two-bedroom units, big enough for six, are $55, double, $10 per extra person. Maid service is included in these rates. The rest of the year, prices are $6 to $7 higher. More pluses for the Kihei Beach: free coffee in the morning; a freshwater pool for swimming; the fact that you're within walking distance of **Robaire's,** a fine French restaurant and one of the better eating places in the area. Three-day minimum stay. For reservations, write Kihei Beach Resort, 36 South Kihei Rd., Kihei, Maui, HI 96753 (phone: 879-2744).

If you choose to stay at the **Punahoa Beach Apartments,** you know that you'll be in good hands. Punahoa is a small place with just 15 units, all of which have private lanais, ocean views, fully equipped kitchens, telephones, and smart, modern furnishings. It's surrounded by gardens, and it's right on the beach, with good swimming and surfing; children love it around the rocks because of the fish. The studio apartments rent for $44 daily in winter (December 15 to April 30) and $33 in summer (May 1 to December 14); one-bedroom units are $53 and $40; the one-bedroom roof garden is $58 and $42; and the two-bedroom apartments are $65 and $47. Punahoa gets booked way ahead with repeat visitors in winter, but accommodations are easier to come by in summer. Five-day minimum stay. Monthly rates are available year round. Write to Punahoa Beach Apartments, 2142 Iliili Rd., Kihei, Maui, HI 96753 (phone: 879-2720).

For those who would like to stay at a resort hotel in Kihei, there's the **Maui Lu Resort.** It boasts a beautiful ocean beach, 30 acres of lush surroundings, a large swimming pool, two tennis courts, restaurant, cocktail lounge, and accommodations ranging from $37 double for standard units to $57 double for deluxe beachfront rooms, plus small studio cottages and others more spacious. All units have color TV, phones, refrigerators, and coffee-makers. Most rooms are air-conditioned, while some are cooled by overhead fans. There are many kitchenettes and some full kitchens. *Note:* Rates are subject to change this year. Write Reservations Manager, Maui Lu Resort, Kihei, Maui, HI 96753 (phone: 879-5808). The nationwide toll-free reservations number is 800/367-5245.

About five miles beyond Kihei, in Wailua, is the **Hotel Inter-Continental Maui,** a 600-room, 16-acre luxury villa that has managed to translate the island feeling of comfort and casual living into a setting of relaxed elegance. Grounds are spacious, vistas are large, and there seems to be no separation between indoors and outdoors. Just about everything one could want from resort life is here, including two beautiful ocean beaches and two freshwater pools. Tennis buffs have 11 all-weather courts (three of them lit for night play), a pro shop, tennis instruction, and clinics available; and the golfers have the 36-hole Wailea Golf Course very close by. There's no chance of getting bored eating here, since there is a slew of restaurants, ranging from the elegance of La Perouse, a seafood specialty dining room, to the relaxed island charm of the inexpensive Makani Coffeehouse. The hotel is *the* evening entertainment spot on this part of the island, with Hawaiian entertainment, dancing, and disco every night.

Using beautiful island woods, rattan headboards, and earthy color schemes of brown and orange or green and yellow, the sleeping rooms continue the hotel's decorative mood. They are large and comfortable, with king or twin beds, private lanais, air conditioning, radio, color TV. Prices go from approximately $55 single, $59 twin in a standard room to $90 and $95 in a deluxe; a third person is charged $10 more. For toll-free reservations, phone 800/432-2673. Within the state of Hawaii, phone: 879-1922 locally, or, in Honolulu, 537-5589.

HOTELS IN LAHAINA: Although the major resort areas of Kaanapali and Napili are not far away, there's a certain ramshackle charm about staying right in Lahaina. Once the capital of the islands, a town with a history as a whaling port and a current free-wheeling ambience that matches those lusty days, Lahaina is a fun-and-games town from morning through night. There are just a few hotels in town, and it's fun—if a bit noisy— to stay at the most famous, **Pioneer Inn,** noted for its salty past, the characters who made its Old Whaler's Saloon a landmark, and a movie career that began and ended with *Hawaii.* It gives you a choice of two wings, each styled to respectfully preserve the charm of the original 1901 building. There are inexpensive rooms without baths here, but they are dark and tiny and not all air-conditioned; I personally opt for the newer rooms. Rates are $27 to $29 for a double in the old building, $29 and $33 for a twin in the new. From the second-floor rooms of the older wing, private lanais overlook the lovely pool area. Singles are $3 less than the above tabs; a third person is $6 extra. (*Note:* There is talk of major room renovation. If this happens, rates may nearly double.) So popular is this place that you ought to reserve 60 days in advance; write to Pioneer Inn, 658 Wharf St., Lahaina, HI 96761 (phone: 661-3636).

If you'd like to settle into your own little apartment right in Lahaina, then **Lahaina Roads** could be your place. The five-story elevator building at the Kaanapali end of Front Street sits in a cool and breezy spot right on a good snorkeling beach; you can look down at the ocean—and watch some spectacular sunsets— from your own lanai. A swimming beach is a half-mile up the road, but there's a freshwater pool right at home. These are condominium apartments, many of them exquisitely furnished by their absentee owners. They are sound-proof with wall-to-wall carpeting, fully equipped kitchens with washer and dryer, large living rooms with convertible couches, and there are phones for free local calls in your room. The baths are divided for dual use and have a square tub with shower. There are outdoor grills on the lawn. One-bedroom apartments go for $43 a day double (they can accommodate up to four people); two bedrooms for $49 double (capable of accommodating up to six); and there is a delightful penthouse (than can house up to eight of you) for $86 for four. Additional persons are $6. Three-day minimum stay. Write them in advance at 1403 Front St., Lahaina, Maui, HI 96761 (phone: 661-3166).

HOTELS AT KAANAPALI BEACH: Just three miles north of Lahaina is what surely must be one of the great resort areas anywhere in the world—**Kaanapali Beach.** Stretched out along this fabled strip of white sand, crystal waters, and gentle, rolling surf, with a championship golf course sloping down to the sea and the West Maui mountains offering spectacular vistas in the background, is a small cluster of luxury hotels. We doubt if you could go wrong at any of them, but each offers something a little bit special. Perhaps the grandest of these resorts is the newest: the $80-million **Hyatt Regency Maui,** which opened in April

1980. Breathtaking is the word for this 815-room seaside caravanserai, which covers 20 acres of prime beachfront and is spangled with eight major waterfalls, Japanese gardens and lagoons, underground grottoes, meandering streams along which swans glide, and an exceptional pool—an entire acre of fresh water that roams under waterfalls and bridges, along gardens and lava rocks, and offers swimmers a sensational 100-foot slide. The atrium lobby, surfaced in Arizona flagstone, is centered around a 70-foot tall banyan tree; surrounding areas are dotted with plantings, gardens, and tropical birds—flamingoes, parrots, peacocks, even penguins. And throughout the lobby and the adjoining luxury shopping arcade (a kind of Rodeo Drive of the islands) is $2-million worth of original artworks, mostly from the Far East and the South Pacific. Such a setup is, of course, a sightseeing attraction; tours for the public are held daily at 9 a.m. and 2:30 p.m.

But if you are a guest at this hotel, you have a wealth of activities to choose from—Robert Trent Jones's 27-hole golf course right at hand, six all-weather surface tennis courts, an underground health spa. Classes and clinics go on all day, in sailing, aquatrimatics (water exercises), hula, pineapple cutting, and backgammon, to name just a few. And dining facilities are as splendid as you would imagine. There are the Swan Court (with real swans) for continental and seafood specialties; Lahaina Provision Company, a garden-like, casual setting for grilled-to-order meats and huge salads; Spats II, an Italian cafe where the pasta is fine, the antipasto bar is huge, and disco rules the night; The Pavilion, for poolside cafeteria dining; and several bars and lounges, including the "sunken" Grotto pool bar. The Sunset Terrace is the scene of frequent luaus, concerts, and other festivities.

As for the rooms, they are spacious, artfully decorated in quiet earth-tones, and provide every comfort: air conditioning, color TV, private phones, full bathrooms, sitting areas, tasteful artworks on the walls. Prices vary according to the view, from golf court to garden to ocean, high ocean, and ocean front. Single or twin, they are $70, $75, $80, $85, and $90. Suites range all the way from $170 for a Club Suite to $700 for the Presidential digs. Each additional person is charged $15; children under 12 stay free with parents; maximum of three in a room.

Toll-free reservations from 800/228-9000. The local phone number is 677-7474.

A long-time favorite at Kaanapali is the **Royal Lahaina**, with

735 rooms and suites spread out on 52 acres of beautiful tropical gardens fronting the beach. There are seven major buildings plus many cottages; one section—Lahaina West—was once a major resort hotel in its own right, and consists of studios and one-bedroom suites with full kitchens. Recreational facilities are magnificent: you can play at 11 tennis courts (including one stadium court), six of them lighted at night (tennis dress is required); golf at the magnificent Robert Trent Jones course that surrounds the hotel or at the Kaanapali Kai course adjacent to it; swim at any of seven pools or in the glorious ocean; sail in a catamaran; and indulge in sauna baths, massages, and a Jacuzzi whirlpool bath when it's time to relax. You can shop at some of the best stores in Maui in two separate shopping arcades, and dine at a bevy of splendid restaurants including the petite **Brasserie by the Sea** for French provincial fare; **Moby Dick's** for seafood as good as it is in New England; **Don the Beachcomber** for Polynesian and Cantonese specialties; **Paniolo Steak House** for choice beef. There are even two grocery stores for those cooking in. There's a Hawaiian dinner show every night at the handsome **Alii Room** (which turns into the Foxy Lady Disco after the show), plus seven cocktail lounges. Once you've settled in here, there's little reason to go anywhere else.

Now for the rooms. There are 19 different categories, and they come in a variety of sizes, shapes, and prices. Even those at the lowest rate—$58 double—are spacious and equipped with color television, air conditioning, direct-dial phone, a small lanai, and a combination bath and dressing room. An important extra: every room has a refrigerator. If you want a kitchen, you can get a studio at $80 or $85 or a one-bedroom apartment at $90 to $150 double. Rooms go up to $75 for a double, while the two- and three-bedroom suites are in the $175 to $300 range (up to four are accepted in the two-bedroom units, up to six in the three-bedroom ones; extra persons $6 each). Cribs and rollaway beds are $6. Deduct $2 for single occupancy. If you wish king- or queen-size beds, the hotel requests that you ask for them in advance. Full American Plan is available at $31, MAP at $24. From December 1 to April 1, expect a surcharge of $5 per category.

There's very little specifically Hawaiian about the hotel lobby or rooms, but step outside and it's all there—the spectacular Maui mountains, incredible views of Lanai and Molokai, and, of course, the sparkling Pacific. For reservations, write Island Holidays Resorts, P.O. Box 8519, 2222 Kalakaua Ave., Honolulu HI 96815.

Walking into the **Maui Surf Hotel** is something like walking into a giant summerhouse; there's bamboo furniture all about, sun colors everywhere, and such a continuity of nature indoors that it's hard to know where the lobby ends and the greenery begins. This is one of the newer hotels in the InterIsland Surf Resorts chain, and it's a winner. The graceful bamboo decor extends into the color-coordinated rooms with their grass-textured walls, Hawaiian piped-in music, air conditioning, private lanais, full tub-and-shower combinations, plus such conveniences as refrigerators, floor-to-ceiling mirrors, ice buckets (courtesy ice), and coffee-makers. Your rate will vary according to the height of the floor and the view: from standard doubles at $65 to superior ones at $71 to deluxe at $78 (these with broad expanses of blue Pacific visible from your private lanai). Suites go from $195 to $395, and there are also adjoining rooms (price of two doubles) for families. Singles are $3 less; no charge for children under 12 staying in the same room with their parents; $10 for an extra adult.

Downstairs, you have the delightful Eight Bells restaurant for breakfast and dinner; the stunning Quee Queeg Room for dinner; and the Pequod Cocktail Lounge, surely one of the most atmospheric watering holes on the planet, built like an old ship and surrounded by a moat. It looks out over a pond filled with water lilies, flashing carp, and waterfalls. Lui William's famed Polynesian show is presented every night in the elegant Kapaa Room, and down at the pool there's the Surfside Restaurant and bar for quick meals and cool drinks. The broad expanse of Kaanapali Beach is just out front, but we predict that if you have little ones with you, you won't be able to get them away from the pool; it's got a cement "island" in the middle that's just great for jumping and diving. A few days here and you may never want to get back to the rest of Hawaii—let alone the rest of the world. Reservations: InterIsland Surf Resorts, P.O. Box 8539, Honolulu, HI 96815. For toll-free reservations, phone 800/421-0811 nationwide; 800/252-0381, California only; locally, 213/937-5800 in Los Angeles and 312/782-9081 in Chicago. The local phone in Maui is 661-4411.

One of the first hotels to be built on the Kaanapali strip, the **Sheraton-Maui** has been blessed with a spectacular location. It is wrapped around a crater called Black Rock (the ancient cliff from which souls of Hawaiians were said to leap to the spirit world beyond), and its main building winds around the rock in a series of descending, curving parapets that are really the balconies of individual rooms. There's also another wing that is more conventionally high-rise. In both buildings, each room is a good size, has its own private balcony or garden and tub-shower combination, plus an optional, $2-a-day refrigerator on wheels. Depending on the view, doubles run from $65 to $95 for rooms in various buildings, the top price being for oceanfront cabanas or "cottages." One-bedroom suites are $125 to $150. These rates apply from December 21 to March 31; the rest of the year, prices go from $59 to $84 for the doubles, from $115 to $130 for the suites. Singles are $3 less; a third person in the room, $10 more; no charge for children under 17.

There's a great deal just to look at in this hotel. The old lobby with the sky for a roof from which you take the elevators *down* to everything is beautiful, with its pool, fountains, and sculpture; off it is the stylish Discovery Room, for continental dining and nightly entertainment. My favorite spots here are the pool and the beaches. The Black Rock Terrace at poolside has a terrific buffet dinner at $8.50, and inexpensive, serve-yourself food the rest of the day. The beach here is my personal favorite at Kaanapali. Snorkeling buffs love the long reef that goes out from Black Rock, and golfers have the Robert Trent Jones Royal Kaanapali Golf Club next door—so everybody's happy. Toll-free reservations: 800/325-3535. The local phone is 661-0031.

A budget hotel on Kaanapali Beach? There's really no such animal, but rates are a bit lower at the **Kaanapali Beach Resort,** and it's also a lovely place, right out on the ocean, with an intriguing swimming pool shaped like a whale, acres of trees and flowers, and a full complement of restaurants and drinking spots. Each room has its own private lanai, is large, air-conditioned, attractively decorated, with the convenience of a refrigerator and color television set with free movies. Considering all these amenities, the price for minimum rooms of $56 in a single, $58 in a double is quite modest. Medium, deluxe, and waterfront rooms and suites go up the scale to $69, $72, and $79 in a double. And for those budget meals, it's nice to know that the coffeehouse offers dinners from about $3.50 to $6. The Kaanapali Beach Resort is owned by the same management that has the Royal Lahaina, and the address to write for reservations is Island Holidays Resorts, P.O. Box 8519, Honolulu, HI 96815. The local phone is 661-0011.

HOTELS BETWEEN KAANAPALI AND NAPILI: Once you pass the big hotels of the Kaanapali area, you're smack into condominium country. Between Kaanapali and Napili, miles and miles of curving coastline are being given over to small apartment hotels that provide every home-away-from-home comfort in an idyllic setting that's nothing like home. Most of these operate exactly like a hotel. Apartments can be rented on a daily, weekly, or monthly basis; full maid and linen service are provided, and the management takes care of all repairs and services. Most do not have restaurants on the premises, but they all have kitchen facilities, and restaurants abound all over the area. *Note.* Since some condominiums do expect you to do your own housework, be sure to inquire about all such details before you send your deposit.

Just about my favorite place here, the **Maui Sands,** is only a mile from the Kaanapali hotels, and has accommodations as comfortable as any $200-a-day luxury suite at about one-third the price. The 76 one- and two-bedroom suites are either set in a beautiful tropic garden or on the oceanfront. These have enormous living rooms with private lanais (great for star-gazing at night), comfortable-sized bedrooms, full electric kitchens, tropical ceiling fans, and color television; a family has plenty of room to really stretch out and relax here. Since each apartment is individually owned, the furnishings are slightly different in each, but all are well-appointed and comfortable. Everything has been newly refurbished. The top accommodation, a two-bedroom apartment overlooking the beach, goes for $77 for four persons. In the garden, it's $62, and near the road, $54. One-bedroom apartments for two people are $55 for oceanfront, $45 for the garden, and $36 for standard. Extra persons are charged $6. Kids love the swimming pool and sunning area, mom appreciates the convenience of the laundry, and everybody loves the beach. Free Hawaiian entertainment once a week in season, cocktail parties every other week, and a cordial reception up at the front desk. For reservations, phone toll-free 800/367-5037, or write to Maui Sands Hotel, P.O. Box 218, Lahaina, Maui, HI 96761. The local phone is 669-6391.

Strangely enough, really good beaches are not so easy to find along this coastline. Many of the apartment hotels are built on rocky beachfronts and guests do most of their swimming in pools. One place that is, however, blessed with a beautiful, reef-protected crescent beach is **Kahana Sunset** on Kahana Bay, about midway between Kaanapali and Napili. There are other things to commend this place, too, notably the 79 units that meander down a gentle hillside and are adequately spaced for privacy, comfort, and good ocean views. I especially like the two-bedroom units, which are like little two-story town houses with twin stairways leading to the bedrooms and two baths; they rent for $75 double. Slightly larger two-bedroom, 2½-bathroom units—called executive town houses—rent for $95 double, and one-bedroom apartments go for $65. It's $6 for each additional person; maximum of six in each unit. All of the units are handsomely furnished and have full electric kitchens with all the comforts a suburban matron might want: dishwasher, garbage disposal, self-cleaning oven, refrigerator and freezer with an automatic icemaker, even one's own washer-dryer. Besides the good beach, there's a freshwater swimming pool, croquet, a putting green, and barbecue pits down on the beach. The Eastman family, long known as fine hosts in this area, are in charge here, and every Friday night they offer a fish fry for their guests. For reservations, write them at Kahana Sunset, R.R. 1, Lahaina, Maui, HI 96761 (phone: 669-8011).

You can also be assured of an excellent swimming beach at a clutch of small hotels coming up now on Napili Bay. Here's where the **Mauian Hotel,** one of the first in this area, is still going strong. Its 44 Polynesian-style units are fitted out with a queen-size bed and two twins to accommodate four persons. They boast fully equipped electric kitchens, private lanais, and plenty of ocean breezes whooshing through. There's a pool for those who can forego the superb beach, a laundry area, even the **Hawaiian Store** next door, an island-style minisupermarket (the shopping carts wear grass skirts) that makes cooking a breeze. There are golf courses and many good restaurants nearby. Rates are $39 to $44 for a single, $44 to $54 for a double; $6 for each extra person; and a 10% monthly discount. Maid service every three days; 10% more for daily service. For reservations, write the Mauian Hotel, Attn. Marge Putt, P.O. Box 1684, Lahaina, Maui, HI 96761; or phone toll-free 800/367-5034. The local phone is 669-6205.

Napili Village, a stone's throw away from the Mauian, is another popular and well-established place in the lovely Napili area. There are just 24 convertible studio bedroom apartments here, each of them capable of housing four, with a folding door creating two separate sleeping areas. Each has a king-size bed and twins, an all-electric kitchen, a large lanai, wall-to-wall carpeting, a radio, and a comfortable living room/eating area. You have a lovely pool and the right to use the beach, just a few steps away, but no beachfront accommodations. The **Hawaiian Store,** mentioned above, is just behind the pool. Rates begin at $37 double or single, $5 for each extra person. A U-Drive agency is located on the premises. For reservations, write Napili Village, R.R. 1, Napili Bay, Maui, HI 96761 (phone: 669-6228).

A true luxury setup on Napili Bay is **Napili Surf Beach Resort,** run by Vivian Lusby, who provides plenty of aloha along with her beautiful beachfront accommodations. Spaciousness and comfort are the big things here: the studio apartments each contain 500 square feet; the one-bedroom units contain 670 square feet. Each apartment has an all-electric kitchen. All units are soundproofed, carpeted, and handsomely furnished. The choice of either the freshwater swimming pool or that blue Pacific is yours. Rates are $37 single and $43 double in the smaller but cozy Puamala garden studios; $51 double in the oceanview studios; and $67 double in the one-bedroom apartments on the beachfronting property. It's $6 for an extra person. On alternate weekends, people come from all around to catch the entertainment, usually the No Ka Oi Four. Write Napili Surf, Napili Bay, Maui, HI 96761 (phone: 669-8002 or 669-8003). Reservations are a must, and a deposit of $100 is required to guarantee space.

Should you happen to have a generous fairy godmother (or godperson, as the case may be) who will grant you a special wish, ask for a stay at **Kapalua Bay Hotel** at Kapalua, near the northern tip of the island. Picture a 600-acre resort complex, surrounded by ocean and bay, by coconut palms and tall pines, by flowering gardens and gentle landscapes at every turn, combining the ultimate in continental hotel service and elegance with the graceful aloha of island living, and you'll get some idea of what Kapalua Bay is all about. It's the newest in the chain of internationally famous Rockresorts (they created Mauna Kea on the Big Island and Caneel Bay Plantation in the Virgin Islands, among others), and as with all of these grand hotels, "no compromise" is the watchword. Kapalua Bay provides three sandy ocean beaches for swimming; a freshwater pool; two 18-hole championship golf courses designed by Arnold Palmer; a "tennis garden" (10 courts surrounded by lush greenery); many dining facilities, including the intimate Plantation Veranda which has won awards from *Travel/Holiday* magazine for gourmet cuisine, the Grill & Bar for informal food and panoramic views, and the Bay Club, just above the beach, for drinks and dining overlooking a spectacular setting—for starters. Buffet lunches served daily in the Mayfair Buffet are among the special treats of the islands (see ahead).

The cuisine at Kapalua, created by Walter Blum, the famed European chef who heads Rockresorts kitchens around the world, is in the continental tradition with island specialties; all rooms are rented on Modified American Plan, which includes breakfast and dinner. And the rooms themselves are gracious beauties, tastefully decorated in subdued South Seas style, all in tones of rust or blue. They have twin or king-size beds, his-and-hers baths, small refrigerators in the dividers between bed and sitting areas, large lanais, and high ceilings (they are reminiscent, in fact, of rooms at the Kahala Hilton in Honolulu and were designed by the same person). Rooms are all the same; only their location makes for a price differential. Standard rooms are $146 per day double; superior, $160; deluxe, $186; suites are $275. An extra person is charged $50 more per day; subtract $15 for a single. At various times of the year, European Plan (minus meals) rates and special golf, tennis, and honeymoon packages may be offered.

Kapalaua Bay also boasts one of the most tasteful shopping arcades in the islands, The Shops at Kapalua, which contains its own little moderately priced European-style Market Cafe.

Write to Kapalua Bay Hotel, Route One, Box 333, Kapalua, Maui, HI 96761. For toll-free reservations, phone 800/225-1739.

Should you prefer your own apartment at Kapalua, the **Bay Villas** are for you. There are 141 of these condominium apartments on the grounds, and they are all beautifully furnished, with sunken tiled baths, wall-to-wall carpeting, washer-dryers, complete kitchens, plus daily maid service. One bedroom and one-bedroom-plus-loft apartments (with 1½ baths) are $85 quad; two-bedroom and two-bedroom-plus-loft apartments (with three baths in each) are $145 for up to six, all with an ocean view; on the oceanfront, the same arrangements cost $97 to $165. Minimum stay: four days.

Write to the Bay Villas, Kapalua, Maui, HI 96761. For toll-free reservations, phone 800/367-5035.

A HIDEOUT IN HANA: Although the expensive and lovely **Hotel Hana-Maui** (rates from about $140 per day, double, including meals), which dominates the Hana region of Maui, is well known, very few tourists are aware that there is also a neat little budget accommodation in the remote little town of Hana. If you can manage to sneak away for a few days from the other attractions of Maui, and want utter peace and relaxation, **Heavenly Hana** could be the answer. Owner-manager Mrs. Alfreda Worst, who has lived in Japan, has created an Oriental feeling about this place, with low railings around the outside lanais, lions at the gate, and beautifully landscaped gardens. There are just four units, modest but clean and comfortable, and each has two bedrooms, a private bath, dining porch, and lanai. Although you enter by your own private entrance outside, the rooms have doors that open into an attractive common lounge. There's good swimming down the beach a way, but the lush tropical atmosphere is enticing, and you might be content to stay here without moving from the spot. If requested in advance, dinner and breakfast service will be available for guests at reasonable prices (there are very few restaurants in Hana). TV is available. Rates are $45 single or double, $50 triple, $60 quad; each additional person $6.50. A minimum stay of two days is required.

Dining in Maui

RESTAURANTS IN THE KAHULUI-WAILUKU AREA: I've always been a fan of Mexican cooking, so I was delighted to find **La Familia** at 2119 Vineyard St. in Wailuku. Repeated visits over the years have kept it on my favorite list of Mexican restaurants anywhere. Owner Tony Habib and his friends have decorated the place themselves and it's charming, with a bent eucalyptus wood ceiling, plants and greenery, and an especially pretty semi-outdoors room facing the garden and gazebo. The menu is also enticing, with all the usual Mexican dishes plus some unusual Mexican vegetarian specialties to serve the natural-foods enthusiasts in the area. They also offer homemade quiches, fresh fish, steaks, and seafood. I finally settled on the chicken burrito, filled with chicken, sprouts, fresh vegetables, guacamole, and a tangy sauce, $5.95, and a delicious order of chile relleno, stuffed with cheese and green chile, fried and topped with sauce, $3.95, both à la carte. The homemade soup and garden-fresh salad were also first-rate. Complete combination dinners run $5.95 to $12.50. And I couldn't resist an extra plate of the homemade flour tortillas to go along with my Carta Blanca. Good wines, and more potent stuff, too. Dinner every day from 5 to 10 p.m. lunch Monday to Friday 11 to 3, from noon Saturday; live entertainment Friday, Saturday, and Sunday nights. Phone: 244-9974.

In a generally desultory dining town like Wailuku, the opening of a restaurant of the calibre of **The Velvet Needle** is good news indeed. Not only does it enjoy one of the most picturesque locations in the islands (in secluded, verdant Iao Valley), but the two-tiered dining room is beautiful, the food imaginatively prepared and decently priced. Whether you sit in the upper room with its South Seas paintings and cozy fireplaces (yes, it can get cool here in the Valley), the lower room with its soft red-velvet sofas and high-backed chairs, or out on the large lanai at umbrella'ed tables, you'll find the food just fine. You can begin or end your meal at the salad bar; it has 19 offerings, a choice of dressings, and costs just $5.95 at dinner, $5 at lunch. Dinner entrees range mostly from $6.95 to $10.95 and are served with fresh homemade bread (vegetables and potatoes are extra, salad bar is $2). Nicely done are the chicken saltimbocca, the Alaskan king crab legs in a wine-and-butter sauce, and the sauteed shrimp Italienne. Lunch is a good buy, with dishes like teriyaki steak, a calorie-conscious zucchini lasagna, and mahimahi amandine, priced from $3.95 to $5.95, including vegetable, potato or rice, and the bread. I can recommend the French onion soup among the appetizers and the unforgettable passion-fruit cheesecake among the desserts. Local people like to gather around the bar during the 4 to 5 p.m. Happy Hour; there's entertainment then, as well as nightly from 8:30. Lunch is from 11 a.m. to 2:30 p.m., pupus and sandwiches from 2:30 to 5:30 p.m., then dinner until 10 p.m., every day. A welcome find. Reservations: 242-6684.

For the best budget dining in this area, try **Naokee's Steak House,** at 1792 Main St. in Wailuku. Come for lunch when every entree on the menu—teriyaki steak, New York steak, mahimahi, etc.—is priced at just $3.50! And that includes rice, vegetables, potato or macaroni salad, and soup. Coffee is extra. At night, many varieties of steak, plus lobster, island prawns, etc., all served with soup, salad, coffee or tea, average $8.75 to $15.75— still good value for the money.

RESTAURANTS IN KIHEI: Those who love really fresh fish should know about the **Kihei Village Fish House,** 1947 Kihei Road, which specializes in deep-sea game fish from local waters, served the day they were caught. The atmosphere is one of island charm—fishnets on the ceiling, walls of Ponderosa pine, rich maroon cloths on the tables, beautiful gardens, and a smashing view of sunset over the ocean. Fish will be served the way you like it—sauteed, poached, char-broiled, deep fried, or baked Hawaiian style—for either $12.50 or $13.50. Along with the catch of the day—maybe red opakapaka or sweet ping snapper—come a basket of hot homemade rolls, tossed salad, a green vegetable, and fried rice with mushrooms and Oriental seasonings. Steaks are available, too, from $10.50 to $12.50. Everything is cooked to order, using no synthetics or shortcuts. The waiters and waitresses are friendly and informative. Try the spicy, chopped shellfish patties called Makena puffs, among the hot appetizers. And treat yourself to a gorgeous dessert: perhaps lemon or Kahula cheesecake, Kihei Mud Pie (with a thick layer of fudge sauce and whipped cream atop coffee ice cream and chocolate-cookie crust), or the delicate mango mousse, in season. Dinner only, from 5:30 to 10 p.m., seven days a week. Phone 879-1545 for reservations.

A great place to cool off on a hot Kihei night, the **Maui Outrigger**, 2980 S. Kihei Rd., is housed in a low-slung wooden frame building directly on the waterfront. You could literally jump from your table onto the beach—but don't. Stay and eat. The food is good and the mood convivial. Fanned white napkins on red tablecloths, flowers on every table, a lively atmosphere at the bar are background to a mostly seafood-and-steak menu that runs from $6.95 for giant salad bar to about $12.50 for Alaskan king crab legs. Honey-dipped chicken, catch of the day, surf and turf (filet and mahimahi) are all crowd-pleasers. This is a dinner-only house, serving daily from 5:30 to 9 or 10 p.m. The bar opens at 3 p.m. Reservations: 879-1581.

Robaire's Wailea, at Wailea Town Center, is a sister restaurant to the older Robaire's, one of Kihei's first restaurants, which offers classic French cuisine. Here the emphasis is on seafood—but à la française, mais certainement. My favorite spot in this lovely dining room is out on the lanai, where I can happily feast on such dishes as ono à la bonne femme (i.e., sauteed with shallot, mushrooms, white wine, and heavy cream), or scampi Dijonais (sauteed in garlic, mustard, white wine, and brandy), or mahimahi à la Provençale (this with tomatoes, mushrooms, and garlic). Most dishes are $12.50 and $13.50, and are served with a light green salad. More modest lunches include quiche with pineapple and sandwiches, from $3.25 to $4.50. For dessert, I can't resist mousse au chocolat. Open for lunch from 11:30 to 3 p.m. Monday to Saturday; for dinner from 5 to 10 p.m. daily. Reservations: 879-4577.

If you're in the Kihei-Wailea area on a Sunday morning between 9 a.m. and 1 p.m., join the local folks who make the champagne brunch at the **Hotel Inter-Continental,** Maui's **Lanai Terrace** a Sunday tradition. The smorgasbord table, stuffed with the likes of fresh fruit, smoked salmon with bagels and sour cream, pickled herring, eggs Benedict, seafood Newburg, wild rice with mushrooms, and chicken livers, plus custom-made omelets, is incredible. A live radio show is broadcast here. Cost of the meal is $9 for adults, $5.50 for children 12 and under, but it should keep you going for the rest of the day.

Also recommended in Kihei: **Kihei Prime Rib House,** 2511 South Kihei Rd. (phone: 879-1954), a rustic South Seas-type building with attractive seating, specializing in roast prime ribs of beef au jus at $13.25, excellent fresh seafood from about $9 to $12.50, served with salad bar, rice pilaf, and homemade bread. Fine wines and exotic drinks. Breakfast, lunch, and dinner served.

RESTAURANTS IN THE LAHAINA-KAANAPALI-NAPILI AREA:

I—and scads of other visitors to Maui—have long had a special fondness for the **Lahaina Broiler** on Front Street, corner of Kapalau. As you sit out on the big, open lanai with the sea smashing against the wall, viewing the South Seas nautical decor and enjoying the delicious food, you know that this is what Hawaii is supposed to be like. Steak and seafood are the big items here, and they are well priced. Dinners, served with soup or salad, French fries or rice, and hot garlic bread, average $7.25 to $11.95 for entrees like shrimp curry, fresh island catch of the day, scampi, and top sirloin. For lunch, one of their sandwich plates—perhaps mahimahi almond sherry, $3.95, or the Captain's Fish Platter, around $6.50, served with rice or French fries and a vegetable—makes a filling meal. The big nautical bar with its plants in "canoes" draws a lively crowd here until Lahaina quiets down, usually around midnight. Phone: 661-3111.

Another place that's immensely popular in Lahaina is **Kimo's,** at 845 Front St., overlooking the water, with glorious sunset views. It's exciting rather than peaceful, and packs in the crowds for good fresh fish of the day at $11.95, top sirloin or teriyaki sirloin, island specialties like huli-huli chicken (breast of chicken marinated in a ginger-shoyu sauce and broiled), or kushiyaki (brochettes of marinated chunks of sirloin and chicken breast), from $7.95 to $9.95. Along with your tasty entree comes a tossed green salad with a good house dressing, long-grain and wild rice, and a basket of freshly baked bread. Special menus for kids, from $3.95 to $5.95. If you have room for dessert, try the Hula Pie—it's supposedly what the sailors swam to shore for—and Kimo's coffee, served up with a bit of macadamia nut liqueur. Phone: 661-4811.

If we're to believe that the sailors swam ashore for Kimo's Hula Pie, then we must also believe that the natives swam from Kimo's to **Nimble's,** at the top of Mariner's Alley, 844 Front St., for their Shaka Pie. Actually, there's a lot more than the luscious chocolate-chip ice-cream pie to paddle on up to Nimble's for; this engaging restaurant is one of the kickiest places in town, with turn-of-the-century decor, scads of antiques and stained glass, baseball and other sporting mementoes, three dining rooms (the one on the lanai overlooking Front Street is the coolest), an enormous and busy bar, a friendly young staff, deeply decolletéed waitresses, and some excellent food at decent prices. (Look for coupons in the tourist papers offering $1 or $2 off on meals.)

Nimble's specialties are fresh fish at about $10 (I highly recommend their ono sauteed in white wine), steak and seafood dishes (from about $9.75 to $12.95), and such local favorites as crêpes of the day (seafood crêpes were tasty), Molokai pork chops, and rack of Colorado lamb. Keiki meals are priced from $4.95 to $5.95. Along with your dinner comes wild and long grain rice, hot breads, and as much of the salad bar as you can handle. Salad bar alone is $6.95, a bit overpriced since there is not really enough to make a full meal on, and canned fruit salad should be banned in Hawaii. But it goes fine with your meal, and so, of course, do the desserts. Homemade island cheesecake with graham cracker crust, covered with strawberries, is great, and the Shaka Pie as good as they say. Nimble's offers drinks from 11 a.m. to 1 a.m.; long lunches from 11:30 a.m. to 3:30 p.m. (seafood chowder, crêpes, burgers, avocado sandwiches, salad bar, from about $2.95 to $4.95), dinner from 5 p.m., and entertainment every night. Phone: 661-0094.

Dining at Nimble's is fun. But one warning: read "The Legend of Alferd Packer" on the back of your menu (he is the restaurant's mascot) only *after* you've eaten.

There are a handful of good French restaurants in Maui. **Chez Paul** at 820-B Olowalu Village was the very first, and it's still one of the very best. It's a small restaurant, simply but tastefully decorated, and the kitchen is excellent, as good as you'd find in many restaurants in Paris. There are just a few dishes on the menu each night, and they may include the very good frog legs sauteed in garlic butter, the delicate braised Belgian endives rolled in ham, or the unusual veal Valdotin, veal baked in casserole with wine sauce, ham, and cheese. Your entree, priced from $10 to $15, comes served with a soup du jour or a crisp green salad, plus two vegetables. If you fancy some escargots or pâté for an appetizer, the chef can oblige. And this is one place where you should save room for dessert, especially the dreamy chocolate mousse! Olowalu is on the Wailuku side of Lahaina, about a 10-minute drive, and Chez Paul is a small place, so keep your eyes peeled for it. It's open for dinner only, from 6 p.m. daily. Reservations are a must: phone 661-3843.

Restaurants come and go with alarming frequency in this area, but one that seems destined to stay forever is the **Banyan Inn** on Front Street in Lahaina, which is still considered the best steak house in town. You'll know you're in the islands when you step into this place, since two walls are nothing but jungle. Dinners are reasonably priced, especially the famous Banyan Inn sizzling steaks, from about $11 to $13. You can also choose from such items as fish freshly caught in Lahaina waters, prime rib roast, and French-fried shrimp, priced from $7 to $11.95, and accompanied by the Banyan Inn special soup (a spicy Portuguese concoction) or fruit cup, a fresh garden salad, vegetable, rolls and butter, and beverage. Lunch is reasonable, too, with à la carte entrees like teriyaki steak, fish, and pot roast under $5, plus salads and sandwiches. French and California wines, champagnes, and exotic Polynesian cocktails are available, too. The phone is 661-0755.

It's a different kind of decor at **Bluemax,** 734 Front St.: posh Victoriana with overstuffed, easy-to-sink-into furniture and a World War I aviation theme. Try it at lunchtime, when you can enjoy homemade soups and gourmet salads (Niçoise, spinach, seafood, $4.25 to $6), a variety of omelets ($4.25 to $5.50), and a crêpe special every day. The chef, who specializes in French country cooking, pulls out all the stops at dinnertime. He'll whip up a neat shrimp thermidor, chicken breast à la Normande, canard à l'orange, veal scallopini piccata, or steak au poivre, all priced around $12 to $13.50. Vegetarians like the vegetable casserole with cheese at $7.25. Desserts are extravagantly good: chocolate mousse, peach melba, and yet another Mud Pie. Lunch is on from 11:30 a.m. to 2:30, p.m., Sunday brunch from 10 a.m. to 2 p.m., dinner from 5:30 to 9:30 p.m., and there's live entertainment every night from 10 on. A swinging spot. Phone: 661-8202.

My favorite eating spot at the Whaler's Market Place is **The Italian Restaurant,** which has a calm and gracious air, unlike the hustle-bustle in many Lahaina eateries. The view is sunset and waterfront, the atmosphere red-checkered tablecloth and candlelight, and the food on the hearty and filling side. A very nice lettuce salad with a choice of dressing (Italian and blue cheese are both good) and a healthy serving of garlic bread precede the entree, which could be Delfino Veronica (mahimahi in white wine and lemon garlic sauce, topped with grapes) or, perhaps, cannelloni pasetto (filled with chicken, cheese, and herbs), both nicely done. I found the chicken cacciatore, however, a bit too heavy and highly spiced. Pasta dishes begin at $4.25, other entrees are $8.95 to $9.95. Service is attentive, the waiters cordial. Dinner is served from 5:30 to 9:30 p.m. Phone: 661-3288.

I suggest you go back to the center of town to feast on the legendary desserts at **Longhi's,** 888 Front St., whose mango cheesecakes, chocolate cake pies, strawberry shortcakes, et al., have inspired poetry and rapture. Desserts run about $2.50 and are big enough and rich enough to share. Just about everything else at Longhi's (new menu daily, depending on what's fresh and in season) is special, too. Dinner about $8 to $15.

I've already told you about many of the fine restaurants in the Kaanapali hotels in the hotel section, above. But there's a new, low-priced winner you should know about, and that's **Apple Annie's Beach House,** just inside the Lahaina-end entrance to Kaanapali Resort. This is the newest in the chain of Maui's popular Apple Annie restaurants, and it's a casual place, smartly styled in island decor, where you can get omelets, salads, pizzas, and Mexican dishes, and reasonable dinner specialties averaging $7 to $9 for such items as mahimahi in varied styles and teriyaki or island-style chicken. It's fun to sit out on the porch and have a few drinks while you wait for your meal. Dinner only, Sunday through Thursday from 5:30 to 12:30 p.m., Friday and Saturday until 1:30 a.m. Phone 661-2160.

A few miles north of Kaanapali Beach, the condominium dwellers have high praise for the food at **Kahana Keyes,** a big, busy place where the atmosphere is most striking around the salad bar, one of the biggest and best on the island. Come early, between 5:30 and 7, when there's a different "Early Bird Special" each night, including salad bar, rice, potatoes or pasta, and such entrees as teriyaki steak, prime ribs of beef, deep-fried catch of the day. The cost is just $6.95. On the regular menu, fresh fish and seafood run $8.95 to $12.95, excellent steaks from $7.95 to $11.95, and house specialties like veal parmigiana and roast rack of lamb from $7.50 to $14.95. Salad bar, of course, is included, along with potatoes, rice, or pasta. Entertainment every night. Phone: 669-8071.

Accustomed as I am to casual dining rooms in the islands, I was totally unprepared for anything as elegant as **Le Tournedos,** a French restaurant in the Napili Shores Hotel with a fountain in the middle of the room, hurricane lamps on the tables, and wide picture-windows mirroring flaming torches and looking out over a floodlit pond, flowers, and rock garden below. The menu is impressive and expensive, concentrating on tournedos, those classic cuts of petit filet of prime beefsteak prepared with a variety of sauces. I can recommend both the tournedos Oscar, filets topped with pink Alaskan crabmeat, green asparagus spears, and sauce bearnaise, $17.75, and the tournedos Marsala au champignon, $15.95. In addition to the various tournedos, the restaurant features such dishes as mahimahi ananas, boeuf Stroganoff, and roast duckling, priced from about $9 to $15. Along with each dinner comes a superb Caesar salad and a very tasty rice pilaf. Desserts are limited to French vanilla ice cream and a light European cheesecake, but they are served beautifully with whipped cream and fresh fruits. *Naturellement,* the house has a fine wine cellar.

The management stresses that men must wear long pants and conventional footwear; women are asked only to "exhibit their good taste." Dinner only is served, from 6 to 10 p.m.; reservations: 669-8077. Incidentally, Le Tournedos is owned by the same people who run Le Bistro and L' Escargot, those formidable French restaurants in Honolulu.

Perhaps the most beautifully open-to-nature dining room in Maui—or in the islands—is the one at **The Bay Club** at the Kapalua Bay resort on the northern tip of this area of western Maui. While the hotel is, indeed, expensive (see above), and dinner will cost about $28 per person for food in the finest continental tradition, anyone with a few dollars in the pocket can have lunch here and enjoy the almost breathtaking views of sea and sky. The Bay Club is situated on a rise commanding a spectacular, multiangled view of the ocean; the feeling is almost of being on board a ship. The atmosphere is serene, with deep, comfortable chairs, wood-and-wicker furnishings, art works, and flowers everywhere. And lunch is surprisingly inexpensive.

A variety of salads, like white tuna in fresh lime mayonnaise, diced Cantonese chicken in papaya nest with chutney finger sandwiches, or a chef's salad go from $4 to $5. A nicely done hot quiche Lorraine is served with salad for $4.95. And for a lunch that feels more like a small dinner, have one of the daily specials at $6.50; it could be ono with meunière sauce or veal Stroganoff on noodles. Lunch is ready from 12 to 2:30 daily.

A RESTAURANT IN HANA: If you're spending any time in Hana, you must not miss the fabulous dinner at the **Hotel Hana-Maui.** Prix-fixe at $16.50, which includes tip, it's a memorable experience. If you are not a hotel guest, be sure to phone 248-8211 for reservations and hope that they will be available. Dinner is served daily from 6:30 to 8 p.m., until 9 on Saturdays. The Polynesian decor, from the lauhala and bamboo ceiling to the tropical garden and open lanais, has a touch of the Mediterranean, designed as it is around an open court. Browse through the comfortable lounges, including a library, and walk through the gardens before you sit down to eat. Dinner is sumptuous and the service is the best. Even the busboy makes his job colorful by filling your water glass with the pitcher held over his head, creating yet another Hana waterfall. The parade of courses starts with a choice of appetizers like crab cocktail or papaya filled with island fruits, proceeds to turtle or clam soup, a choice of salads, and usually a choice of three entrees. I passed up the turkey and chose bacon-wrapped char-broiled filet mignon and mahimahi steak—and was offered second helpings on the steak! A delicious passion-fruit chiffon pie topped the meal. If you fancy something different, call the chef 24 hours in advance and give him instructions for your own favorite entree.

The Sights and Sounds of Maui

Millions of years ago, the sea bottom between the islands of present-day Hawaii and Oahu erupted with surprising frequency. The results of Pele's work can be seen now as the islands of Molokai, Lanai, Kahoolawe, and Maui. The island of Maui, though, is by far the most glorious result of this constant volcanic action. The western end began as a separate island, with mountains that rise like leavened dough and fold upon each other as they run and spill at golden shores into the pounding surf. The eastern side of the island would have gained renown on its own by virtue of its awesome **Haleakala Crater,** where the

Buffet Bravos

Where do Maui families go when they want to celebrate something special? To Sunday brunch at the **Mayfair Buffet** of the Kapalua Bay Hotel, of course—and so should you. Actually, you can go any day between 12 and 2:30 p.m. (avoiding the Sunday crowd) and feast on what is surely one of the most glorious spreads in the islands, $11 and not overpriced. The international chefs at Kapalua go all out for this one, proudly spreading their tables with gourmet treats, not the usual buffet table fillers. On a recent Sunday I counted seven hot entrees alone, including seafood Newburg, quiche Lorraine, sweet-and-sour pork, zucchini with mozzarella, and roast beef. The salad table numbers 25 entrees, the cold fish and meat spread includes sashimi and other island delicacies and crab legs every day. Tropical fruits, fresh fruit salads, and homebaked island breads (including Hawaiian sweet breads) grace the fruit table. And all this is prelude to the vast array of desserts—eclairs and lemon meringue pies and chocolate mousses and babas au rhum and such—all set out against a wall of flowing water. You eat as much as you want, and then come back for more—and more. The dining room, overlooking water and gardens, is a perfect setting for this fantasy meal. Don't miss.

sun rises as it must have on the first day of creation. But as time went on the two volcanic fountains feeding the growing islands caused the two land masses to meet and melt into one single island, creating the Maui that now exists. The ancient Hawaiians believed, though, that their own special god, Maui, pulled up both ends of the island from the sea bottom with his fish hooks. In any case, both versions of paradise are one for you to explore and enjoy, driving over modern roads with a minimum of effort. Plan on at least three days to see Maui: the first to explore Kahului, Wailuku, and Lahaina; the second to see the windswept wonder of Haleakala; the third either for the beach or for an excursion into the lush, tropical rain forest of Hana.

THE FIRST DAY—FROM KAHULUI AND WAILUKU TO LAHAINA:

Let's suppose you begin your trip at the Kahului Airport. Head west on H-32, take a left and continue into **Kahului** proper. **Kahului** is important to Maui because it has the only deep-water harbor on the island (sugar is shipped from here), and there are several resort hotels on the waterfront. If you haven't gotten your muumuu yet, or if your child wants a swimming board, or you're just plain in the mood to shop, you've come to the right place. There are no less than three big shopping centers here. **Kahului Shopping Center** has a few good shops for Hawaiian wear, a large drugstore, and a few restaurants. A little newer, **Kauhaumanu Shopping Center** is a giant complex, with Liberty House, Sears, and other major establishments; most of the shops are designed for the local people, but a few are slightly unusual, like one selling Japanese stationery and school supplies. The Center for Performing Plants is worth a stop. **Apple Annie's** is a neat little place for drinks and tasty food—omelets, burgers, Mexican specialties—and an apple dessert. Newest of the shopping centers is **Maui Mall,** where, in addition to huge branches of Long's Drugstore and Woolworth's (both good for reasonably priced souvenirs), **Pieces of Dreams** offers handicrafts, artful cards, and jewelry of merit. There's often entertainment here by Maui musicians. Restaurants abound: favorites are **Farrell's** for ice-cream specialties and light food and the **Pizza Factory Restaurant** for pizza and cool drinks under the Tiffany lamps.

Back in the car, continue to drive to Wailuku along the valley floor on Kaahumanu Avenue; you'll pass both the Maui Pineapple Company (pineapple is important to the island's agriculture) and Maui Community College, a rapidly growing educational center on the island. **Wailuku,** the civic and business center of Maui, is Kahului's older sister. Market Street is the local business area, and Vineyard Street is where you'll find a health-food store, bookstore, and other establishments under the banner of the Hare Krishna people. Wailuku also has several beautiful new state and county office buildings, and it's past these that you turn left on Iao Road for a look at the **Hale Hoikeike,** showcase for the Maui Historical Society. Relics here date from prehistoric times to the annexation. Hours are from 9 a.m. to 3:30 p.m. daily, and admission is $2 for adults, 50¢ for students.

Keep right on in the direction you are headed for a drive through magnificent Iao Valley. Watch, on the right, for a mountain that looks uncannily like the profile of John F. Kennedy. Then proceed to **Iao Needle,** a 1200-foot finger of lava scratching at the sky and draped in green cloaks of luxurious foliage that are common to this rainy valley. In fact, the clouds are likely to be heavy and brooding here, as if the local spirits were still mourning the slaughter that went on in this valley in 1790, when Kamehameha's men, armed with cannons, devastated the local forces of Kalanikupule. On the way to the Needle Lookout, do make a sidetrip to **Kepaniwai Park,** once the scene of a bloody battle in Hawaiian history, today a gardeny spot where local kids happily play in the swimming and wading pools.

On to Lahaina

Provided you haven't gotten lost in the shopping centers or stood gazing at Iao Needle for too long, this portion of your trip should not take much more than an hour. Now you can continue on to **Lahaina,** 22 miles from Kahului Airport on a road that curves along the western end of the island and allows you to survey some of its glorious beaches. Trace your way out of the valley, back to the outskirts of Wailuku, and take a right onto H-30 out of the city environs through the cane fields to where the road meets the ocean at Maalaea. (If you were driving to Kihei, you would have made a left a little while back, onto Route 31. There's not much in the way of sightseeing here, but you could have a swim at Kamaole Beach or Kalama Park and do some shopping at newly expanded Azeka Place.) Now every turn in the mountain road surprises you with oceanscapes that get more and more wild and spectacular. After you pass the lighthouse, watch for signs pointing to **Kahoolawe;** you can get a view of this smallest island in the chain, which is used at present as a bombing target by the navy. Continue on, passing a never-ending stretch of beach on your left; at some points the high-tide surf splashes right up onto the shoulder of the road. Soon you arrive at a busy intersection where Lahainaluna Road crosses the main highway. Turn toward the ocean and you're right in the heart of Lahaina, once the royal capital of Hawaii, the whaling center of the Pacific, and the scene of some of the most colorful—and violent—history of the islands.

Today the Lahaina Restoration Foundation is restoring many of the buildings and relics that remain from the old days when royalty walked the streets and whalers brawled in them. You can already explore **Baldwin House,** on Front Street, home of the devoted missionary Dwight Baldwin, who also doubled as a surgeon and doctor for Maui and its smaller islands. The Baldwin House has been lovingly restored, and a visit—personally guided—will give you a good insight into the incongruous blending of New England and the South Seas that marked the missionary lifestyle. Admission is $2 for adults, $1 for children.

The Foundation also sponsors "The World of the Whale" exhibit aboard its floating museum **Carthaginian,** anchored just opposite the Pioneer Inn. The exhibit features a real 19th-century whaleboat discovered in the wilds of northern Alaska, and various multimedia displays on whaling, whales, and the reef life of Hawaii. Open daily; admission $1 for adults, 50¢ for children 12 and under.

Across the street from Baldwin House is the **Lahaina Library,** standing in the midst of what was once the taro patch of Kamehameha III. Behind this spot excavations are currently going on for the foundations of his royal palace; you can now view some of these foundations through glass panes on the ground level. Just behind that you can stand on the edge of the wharf at historic **Lahaina Roads** and maybe see a black stone in the ocean, the **Mauola Stone,** which was believed by the old Hawaiians to have sacred healing powers. Anyone who was ill could lie on top of the stone and be washed clean of his malady by the action of the waves. (Don't bother jumping in; it's only a legend.) It's interesting to gaze out across the water at the islands of Molokai, Lanai, and Kahoolawe, and to realize that you're on the precise spot where the whaling ships used to drop anchor over a hundred years ago. This spot is especially memorable at sunset, when half the island's population, it seems, turns out to watch the sun turn the sky to golden fire.

Turn left before you get to the town square and you'll end up at the **Pioneer Inn** (which you saw in the movie *Hawaii*), a hotel-hideaway that's been attracting beachcombers, movie stars in disguise, and other assorted notables for over half a century. It's been renovated now, but the old lazy, South Seas nautical charm is still there. and it's fun to stop for a drink or a bite in its Harpooners' Lanai.

Across the street from the Pioneer Inn is a banyan tree that has been reaching out and monopolizing the town square for many years now. The locals will hotly defend its rank, size-wise, in comparison with other banyans in the world. It *is* big. The **Court House** faces the ocean behind the tree, and at the end of Wharf Street you'll find the reconstructed remains of an old fort that once stood someplace in the vicinity of the banyan tree. Rebuilding it at the original site would have meant that the tree had to go. Never! The tree remained, and the ruins of the fort were relocated.

Just off Front Street, on Prison Street, you'll get a taste of what awaited the whalers in town after the sunset drums were beaten each evening. You see, the whalers were not exactly popular among the kings and missionaries of Lahaina. For too long it was the habit of the native women to swim out to the ships with their own particular brand of aloha. When the missionaries decreed the end of such abominations, the sailors replied with riotings and burnings, even shellings of the mission house. So the custom developed that any sailor found ashore after the sunset curfew was immediately clapped into jail, where he might awaken the next morning to find his ship gone. **Hale Paahao,** the old stone jail, is still there.

You should also have a look at an important cultural contribution made to Lahaina by another group, the Japanese. Drive along Front Street and turn left on Ala Moana Street until you come to the Lahaina Jodo Mission. Here an enormous statute of Amida Buddha presides over the **Buddhist Cultural Park,** complete with a temple and a pagoda in the best tradition of Buddhist architecture. The statue was brought here from Kyoto to celebrate the centennial of Japanese immigration to Hawaii. There's an almost palpable serenity to this place, so drink it all in before you get back to the swinging world of present-day Lahaina.

Shopping Lahaina

Even more fun than seeing the historical sights is seeing the contemporary shops. New boutiques open almost weekly, it seems, and the place is a shoppers' mecca on the order of San Francisco's Sausalito. To get an idea, walk along Front Street for a few blocks and you'll find the likes of the **South Seas Trading Post,** with many rare and unusual items from the South Seas and the Orient. Note the extraordinary necklaces from Kathmandu, along with necklaces carved out of coconut from Samoa and authentic grass dance skirts. Also note the section dealing with rare New Guinea artifacts. . . . You can pick up whaling mementoes of Lahaina at **The Whaler:** carvings of scrimshaw and ivory, boxes, prints, plus other nautical memorabilia. **Far Out Fits, One World Family,** 726 Front St., has handcrafted clothing for kids and grownups; books, toys, cards; and **Endeavour Imports,** 762 Front Street, brings in lovely things from Thailand, Indonesia, and India.

The Wharf at 666 Front St. is a nifty little shopping world in itself, with scads of quality boutiques, fast-food and sit-down restaurants, a fountain and stage area for free entertainments, and a glass elevator that the kids will love riding. Kids will also like **Geppetto's Workshop** for handcarved toys, marionettes, and stuffed animals; men and women can pick up a cool summer hat at **The Maui Mad Hatter;** and everyone should love the artful butterflies at **Julie's Butterflies,** the exquisite gifts at **Alberta's Gazebo** and **Spanky and Our Gang,** and the masterful examples of the craftsmen's art at **Following Sea.**

A short walk or drive from here, at 505 Front St., **Whaler's Market Place,** designed to look like a group of Nantucket cottages, is another multifaceted attraction, with shops, restaurants, and a well-recomended Wednesday-night luau. Trade the way the whalers did at the **General Store,** the way they didn't at places like **Eenie Meeni Bikini** and **Jade & Jewels,** among scores of others. As you may gather by now, serious shoppers could pass eternity here, but I suggest at this point that you take a short train ride (or drive) to Kaanapali and another exciting shopping complex, **Whaler's Village.**

The train ride is aboard the **Lahaina-Kaanapali & Pacific Railroad,** a replica of a railroad that carried cane between the villages of Lahaina and Kaanapali from 1890 to 1920. Now it carries visitors, especially those based at the Kaanapali hotels, who use it whenever they went to run into Lahaina. The train clickety-clacks through some perfectly beautiful scenery, the mountains on one side, the sea on the other. (Kids really dig it, especially the ferocious toot of the steam whistle.) One-way fare is $3 for adults, $1.50 for children 2 to 12. You could also just make a round trip if you like ($5, adults; $2.50, children), and find yourself back in Lahaina.

Whaler's Village is a "shopping center" that's also a museum, designed to recapture the late 19th-century years when both Lahaina and Kaanapali were major whaling ports. The decor is a combination of New England and Polynesia, and outdoor displays document the history and biology of whales and whaling. If you're lucky, you may catch sight of some humpback whales playing offshore; they are regular visitors December through May. The shops here are among the best in the islands. **Ka Honu,** for example, imports one-of-a-kind native handicrafts from the South Pacific. They cater to collectors (New Guinean masks and statues, ships carved out of whalebone, authentic Hawaiin quilts and the like), but they also have plenty for the less specialized shopper (scrimshaw, tapa, fans, Hawaiian rhythm instruments). Prices begin at $1, go up to about $5,000. . . . **Godber's Indian Arts Store** has an enormous selection of American Indian artifacts—silver and turquoise jewelry, Indian pottery, Navajo rugs and sand paintings, Hopi silver, many handmade dolls, drums, beaded purses. . . . **Pier 49** has a stable of local artists who create scrimshaw works of high quality, working on ivories from nonendangered species, i.e., fossilized walrus and mastodon. They also have two outlets in Lahaina. . . . **Super Whale Children's Boutique** has one of the best selections of kids' clothes we've seen anywhere in the islands, and the size range runs from infants through 14 for girls, up to 18 for boys. There are other Super Whales at the Pioneer Inn in Lahaina and at Wailea Town Center in Kihei.

The Village Gallery is outstanding, displaying unique art forms in many media. . . . So, too, is the **Narwhal Shop,** with most artifacts having to do with whaling, all in flawless taste. . . . Check the fine collection of books on Hawaii and many other subjects in the attractive **Book Cache.** . . . Buy an aloha shirt or a muumuu or some island jewelry at the tasteful branch of **Liberty House.** . . . And end with a banana daiquiri at the swinging **Rusty Harpoon** or a swim at lovely Kaanapali Beach, just beyond the shops.

On to Kaanapali and Napili

Back in your car, you can drive out of Lahaina in the Napili direction, or you might want to take Lahainaluna Road to its beginning at the **Lahainaluna High School,** walk through the pleasant campus, and see the first printing press on the island. In any case, your path will continue to lead you west as you follow either Front Street or H-36 to the point where the two converge at the site of the **Royal Coconut Grove,** an ancient spot favored by royalty, whose restoration is another on a long list of projects of the Restoration Foundation.

Continue on H-36 and you'll pass the incredibly beautiful setting of the **Kaanapali Beach Resorts.** It's worth your time to take a guided tour of the glamorous new Hyatt Regency Maui (9 a.m. or 2:30 p.m.), or walk around on your own, admiring the gardens and plantings and the colorful birds that abound in the lobby and on the grounds. The shops here are noted for their architectural details (extraordinary ceilings, one in stained glass; railings of oak and teak, copper and brass), as well as their luxury offerings: luggage from Lloyd and Carver, men's clothing from Brendan Shane, jewelry from Gold Point, and African Exotica from Elephant Walk, among others. Most impressive of all are the works of original art and sculpture in the passageways between the shops. You can swim anywhere along Kaanapali (beaches are public property), or drive on to **Honokawai Beach**

Park, a mile or so ahead, where you could take out your picnic lunch. Several miles farther up the road, almost at the tip of the island, you'll come to the magnificent **Kapalua Bay Resort.** Here I suggest you get out, survey the grounds, maybe have a drink at The Bay Club, and admire the beauty, natural and man-made, all around you. Admire the beauty, too, of **The Shops at Kapalua,** a graceful setting for high-quality boutiques. A visit to **La Trouvaille,** for example, brims with the excitement of crafts and artifacts—Balinese temple ornaments, Chinese opium pillows, rare masks from the South Pacific—collected by owner Joan McKelvey. **By the Bay** has extremely tasteful mountings of shells and coral for indoor decor; I like their branch-coral trees on koa-wood bases. **Ka Honu** is here with South Seas crafts, **Mandalay** with ancient Buddhas, and **Auntie Nani,** a branch of Super Whale, with a young teen department and lots of hand-made-on-Maui fashions. **The Market Cafe** has gourmet kitchen gadgets, cheese and deli sections, and, behind the swinging half-door, a real little cafe, where a well-deserved cup of cappuccino can bring your shopping labors to a close.

The good road continues just a few miles farther, to Honoko-hua; from there you'll have to double back the way you came, since the road continuing around the island is much too rugged for a small car.

THE SECOND DAY—HALEAKALA: Now you're set to visit Maui's Valhalla, **Haleakala,** the home of the great god Maui, and, just as the proper home of a god should be, this is an awesome place. To reach it you'll have to drive 1½ hours from Kahului, part of it on a snaky highway high above the clouds. But it's worth whatever effort you have to make to see this sleeping giant, whose crater alone is 7½ miles long, 2½ miles wide. And it makes it even more exciting, as you scale its 10,000 feet, to know that the volcano is sleeping, dormant—not dead or extinct as is Diamond Head (or at least hope it is). In other words, it *could* erupt in front of you. But don't panic; Pele has not visited here for some 200 years.

As of this writing, construction is going on that closes the Haleakala road between 11 a.m. and 9 p.m. on weekdays. That means that you have to get up very early to make the trip and be back down in time. (Phone 572-7749 to check on road and weather conditions; you'll want to go on a clear day. Actually, the best time to see Haleakala is at sunrise; few things on earth can equal this sight, when it seems that the sun has risen only for you. Bring along a warm sweater, since it gets cool up here. And since there are no restaurants or gasoline stations once you pass the lower slopes, be sure to gas up, and you may want to bring a breakfast picnic.

Starting from Kahului, drive east of the city and follow the signs to the junction of H-36 with H-37. Continue on the Kula Road (H-37) and then to H-337, the Upper Kula Road. This is easy driving, but once you turn off to the left, on Route 378, you're on Haleakala Crater Road, and it's a winding two-way highway through the clouds. Check in at park headquarters to get maps and a general orientation. Camping, horseback riding, or hiking in the crater, over the same routes that once served as the main avenue of travel between the two ends of the island, is a magnificent experience. The rangers can give you all the details.

If, however, like me, you do most of your hiking in a car, there's still a great deal to see. You can get wonderful views of the crater at both **Leleiwi** and **Kahaluku** lookouts. If you're one of those lucky types who arrive when the sun is strong at your back, the clouds overhead misty, you might get to see your own shadow in the rainbow, a phenomenon known as the **Spectre of the Brocken.** And you may also experience the phenomenon of the double winds. The wind will be blowing right in your face as you view the crater, but then, if you just go back to the road and turn to face the other way, the wind will again be in your face. The effect is caused by the curling of the wind jets as they flow over the lip of the crater.

With or without spooky side effects, the view of Haleakala is awesome. You may also see some of the magnificent silversword plants that bloom in the lava between June and October. As tall as a man, they blossom once, producing purple-and-golden flowers, and die—leaving their seeds to grow again in the lava rock.

Now hop back into your car again and drive to the **Haleakala Observatory.** Here your gaze encompasses some 30,000 square miles of the Pacific; and below you the crater, its kaleidoscope of colors changing with the sun and the clouds, creates an incredible light show that technology could never approach. Now take the Skyline Drive another half-mile to **Red Hill,** the summit of Haleakala and the home of a satellite-tracking station. Stop a while to pay homage to the great god Maui, and down you go, to warmer climes and the golden valleys below. On the way down the slopes, stop in for a great lunch at **Kula Lodge** in Kula.

Then watch the road for a sign directing you to **Willy Fong's Little Museum and Hobby Shop,** where Willy, a charming gentleman in his 80s, handcarves jewelry made of rare Hawaiian woods, and sells them for modest prices. **Bullock's of Hawaii** in Pukalani is another possible stop, for a snack plus excellent woodcarvings, handicrafts, muumuus, and distinctive souvenirs. A possible sidetrip, just a few miles off to the right, is a visit to the little cowboy town of **Makawao.**

THE THIRD DAY—HANA: Whether or not you decide to go to Hana depends on what kind of driver you are. Don't say I didn't warn you. It's rugged driving on a narrow, cliff-hanging road with many blind turns and pot holes aplenty (especially on the last stretch, from Hana itself to the Seven Sacred Pools). There are no restaurants or gas stations. The views of dense tropical forests and cascading waterfalls are sensational, though, and, if you have the strength for it, well worth the effort. If it's all too much, relax and return to any of the dozen beaches we're sure you've already found.

If you do opt for Hana, head out of Kahului on the same road you took to Haleakala, but continue on Highway 36 and stay on it all the way. Coming up soon is **H.A. Baldwin Park,** a favorite picnic camping spot. Further on you'll pass through **Paia,** a neat little natural-life-style town where you might want to get some picnic fixings at Pic-Nics on Baldwin Avenue, or stop to see the imposing Japanese temple, complete with an immense gong. From here on out it's just you and nature and maybe a few other cars en route to Hana. Pineapple fields drop out of sight after a while as you swing and fly around the inside faces of many valleys, with waterfalls spilling over the mountaintops, rivers running under the roadway, and lush vegetation all around. The white-and-yellow ginger blossoms all along the way are so thick that the air is yellow and perfumed with their scent. (It's illegal to pick them, though, so just admire them from afar.) One is constantly tempted to stop at a particular waterfall and admire its unique beauty, but I suggest that you keep right on until you get to **Keanae Park,** resplendent with flowers and shrubs. You can also pull over for a lookout view of **Wailua** and **Keanae** villages, or even take a sidetrip through them. People here still live in the same style their ancestors did many generations back. **Pua Kaa Park** down the road is another place to stop for a look-see. One more possible sidetrip before you get into Hana proper is over a bumpy left-turn road that leads the way to the **Waianapanapa Cave** where poor Popoalea was slain by her jealous husband; the water is said to still run red with her blood every April. Your first vision of "Heavenly Hana" may be a letdown, though, if the black-sand beach is not as neat as it should be (it wasn't on my last trip). But you should walk around the town for a while and soak up the atmosphere. A must on your list of sights should be the **Hasegawa General Store** where, it is reported, you can get anything and everything your heart desires (just like at Alice's Restaurant) in one tiny shack. A song was written about the store several years ago, and it has not changed in spite of all the hullaballoo.

Besides such novelties as this, you'll walk in the footsteps of illustrious ghosts in Hana. Captain Cook and his men dropped anchor here. The Hawaiian monarchs made this their vacation territory (they always picked the best places), and the missionaries were only too glad to follow them to enforce their teachings. If you're in a historical mood, you can even see the place where Kaahumana, the favorite consort of Kamehameha, was born.

The main industry of Hana is lovely and expensive **Hotel Hana Maui,** where you can treat yourself to dinner (see "A Restaurant in Hana," above), or a superb buffet lunch. Or have a picnic, or an inexpensive lunch at **Tutu's Snack Shop** on the beach on in the hotel's coffeeshop. If you've still got the strength for more of this rugged driving, continue past Hana, about nine miles farther, to the site of the **Seven Sacred Pools.** Here one pool feeds into another and so on, creating an enchanting spot for a swim. And, of course, in true Hana fashion, there are waterfalls all along the way to the pools. Return home the way you came, since the road tapers out beyond this point and becomes just a dirt path. Driving home is a bit easier, since you are on the other side of the road. The view is also extra-special from that vantage point. Return time should be about three hours, but do drive carefully. End your day, perhaps, with a super dinner at **Mama's Fish House,** a big favorite with the local people for super-fresh fish; it's moderately priced and on the waterfront, just outside of Paia, on Highway 36; open 5 to 9:30 p.m.

Chapter XI

THE GARDEN ISLAND: KAUAI

WHERE DO HONOLULU RESIDENTS go when they want to get away from it all? To a magic island that any visitor can reach by putting down $32 and spending less than 20 minutes on a jet. Ninety-five miles northwest of the bustling freeways and crowds of Honolulu is a verdant little island that seems to have been sleeping in the tropical sun for centuries. It exudes a peace and tranquility that is decidedly not of the 1980s.

And yet, with its comfortable hotels and restaurants and golf courses and nightclubs and shopping centers, you couldn't exactly call Kauai behind the times. The only thing old-fashioned about it is the openheartedness of its people, the lack of pressure, the gentleness that is everywhere.

To my way of thinking, you should have at least four days to spend here, to discover the myriad beauties of this jewel-like island. For nature has been good to Kauai, creating craters and canyons (**Waimea Canyon** is even more spectacular, in some ways, than the Grand Canyon), mountains and rivers, glorious stretches of sparkling sand and graceful, palm-fringed beaches. The oldest of the islands in the Hawaiian chain, Kauai was born from the sea millions of years ago by violent volcanic eruptions occurring far below the ocean floor. Pele, the Hawaiian goddess of volcanoes (who, incidentally, is still revered by more than a few natives), made her first home here before moving on to the other islands; Kauai's volcanoes are now extinct. The centuries have turned the red volcanic earth green and glorious, and abundant rainfall has earned Kauai the title of "The Garden Island." But don't despair; rain falls where it's needed here, and only occasionally on tourists. Mount Waialeale, 5240 feet high, receives something like 486 inches of rainfall a year, making it the second-wettest spot on earth. Other areas just a few miles away receive fewer than 20 inches. It rains in Kauai, but not enough to spoil your fun.

KAUAI—PAST AND PRESENT: Kauai has always been attractive to visitors. The very first were the Menehunes, who, according to legend, were here long before the Polynesians ever dreamed of leaving the South Seas. No one knows where these two-foot-tall gremlins came from (could they be the descendants of the lost colony of Lemuria? could a flying saucer have deposited them?) but, whatever their origins, they accomplished remarkable engineering feats whose remains you can still examine. In about 750 A.D., the first Polynesians arrived, beaching their outrigger canoes on the banks of the Wailua River, on Kauai's north shore. It was along this side of the island that religious temples and villages sprang up. (Interestingly, an international yoga group recently chose this area as its headquarters; seems the vibrations are still special.) You can explore the remnants of these *heiaus* (temples) on the Wailua (sacred) River today. Captain James Cook, the next notable visitor to the island, was heartily greeted on the southern shore, at Waimea. This deep-water harbor had become a favorite of the *alii* (royalty) who ruled here in pre-Cook days.

Kauai is proud of the fact that it is the only one of the Hawaiian Islands that was not conquered by Kamehameha the Great. The island was ceded to Kamehameha's federation in about 1790, and from then on, its importance as a political power declined. The **Koloa** section of the island, though, is notably proud of its own contribution to Hawaiian politics, Prince Jonah Kuhio, Hawaii's first representative to Congress (1902-1922), and the much-beloved "People's Prince." (Kuhio Beach and Kuhio Avenue in Honolulu were, of course, named for him.) Each March 26, his birthday is celebrated with great pomp and pageantry, not only on Kauai but all over the islands.

The modern world is rushing in on Kauai, as it is all over Hawaii, but it is still a haven of peace and beauty. To see it properly, you will have to rent a car since there is a minimum of public transportation. There are sightseeing limousines and a limited bus service, but the best way to see the island is on your own. Seven or eight car-rental places are lined up in a stall across the road from the airport lobby at Lihue, and many rent inexpensive cars. Try Wiki-Wiki Wheels for some good bargains. **Tropi-**

cal **Rent-a-Car** and **American International Rent-a-Car** offer good deals on flat rates.

Please note that the area code for the state of Hawaii is 808.

Hotels in Kauai

HOTELS IN LIHUE: The minute town of Lihue, since it is a convenient halfway point on the two major sightseeing excursions around the island, is a good tour-base. It is here that you will find the hotel that, because of its size, proximity to the airport, and quality and quantity of facilities, is pretty much the island's tourist center; it's the **Kauai Surf** (phone 245-3631). The hotel is actually about a mile south of the Lihue town limits, right on splendid Kalapaki Beach, which overlooks Nawiliwili Harbor. The two high-rise buildings with their 620 rooms are in an ideal setting for a Hawaiian escape, surrounded by 187 acres of garden and beach. You can't ask for more activities or conveniences. You can enjoy tennis (there are eight regulation courts, plus two paddle tennis courts and a pro shop), riding, canoeing, sailing surfing, snorkeling, hula lessons, the 18-hole Kauai Surf Golf and Country Club; you can even take a helicopter flight or make a river safari. The scenic pool and its "sunken cocktail lounge" overlook the beach. You can dine in the Outrigger Dining Room, have an early bite in the Surfside Snackshop, or try the exquisite Golden Cape Rooftop Restaurant or the Surf 'n' Sirloin Steakhouse. Superb seafood dishes are offered in the beachside Fisherman Restaurant. Since you are not within easy strolling distance here of other restaurants, the $28-a-day American plan is quite convenient.

Now for the rooms. All are large and interestingly decorated, with water and mountain views everywhere. Double occupancy starts at $52 and goes to $58, $65, and $72 for superior and deluxe rooms. During the "peak" winter season, rooms are about $5 more. Perfectly delicious cottages (perched atop ocean cliffs), suites, and penthouse apartments can also be yours, if you can go from $235 to $455 a day, double. Single occupancy is $3 less; a third person, $10 more; children under 12 and cribs free; maximum of three in room. A lovely choice.

Toll-free reservations: 800/421-0811 nationwide; 800/252-0381 in California; in Honolulu, call 922-1636.

For all the comforts of a condominium apartment right at Nawiliwi Harbor, just down the road from Lihue and very close to all the activities at the Kauai Surf Hotel, there's the **Banyan**

Harbor Resort, 3411 Wilcox Rd. (phone: 245-8537). Each of the 148 units in this new building is either a one- or two-bedroom apartment, smartly furnished in island decor, with plenty of space to move around in and a complete kitchen with its own dishwasher, washer, and dryer. You can play tennis at their court (bring your own racket), swim at the pool, and, when it's time for the ocean, stroll or drive over to beautiful Kalapaki Beach. The Kauai Surf Golf Course is across the street. No restaurant on the premises, but the Menehune Shopping Village, close by, has several.

Rates vary according to season (higher rates from December 15 through April 4), and go from $45 to $55 for a one-bedroom garden view apartment to $50 to $60 for a harbor view, $55 to $65 for a bay view, all double occupancy. Two-bedroom apartments, based on quad occupancy, are $55 to $65, $60 to $75, $65 to $85. An additional person over 12 is $7, and rollaways and cribs are also $7. For toll-free reservations, phone 800/854-2868 nationwide, 800/532-3744 in California.

Tucked away at 3115 Alahai St., near the Lihue Shopping Center, is the **Ahana Motel Apartments,** my favorite budget choice in the area. Mr. and Mrs. Sau Ahana have long provided simple-but-sparkling-clean accommodations here, and their faithful following keeps returning year after year. Prices for these plainly furnished, homey units, all with television and many with kitchens, are unbelievably good for this day and age. Single and double rooms without kitchenettes are $14 and $15; a one-bedroom apartment or studio for two is $18 single, $21 double, and various combinations of rooms with and without kitchenettes can be worked out to accommodate large families with children. Newer two-bedroom apartments, each with *two* bathrooms, rent for $36 for four. There is a charge of $4 for each additional person. The units are set in back of the main house on this quiet side street and offer peace and quiet aplenty. Beautiful Kalapaki Beach, a very short drive away, is yours to swim in. Many of the regulars here are golfers, since the Kauai Surf Golf Course is a few minutes' drive away, and the expansive Wailua Golf Course is not far along Highway 56, nor is lovely Lydgate Beach. Write well in advance for accommodations. The address is P.O. Box 892, Lihue, Kauai, Hawaii (phone: 245-2206).

HOTELS IN THE WAILUA-WAIPOULI AREA: It might be said that no hotel in the islands is as Hawaiian as Kauai's **Coco Palms**

Resort, close to the sea at Wailua Beach and a few miles north of Lihue. Here you can live even more graciously than did the Hawaiian royalty who once strolled along the banks of the palm-fringed lagoon around which the main hotel building and small cottages are spread. The evening torchlighting ceremony is an authentic moment relived—as the conch shell blows, the canoes arrive, and, one by one, scores of torches are ignited. Whether you dine by torchlight in the Lagoon Dining Room with its ancient fire pit, in the Coconut Palace Dining Room, or in the Flame Room for succulent steaks, you have the feeling that you are there by invitation of the old Hawaiian *alii.*

The royal colors of red and gold are predominant from the vaulted lobby to the extravagantly decorated rooms and cottages. Minimum, medium, and deluxe rates, for two, are $51, $61, and $64 from June to Late December; there is an additional charge in the winter. The higher-priced rooms have unique outrigger beds that even include the paddles! A variety of romantic luxury suites, popular with honeymooners, is also available, such as the Queen's Cottage at $80 and the King's Cottage at $85, the Prince of Hawaii Cottage at $110, and others, up to the Coconut Palace at $225 for four people. (Some of these are more lavish than a movie set. Would you believe shell basins and lava-rock bathtubs, some outdoors in secluded little nooks?) For single occupancy, deduct $3; extra persons are $6; American Plan is available at $27 per person, MAP at $21.

There's little chance of getting bored at Coco Palms, even if you scarcely leave the grounds. There are nine tennis courts and a tennis pro, the 18-hole Wailua Golf Course nearby, a shopping arcade, and three beautiful outdoor pools. Shows every night in the Lagoon Dining Room. The only disadvantages that I can see are that you must cross the road to get to the beach, and the ocean can be a bit choppy at times. Otherwise, perfect. Write to Island Holiday Resorts, P.O. Box 8519, Honolulu, HI 96815. The phone in Honolulu is 922-6121.

About a mile past Coco Palms, on the ocean side of the road, Island Holidays runs a more moderately priced hotel that is also very pleasant, the **Kauai BeachBoy.** Rooms here go from $42 to $47 single, $44 to $49 double. And there's nothing skimpy about the rooms. Facing either the gardens or the sea, each of the 242 units has its own lanai, is air-conditioned, has two double or twin beds, a color TV, a small refrigerator, a lovely, large dressing room with a mirrored closet, tiled bathroom with stall shower, and smart decor throughout, from the Polynesian-print spreads on the beds to lamps with coconut bases. There is a huge, almost Olympic-size swimming pool, the Pool Bar and Broiler Restaurant, and a nightclub close to the water. Of course, there's the beach, and Kauai's purple mountains in the background (from your room you might catch a view of the island's legendary "Sleeping Giant" cliff formation). **The Market Place,** a Hawaiian-style shopping village, is just across the street. For reservations and information, write to Island Holidays Resorts, P.O. Box 8519, Honolulu, HI 96815.

Right next door to the BeachBoy is the also very attractive **Islander Inn Kauai.** The three-story buildings, grouped around a free-form pool, provide a plantation feeling, and ironwood trees form a protective windbreak against the sea. Entering the lobby, you could easily imagine yourself in a gracious Georgia homestead if it were not for the vivid, lighthearted colors and Polynesian art reflecting the spirit of the islands. The large air-conditioned rooms are furnished with your choice of two double beds or three "long boy" twins. Closets are roomy, and the bath is divided for dual use. Rooms are decorated in either blues and greens or golds and oranges. Angled courtyards give privacy to the lanais. Superior rooms are $39 single, $42 double; superior ocean front, $43 single, $46 double. It's $6 per night for a third person, with a limit of three people to a room. For reservations, write InterIsland Resorts, P.O. Box 8539, Honolulu, Hawaii. Or phone the main office in Honolulu toll-free at 800/367-5360.

The newest hotel in the Coconut Plantation area is a spacious, sprawling, island kind of place called **Holiday Inn-Kauai Beach.** Yes, it's a Holiday Inn, with all the comfort and convenience that the name implies, but its decor and feeling are true Hawaiiana. Emphasis is on the arts and artifacts of Polynesia, from the stained glass Hokule'a (the hotel has chosen the legendary Polynesian canoe as its logo) and the mural *The Floating Island* by noted artist Herbert Kawainiu Kane in the lobby, to such meticulous details as authentic tapa designs carved on the doorknobs of each individual room. The setting is a beautiful one, with groves of coconut palms, Norfolk pines, flowers, and tropical vegetation all about. The hotel is set on 10½ acres of Waipouli Beach, fine for snorkeling but a little rough for swimming; guests can use the large waterfront pool or be driven to a good swimming beach nearby.

As expected from a Holiday Inn, dining and entertainment facilities are top-notch, beginning with full-time room service. The Voyage Room serves a splendid noontime buffet, plus breakfast and dinner; Cook's Landing sandwich bar poolside is the place for sandwiches plus drinks and pupus; and there's an authentic Polynesian feast and show Tuesday, Thursday, and Sunday evenings in the Luau Halau. And within easy walking distance are all the restaurants and shops of the Coconut Plantation Market Place.

Rooms at Holiday Inn-Kauai Beach have all been tastefully decorated with authentic Polynesian touches, and over 70% of them have an ocean view. From December 20 to April 4, singles are $52 to $75, doubles $60 to $75; the rest of the year it's $48 to $72 single, $58 to $72 double. An extra person is $8, a rollaway $6. For reservations, write Holiday Inn, Kauai Beach, Coconut Plantation, Kapaa, Kauai, HI 96746, or call your local Holiday Inn reservation office. The phone number in Kauai is 822-3455.

If you'd like to settle into this area and have a place with your own kitchen, you can't do better than at the **Plantation Hale Hotel** in the Coconut Plantation complex, which has three swimming pools and some of the most eye-catching, luxurious rooms I've seen in the islands. The hotel is of the cluster type; there are several two-story buildings grouped around the three pools. Within are 160 air-conditioned units, all exactly the same. Each consists of a living room with sofa bed and a bedroom with two more double beds, all expensively decorated with beige carpeting and beautifully made cane furniture; a dressing room complete with built-ins; a large bathroom with tub and shower; a private lanai, and a full kitchen with a pass-through to a counter in the living room. From December 19 to April 3 it's $60 double or single, $50 the rest of the year. Although it has no restaurant, it is directly adjacent to Coconut Plantation Market Place with its several eating places, and there are other excellent restaurants less than a mile in either direction. For reservations, write Plantation Hale, Coconut Plantation, Waipouli, Kauai, HI 96746; the phone is 822-4941.

HOTELS IN THE POIPU-KUKUIULA AREA: On the dry and sunny leeward side of Kauai, about 14 miles south of Lihue, is a glorious area that comes as close to the real Hawaii as you can get. Around every bend another little garden curves down toward the sea, and the white, sandy beaches look out on a crashing, spectacular blue-green surf. Swimming is ideal here. If you want to settle down in Kauai, this, in my opinion, is the place to do it. But even if you have just a few days, it's a convenient base for island sightseeing.

Right on Poipu Beach, surely one of the loveliest in the islands, is the deservedly popular **Sheraton-Kauai Hotel**—so popular, in fact, that a $20 million, 232-room addition to the 170-room hotel is being built at the time of this writing. The atmosphere is island-beach all the way, with every one of the rooms in the sprawling, low-slung, Polynesian-style wooden buildings commanding at least some degree of ocean view and having a private lanai from which to enjoy it. All newly refurnished and redecorated, the rooms are decent-size, have TV and radio, air conditioning, doubles or twin beds (no king size), and small refrigerators for an extra $2 a day. Entertainment and dining facilities are quite special: the Outrigger Room features Wednesday and Saturday night Kamaiiana Buffets and Polynesian shows, with beautiful luncheon buffets daily; and between the Outrigger Room, the Drum Lounge, and the Mokihana Lounge, there is always entertainment at night. Tennis and golf are nearby, a large pool overlooks an ocean front, and the beach, the glorious beach, is right here. Rates go from $67 to $82 double from December 21 to March 31, from $57 to $72 the rest of the year. Subtract $3 for a single; add $7 for a third adult; children under 18 free with parents; maximum of three in a room except on special request direct to hotel.

For reservations, call toll free 800/325-3535 from mainland U.S.; 800/268-9393 from eastern Canada; 800/268-9330 from western Canada. Or write Sheraton Hotels in Hawaii, P.O. Box 8559, Honolulu, HI 96815.

Both the **Waiohai** and **Poipu Beach Hotels,** Island Holidays' contenders out in this area, are in the process of transition. By the end of 1981 a brand-new Waiohai should have risen from the rubble of the completely razed old one. Poipu Beach will be renovated and absorbed into the new hotel as its family wing; meanwhile, it is still there, and pleasant as always. I've always liked the rooms here; they are large and nicely furnished, each with twin beds or a double bed and color TV. And every room has a compact little kitchenette as well as a dressing room—all of which make for very easy, very comfortable living. Every room is the same, but from December 20 to April 1, those that have a mountain view rent for $51 double, those with an ocean or pool view go for $55 and $61. The rest of the year rates are $5 less. Single occupancy is $2 less in each category, and there is a charge of $6 per extra person. There's a pool, of course, but you can practically fall out of your room onto the beach—it's that close.

For reservations and information on either Waiohai or Poipu Beach Hotel, contact Island Holidays Resorts, P.O. Box 8519, Honolulu, HI 96815.

Nestled between the Sheraton-Kauai and Poipu Beach Hotels is what might well be the ultimate condominium resort in the islands. This is **Kiahuna Plantation,** which lives up to the translation of its name: "a special place." Some 333 beautifully furnished one- and two-bedroom beachhouses covering 20 acres ramble down to the water (only a few are at water's edge), and more are in the works; within 15 years there will be 1200 units in this condominium community. The luxurious, fully-carpeted apartments have space to spare and a decorator's fine touch everywhere—in the sparkling tones of yellows and greens, the bamboo furniture, the hangings and decorations. They are all air-conditioned, have either a queen or two twin beds in the bedrooms and queen-size hideabed sofas in the living rooms, and overlook garden or ocean vistas. All electric kitchens are equipped with every convenience, and there is daily maid service (not always the rule in condominiums), but no TVs. Right at hand is the delightful Plantation Gardens Restaurant (see ahead) for continental dining.

Both tennis and beach buffs consider Kiahuna a mecca of sorts: the net set for ten championship courts, some of them lighted, all free, with a pro shop, snack bar, and swimming pool by the courts; the beach bums for the fine sand and mild-to-wild surf of Poipu and nearby Brennecke beaches. Swimming, shelling, snorkeling, scuba diving, and surfing are all good here, and Beach Captain Marge Oberg, women's world champion surfer, is available to give surfing instruction.

Kiahuna is expensive—very. One-bedroom apartments, which can sleep four, are $79, $99, $139, and $169 double occupancy. Two-bedroom apartments, which can shelter six, are $138, $158, and $198 for up to four; there is an additional charge of $8 per additional person. For reservations from mainland U.S., phone toll-free 800/367-5020; from Canada and Hawaii, call collect 808/742-6411; or write Kiahuna Plantation, RR One, Box 73, Koloa, Kauai, HI 96756.

If you're looking for a luxury apartment with a home-away-from-home feeling, the **Sunset Kahili Apartments** could be just right for you. Although they are situated on a bluff, there is a fine sandy beach just two blocks away. You have your choice of a one- or two-bedroom apartment. In either case, you'll have a fully equipped kitchen including a dishwasher and a laundry washer-dryer. Each apartment has beautiful, thick-shag wall-to-wall carpeting, floor-to-ceiling draperies, and a private lanai overlooking the swimming pool and blue Pacific. There's a four-day minimum here: $60 per day for two people plus $5 extra per person in the one-bedroom apartments; $80 per day for four people plus $5 per extra person in the two-bedroom apartments. Rates are lower for extended stays. For reservations, write Sunset Kahili Apartments, R.R. 1, Box 96, Koloa, Kauai, HI 96756 (phone: 742-1691).

THE GOOD LIFE AT HANALEI: Located on a lush green plateau that extends from the mountains through some 11,000 acres of rolling pastures, river valleys, and undeveloped forest lands down to spectacular white-sand beaches, **Princeville** at Hanalei is a mulimillion-dollar planned resort where the living is easy and the outdoor recreational facilities unmatched. Accommodations are deluxe, with low-rise designs prevailing in the existing 475 units. Another 600 units are under construction, and a Marriott hotel is to be built here. Described as "Paradise Improved" by Dan Jenkins in *Sports Illustrated,* Princeville is perfect for anyone who loves the sporting life.

Special golf and tennis packages are available, with prices starting at $36 per person for a two-night tennis package, $46 for a two-night golf package. Golfing is on a spectacular 27-hole Robert Trent Jones, Jr., course, and there are six outdoor tennis courts. Other activities range from swimming, sailing, and snorkeling to trapshooting, horseback riding, and helicopter rides. There are four restaurants on the property; the Princeville Lanai Restaurant presents a twice-weekly Polynesian extravaganza.

Condominium units are beautiful from the outside, constructed of natural wood with peaked, shake-shingled roofs. Inside they are luxuriously appointed, and no expense has been spared in the decor. Some have fireplaces and sunken Japanese-style tubs. They all include fully equipped kitchens, washers and dryers, beautiful furniture. Many of the units are centrally managed by Princeville Corporation, with prices beginning at $60 per day for a one-bedroom apartment with ocean views. For reservations, contact Princeville Reservations Office, 225 Queen St., Suite 200, Honolulu, HI 96813. For toll-free reservations from the mainland, phone 800/367-5340; in Honolulu, call 524-5972.

Picture-perfect Hawaii is what I'd call **Hanalei Bay Resort,** a separately owned and managed luxury condominium hotel in the Princeville complex. The setting is a spectacular one, with the lobby and outstanding Bali H'ai Restaurant (more about which ahead) on the top level, and low-slung buildings winding down 20 acres to the white sands of Hanalei Beach below. Tennis players have 11 championship courts (three of them lighted), full pro shop and teaching program; golfers get a discount at the 27-hole Princeville "Makai" course surrounding the property. There are also two swimming pools and sauna, and good swimming in the ocean, which is, however, a long walk from many of the apartments (a roving jitney provides continual service around the sometimes steeply sloped complex). Inside the buildings, which are named "Hibiscus," "Bouganvillea," and the like, to correspond with the flowers growing outside their doors, are exquisitely furnished studio and one- and two-bedroom apartments, all with plentiful space, rattan furniture, beautiful dressing rooms, large baths, air conditioning, complete electric kitchens, and coral fronds and other artful decorations on the walls. Prices for mountain-view apartments are $48 studio (one to two), $75 one-bedroom (two to four), $115 two-bedroom (four to five). For ocean-view apartments, the rates are $53 studio, $80 one-bedroom, $125 two-bedroom, $165 three-bedroom (six to seven). Add $8 more for a rollaway bed.

For reservations, write to Hanalei Bay Resort, P.O. Box 220, Hanalei, Kauai, HI 96714. The local phone is 826-6522.

Dining in Kauai

RESTAURANTS IN LIHUE: Whether or not you're based in Lihue, you'll undoubtedly come into town and want to spend some time at the Lihue Shopping Center, which is as good a place as any to start your Kauai dining adventures. Here you'll find the simply appointed but spotless **Judy's Okazu Saimin,** where Judy herself is always fluttering around to add true warmth to the atmosphere. Saimin comes in a variety of sizes here, and meals come in a variety of courses. If you're really hungry, ask Judy to treat you to a nine-course meal. She'll clap her hands; and then, duck—for you'll be the guest of honor at an enormous Oriental repast. These meals will usually run about $11 a person (for four or more people, and must be ordered in advance), but you won't need to eat for a long time after. Or try the seafood dinner, which consists of mahimahi and a variety of tempura—shrimp, fishcake, and egg—about $6.25. Judy's cooking is great. The place is open from 10:30 a.m. to 2 p.m. and again from 5:30 to 8:30 p.m. (until 10 p.m. on weekends). Closed Sundays.

Here's another one of the few places to eat in Lihue proper and, praise the skies, it's a good place to eat. Turn onto the one-way street running next to the Kress store in downtown Lihue and you can't miss the **Lihue Barbecue Inn,** 2982 Kress St. Owner Henry Sasaki is constantly redecorating this popular *kamaaina* place; now it has air conditioning, dark-red booths, a low ceiling, and wall-to-wall carpeting. But the food is the thing here, with Japanese, Chinese, and American meals available. You could bite your nails at dinnertime (no nutritional value in that) choosing among dishes like fresh corned beef and cabbage, broiled teriyaki butterfish, teriyaki steak and shrimp tempura, baked salmon steak, seafood platter, and Chinese platter, from about $5 to $8. There are also a few higher-priced specialties like island T-bone steak and lobster, up to about $11.95. Lunch is cheaper, $3.25 to $6.95 for a complete meal. There's a bar, too. And the mood is always friendly. Open every day but Sunday for breakfast, 8 to 10:30 a.m.; lunch, 10:30 to 1:45 p.m.; dinner, 4:30 to 8:45 p.m.

For the best steak on Kauai, I vote for **J. J.'s Broiler,** just down the main Highway 56 from the Lihue Shopping Center, on the road leading to the sugar mill. And from the number of local people who frequent J.J.'s, I'm not alone in my opinion. My favorite spot in this smartly styled restaurant is the courtyard with its statues. Specialty of the house is the Slavonic steak, $8.95, with an exquisite flavor. The price includes salad bar helpings, garlic bread, and soup. Or, you might have the beef kebabs, mahimahi, teriyaki steak, top sirloin, or lobster, priced from $6.95 to $12.95. Salad bar and soup alone is $4.95. Dinner and cocktails from 6 to 10 p.m. Reservations recommended (phone: 245-3841).

The most elegant restaurant on Kauai? We'd vote for the **Golden Cape,** in the penthouse of the Kauai Surf Hotel, a magnificent, ornate Victorian-style restaurant overlooking a curve of ocean. It takes its name from the exquisite yellow-feather cape displayed in a glass case at the entrance. Within, rich dark-red carpeting matches the leather banquettes, and soft-red lanterns complement the pink tablecloths and burnished brass samovars. Everything is à la carte, and beautifully prepared; you might try breast of chicken or shrimp scampi (large Pacific shrimp) or veal piccata Neapolitan—all are excellent. Entrees run about $10 to $16. The sommelier will visit you with his extensive wine list, and the staff endeavors to make your dining experience special. Save room for .dessert, which promises such temptations as crêpes Kahlua (coffee ice cream wrapped in crêpes and topped with dark fudge sauce) or apple whiskey delight (apple baked with a whiskey custard sauce and almonds) served in a snifter. The Golden Cape serves dinner only, from 6 p.m., when live entertainment and dancing also get under way. Reservations are a must (phone: 245-3631).

Where do the local people take guests when they want to treat them to something special? To one of the nicest places around Lihue town, the **Hanamaulu Cafe,** two miles north of Lihue on Highway 56. While the indoor part of the cafe looks like just another pleasantly ordinary Oriental restaurant, the garden is something else again. Individual Japanese tearooms look out on a beautiful garden with stone toros, bonsai, carp, all in a tranquil and moody setting. The nicest thing about all this is that you don't need a minimum group to get one of these *ozashiki* rooms (but it is a good idea to make reservations), in which you can order anything on the menu, even the $5 plate dinners. There's also a deluxe plate dinner at $6, and a variety of à la carte Oriental dishes at $4.50 to $5.50. Or treat yourself to a multicourse Oriental banquet for about $10 per person. Cocktails are available. The food is subtly seasoned—delicious! Reservations 245-2511.

If you're like me and the mere thought of Mexican food makes your mouth water, don't just sit there, hasten to **La Luna** at 4261 Rice St., a casual *fonda* with a spacious, covered outdoor dining area, a smartly decorated interior, a big bar, and lots of tasty dishes reasonably priced. You might as well start with a margarita magnifica or a tequila sunrise while they're fixing your appetizers: perhaps the super nachos or quesadillas at $3.50. Then on to combination plates ($3.75 to $5.25) and specialties like relleno combination, enchiladas rancheros, and tostada suprema, $4.50 to $6.25. La Luna is open every day from 11 a.m. to 11 p.m., and there's live entertainment Tuesday through Saturday nights from 7:30 to 12. It could be Mexican music, it could also be country western—or whatever. Phone: 245-9173. *Simpatico.*

RESTAURANTS IN POIPU AND HANAPEPE: A spot as much favored by locals as tourists, **Plantation Gardens Restaurant** sits majestically in a seven-acre botanical paradise of cacti and rare plants. Part of Kiahuna Plantation (see above), the restaurant is a restored 19th-century plantation manager's home, an incomparable setting for dining on gourmet cuisine. You could begin, for example, by having a drink in the Poi Pounder Room (where Hawaiian calabashes and stone tikis are displayed in antique French armoires), or outside in the garden. Then on to dinner, perhaps in a Victorian drawing room, or in the main dining room, open on three sides to look out over lily ponds, cactus gardens, palm trees, and the blue Pacific beyond. Many dinner entrees are of continental inspiration with an island flavor: roast duckling with diced papayas, avocados, and other vegetables accompanied by a light teriyaki sauce, or oven-baked filet of red snapper topped with a shoyu cream sauce. They run from $8.75 for a vegetarian platter up to $15 for gulf shrimp à la Provençale. Appetizers include very French escargots with chablis and garlic butter, as well as sashimi, offered in the traditional Japanese manner. Desserts are lavish: I'd brave the waves for "Naughty Hula Pie," an island chocolate-cookie-crust ice-cream pie favorite. Lunch, 11:30 to 2 p.m., offers sandwiches, big salads, and specials such as Tutu-Wahine's omelets, Koloa beef ribs, and locally bred prawns, from $4.50 to $7.50. Breakfast, too. Dinner from 6:30 to 9:30 nightly. Reservations: 742-1695.

Whaler's Cove, part of the Poipu Village Resort, has one of the most scenic settings in the Poipu area, its lanai dining room jutting out over the old Koloa Boat Landing. Service was slow and some of the fish dishes cooked to the point of dryness the night eight of us dined there, but the place holds promise once a few kinks are ironed out. Recommended among the appetizers are the steamed clams with garlic bread and very tasty escargots en croute. Among the entrees, which run from about $8.95 to $13.95, fresh island prawns stuffed with a blend of crabmeat, shrimp, and mushrooms in a sherry sauce and topped with a butter crust were flavorful, as was the seafood combination plate. Catch of the day was a juicy ahi at $12.50, nicely done. Natural-food fans can choose from at least three entrees among the Vegetarian Variety (perhaps eggplant parmigiana, stuffed zucchini, or fettucine Alfredo), all about $5 with soup or salad; and there is a different Chicken Que Será Será dish every night for $8.95. Desserts like freshly baked cheesecake and macadamia pineapple pie are on the lavish side, and even more lavish and luscious are the coffee liqueur specialties—one taste, for example, of Café Lorraine (Grand Marnier, Kahlua, and coffee with whipped cream) sets the whole meal to rights.

Dinner is served daily from 5:30 to 10:30 p.m., entertainment begins at 9 Wednesday through Sunday. Reservations advised: phone 742-6655. Lunch, which consists of sandwiches, egg specials, and fish salads, $3.85 to $6.25, is on from 11 a.m. to 2 p.m., breakfast from 9 a.m.

Visiting Waimea Canyon is a Kauai must, and another Kauai must is stopping at the **Green Garden Restaurant** on Highway 50 in Hanapepe for a meal either before or after. Green Garden is a longtime *kamaiiana* favorite (it has been run by several generations of the same family for over 30 years), and it manages to serve delicious food at moderate prices in a spirit of real island aloha. The place does look like a garden, full of plants and flowers, done in a bamboo-and-white motif. The menu is a combination of Oriental and American dishes, with special kudos for the selections from the kiawe wood char-broiler, from $4.75 to $9.75. These include pork chops brushed with butter or teriyaki sauce, "butterflied" rock lobster tail, suniyaki (char-broiled beef kebab brushed with teriyaki), and steaks, from $5.95 up. They are served with fruit cup or homemade soup, tossed salad, and coffee or tea. Most complete dinners run $4 to $5, with such main-course choices as shrimp tempura, boneless teriyaki chicken, sweet-and-sour spareribs, with all the extras. And you could also declare a special holiday and have a nine-course Oriental dinner on about a half-hour's notice! The Green Garden's homemade pies are a must: even the strongest will falter at the sight of their coconut cream or chocolate cream or their famous macadamia nut and lilikoi pies.

The Green Garden is open from 6 a.m. to 2 p.m. and from 5 to 8:30 p.m., but closed Tuesday evenings.

RESTAURANTS IN THE PRINCEVILLE-HANALEI AREA: Right in the little town of Hanalei itself, next to the Hanalei Trader shop, is a restaurant I am partial to called **The Dolphin.** Tiki poles provide a striking entrance. Inside is more beauty; tapa-topped lacquered tables, glass-float lights, a redwood interior with a dramatic inlaid mural. It's obviously a place to pamper yourself, and the food will not disappoint. There is fresh fish almost daily, nicely prepared, like broiled mahimahi at $8. Other favorites, from $8 to about $16 (for charbroiled lobster), include Hawaiian chicken and an excellent New York cut of teriyaki steak. All entrees are served with family-style salad, steak fries or rice, and hot homemade bread. Homebaked desserts are another plus for the Dolphin (they've got a whopping-good Mud Pie), as well as solid appetizers like ratatouille and New England clam chowder. Dinner only.

Princeville at Hanalei, the gracious resort complex, has a restaurant that matches its charms called **Princeville Lanai Restaurant.** You'll feel as if you're dining in a wonderful private chalet, thanks to the high cathedral ceiling, the panoramic view through the open-air wall overlooking Hanalei Bay, and the natural wood and earth colors complementing the soft lights and spectacular scenery. Happily, both food and service are on a par with the setting.

Dinner is a well-priced package, since all entrees, which range from $8.95 for chicken Kilauea to $14.50 for Malaysian prawns à la scampi, are accompanied by a choice of soup or tossed green salad, fresh vegetables, country-style baked potatoes or rice, and assorted breads and butter. My favorites here are seafood specialties: The chef does a beautiful poached salmon, and there is always fresh catch of the day at $9.75, plus a hot vegetarian entree, and a beautiful salad bar, $6.95. A friend who lives in the neighborhood swears by the pumpkin bread Aunt Jenny often bakes for dinner and by her homemade banana muffins with raisins for breakfast and lunch. Polynesian shows are scheduled several nights a week.

Lunch is also pleasant but less elaborate, featuring the likes of mahimahi sandwiches and "Salade Hanalei" (baby shrimps, asparagus, beansprouts, and house dressing). The Lanai also serves breakfast for those lucky people living nearby. At dinner reservations are a must: phone 826-6228.

My favorite restaurant in this area—indeed, in all Kauai—lives up to the aura of its name: **Bali H'ai.** Located in the Hanalei Bay Resort at Princeville, on the site where *South Pacific* was filmed in 1957, this lanai restaurant with its angled roof, colorful banners, bamboo-backed cane chairs, and soft colors overlooks magical vistas of Hanalei Bay and mountains. While you're feasting your eyes on the scenery, you can also feast on imaginatively prepared food. Dinner entrees, which run from about $9.50 for ginger chicken simmered with pineapple and snow peas on up to $14.50 for rack of lamb, are accompanied by freshly baked dinner rolls, garden salad, and baked papaya. Choice selections: baked salmon Bali H'ai in pastry shell with spinach and cream sauce; broiled New York steak, and scampi. For appetizers, try something unusual: Camembert cheese tempura-fried and served with fresh fruit and mustard sauce. Have the banana cream pie for dessert. There are Polynesian shows Sunday and Thursday.

Lunch is also lovely, with a fresh fish entree at $6, crêpes, salads, and sandwiches. Sunday brunch, served from 8 a.m. to 2 p.m., features champagne punch, fresh tropical fruits, and baskets of "sumptuous breakfast pastries," and costs $7.75 for adults, $5.75 for kids. Reservations for dinner, please: phone 826-6522, extension 18.

RESTAURANTS IN THE WAILUA-WAIPOULI-COCONUT PLANTATION AREA: For an elegant evening in Kauai, head for the luxurious **Coco Palms Hotel.** Arrive about 7:30 to see the impressive torch-lighting ceremony, done with great authenticity and a true feeling of the olden days. Then proceed to the Lagoon Dining Room (dinner seating from 8:15 to 8:30), where you dine in style on good continental cuisine. The menu changes every night, but typical appetizers include lomi lomi salmon, tropical fruit, and potage St. Germain. Your main course could be roast capon or teriyaki steak, Polynesian shrimp tempura or Wailua beef brochette. You'll also get salad, vegetables, and potatoes with your main dish, and a choice of dessert—perhaps orange chiffon pie or the famed Coconut Palms sundae (vanilla ice cream with coconut syrup and coconut topping), for an all-inclusive price, from $10.25 to about $16. Around about 9, when you're sipping your coffee, the evening show gets under way; it's always pleasant, featuring either a Mormon church singing or dancing group or local Hawaiian entertainment by Larry Rivera and his group. There is no cover charge. Reservations: 822-4921.

Another good Coco Palms possibility: the buffet brunch every day from 10 a.m. to 2 p.m., $6.50, filling and delicious.

Very popular in the Coconut Plantation area is **The Spindrifter** (you may have dined at one in Honolulu or in Kona). The Kauai version is a charming and comfortable place with high-beamed ceilings and soft light from hanging leaded-glass lanterns. The menu is mostly steak and seafood, but with a Mexican touch; I like the steak-and-enchiladas plate at dinner, as well as the more usual fried chicken or steak and scampi. You can eat hearty here, because along with your main course, priced from $7.75 to about $13, come a few turns at an excellent salad bar, plus soup from the kettle, hot bread and butter, and steamed rice. Lunch features lots of good burgers and omelets, plus salads and a Mexican entree, stuffed quesadilla: a combination of cheese, tomato, beef, chili peppers, and tangy sauce on a grilled flour tortilla. Ole! Hawaiian and contemporary music every night. Reservations: 822-3451.

In Coconut Plantation itself there are scads of snackbars where you can put together an ethnic picnic, choosing from Oriental, Filipino, Mexican, Italian, and American foods. The best "real restaurant" here is **Buzz's Polynesia,** noted for its salad bar, Hawaiian luau plate ($8.50), beef and seafood dishes, and a charming island atmosphere. Open almost all day.

After Dark in Kauai

Nightlife in Kauai is where you find it. There's nothing spectacular enough to warrant a 40-mile drive, but wherever you are, something will be going on—perhaps Hawaiian entertainment, rock music, or just soft sounds to sip your cocktails by. Most of the big hotels provide Hawaiian shows for their dinner guests. And I should tell you that here in the neighbor islands Hawaiian shows are usually relaxed, informal affairs, much less pretentious than those in Waikiki. Besides, you'll probably recognize the faces of the entertainers; they may be the hotel clerks or busboys or cab drivers you met during the day! In the islands, everybody dances, everybody sings, and surprisingly well. Unless it's a dinner show, a drink or two gets you a ringside seat for the action; unless there is name entertainment, there's usually no cover or minimum charge.

LIHUE: **Club Jetty,** at Nawiliwili Harbor, alternates between live band and disco until the wee hours; you may catch a Polynesian show here on weekends. . . . Best Polynesian show in town is the one at the **Planter's Bar and Lounge** of the Kauai Surf Hotel, a glorious spot perched over the water. It's on every night at 8:45. At the same hotel, **Destination Disco** is just that, one of the most popular disco spots in town. And there's dancing every night in the Surf's **Golden Cape Room.**

COCONUT PLANTATION-WAILUA-WAIPOULI: There's a lot of action at the hotels out here. At the **Holiday Inn Kauai Beach** there's entertainment from 9 every night at **Cook's Landing,** plus terrific luaus on Tuesday, Thursday, and Sunday. Admission of about $20 for adults, $12 for children includes one-hour bar, buffet dinner, and show. . . . another top luau is held on the same nights at the **Kauai Resort Hotel**, for $20.50. . . . The **Lagoon Dining Room** is the place for the Coco Palms dinner show, every night at about 9: it's either the Mormon church singing and dancing group, or Larry Rivera. . . . A swinging disco called the **Boogie Palace** packs in the crowds at the **Kauai BeachBoy Hotel,** every night from 9 on. There's a $1 cover most nights. . . . Newest disco is the **Kauai Observatory** at Waipouli Plaza, a mile past Coconut Plantation, with live music from 8 to 10 p.m., disco until 4 a.m., and big-screen TV and "celestial projection" show all the time. Cover charge $1 weekdays, $2 weekends. . . . "People of Paradise," an excellent ethnic dance show, is presented nightly at **Paradise Pacifica,** behind the Wailua Marina. Admission is $8 for adults, $4 for children under 12. You can also combine the show with the exciting, ethnic "Luau Pacifica" for a total price of $20; children under 12, half price.

POIPU BEACH: Count on good entertainment in the **Drum Lounge:** Norman Young is usually on hand, joined by either Wally and Polei or Hawaiian Time. The show starts about 9:15 p.m.

HANALEI: You can catch Polynesian shows on Sunday and Thursday at **Bali H'ai** in the Hanalei Bay Resort, several nights a week at **Princeville** at Hanalei. . . . **Tahiti Nui** is a local place that swings when the mood is right. There's local impromptu entertainment at various times, including the Friday night luaus.

The Sights and Sounds of Kauai

Since you cannot circle entirely around the island of Kauai and see it all in one day, you must plan on at least two full-day sightseeing excursions. The trip to **Waimea Canyon** (the southern and western route) is best made on a clear day; call the weather bureau before you go. If it's foggy, take the eastern and northern trip first. Both trips are about 40 miles each way, and since each offers a full share of gorgeous little beaches as well as awesome natural wonders, you should plan to leave early in the morning, pick up a box lunch in town for a picnic (or check the restaurant selections above), throw your bathing suits and suntan lotions into the backseat, and head off for an adventure.

WESTWARD TO THE CANYON: Get thee to Lihue, the center (for all practical purposes) of the island and the site of a delightful shopping complex in the center of town. Nearby, at 3016 Umi St., Suite 207, you will find the offices of the Hawaii Visitors Bureau, where lovely Maile Semitekol and Sue Yoshishige can help you get oriented.

Your next stop in Lihue should definitely be the **Kauai Museum,** a two-building complex at 4424 Rice St. housing a splendid collection of Hawaiiana (quilts, calabashes, furniture, artifacts, etc.) as well as the permanent exhibit, "The Story of Kauai," which includes a six-minute film shot from a helicopter and showing rarely seen parts of the island. Note the Museum Shop, with many fine Hawaiian and South Pacific items. Open weekdays 9:30 to 4:30; Saturday, 9 to 1. Admission is $2 for adults; children under 17, free with an adult.

Now cross Eiwa Street and walk to the site of the new **Civic Center** whose daring architecture is strikingly modern in this setting. Back in your car now, follow Rice Street until you almost reach its junction with Highway 50. To your left is the quaint little **Haleko Drive** and four restored homes once belonging to sugar plantation workers, which now house several restaurants, including the cozy little **The Egg and I.**

Now follow Highway 51 to **Nawiliwili** (the place where the willow trees grow). Once one of the most bustling harbors in the island, it is just a shadow of its former self. Biggest attraction here is lovely Kalapaki Beach, one of the best in Kauai, the town beach that residents share with guests of the Kauai Surf Hotel.

After a swim here (highly recommended), walk across from the Kauai Surf Hotel to the **Menehune Shopping Village,** which ought to be better patronized than it usually is. It has some pleasant resort and island craft shops, a good bookstore, and a terrific steak-and-salad bar house, **Cork 'n' Fork.** Locals also like **Rosita's** for Mexican food and **Ritz Cafe** for sophisticated snacks: crêpes, yogurt, lox and bagels.

Poipu

About 14 miles out of Lihue you head into the tranquil **Koloa** region of Kauai; swing off the main drag onto Highway 52 and follow the markers to Poipu Beach. On Kiahuna Plantation is a remarkable botanical garden, **Moir's Gardens.** The Hawaiian name for the gardens is **Pa'u A Laka,** the Skirt of Laka, goddess of the hula and sister of the volcano goddess Pele. It is believed that this site was once the training grounds for her disciples. The place abounds in history as well as horticultural beauty (a cactus garden, an orchid garden, a plumeria plantation), and you are invited to walk through the gardens free; markers identify plants.

An Adventure Off the Beaten Path

Just before you reach the pier at Nawiliwili, turn off Highway 51 and take Route 58 to the **Menehune Garden,** where you can explore flowers, plants, and herbs of old Hawaii: gracious "Aunty Sarah" Kalikea will show you the grounds. Admission is $2 for adults, 50¢ for children under 12. Then, back to the pier until you come to a narrow road leading up into the mountains and the site of the **Alekoko Fishpond,** reputedly built by the Menehunes in one night (regular little workers, weren't they?). If you're lucky enough to arrive when a tour limousine is not here, you will be able to enjoy the unearthly quiet of this area. This is peace that you can almost drink.

Now you continue on to the glorious **Poipu Beach** region. Although luxury hotels abound along this stretch of crystal and golden sand, the very best beach, the one to which even the hotels send their guests, is the Poipu public pavilion. It's the perfect place for a picnic and a swim.

Continue along the Poipu shore highway and you will come upon the monument, on the right side of the road, commemorating the birthplace of Prince Jonah Kuhio Kalanianaole, who represented Hawaii in the U.S. Congress from 1902 to 1922. Up the road, the **Kukuiulua Small Boat Harbor** is the best place to take in, in one swoop, the grandeur of the south shore of Kauai. Set your sights now for the **Spouting Horn** blowhole on your right, and then drive on down the highway to see it close up. A lava tube under the black rock funnels the force of the waves into a veritable geyser; the effect is spectacular.

Back on Highway 50, now, watch for the HVB marker and the sign indicating **Olu Pua Gardens,** just past the junction of 50 with 54. Here you'll find another horticultural fairyland (they really mean it when they call Kauai the "Garden Island"). On 12 acres of land that was once a plantation manager's estate is an island-within-an-island of floral beauty. Your $3 admission charge entitles you to stay as long as you like and explore the varied gardens.

Back on Highway 50, you'll come to the HVB warrior pointing directly to the lush and lovely valley of **Hanapepe**. It's a fine miniature of some of the grander valleys you'll see on Kauai. If you're hungry, stop for lunch at the **Green Garden**. The **Salt Pond Pavilion** is a good spot for a picnic lunch and a swim; turn toward the ocean on Highway 543 outside Hanapepe. Down the other fork of the highway are located the ancient salt ponds where the *Hui Hana Paakai O Hanapepe* still practice the ancient art of salt-making. These drying beds are almost 200 years old.

On you go now, hurtling into the historic town of **Waimea** where Captain Cook first landed in 1778, looked around him, and claimed the Sandwich Islands for England. You'll first pass a state marker indicating the site of a Russian fort where a member of the Alaska Fur Trading Company, hoping to capture the island for his czar, built—and watched crumble—the walls of his six-pointed fort. Parking facilities have already been built, but until the complete fort is restored, there's not much to detain you here.

Now watch for the sign leading through a quiet valley up to the site of the **Menehune Ditch.** Those busy little gremlins were at it again. Here they built an aqueduct to feed mountain water to the highlands of the valley. All that remains are cut stone bricks, two feet higher than the road and 200 feet long, inscribed with markings whose significance the archeologists can only guess at.

To the Canyon

Just outside Waimea, take the Waimea Canyon Road on your right. Don't continue to Kekaha, since most of the beautiful beach here, the area's major charm, has been closed off by the army. Winding and doubling back in the most vicious of manners, the Waimea Canyon Road carries you higher and higher into the cool, crisp **Kokee** region, 3600 feet above the green seas of Kauai. The scenery is spectacular: on one side stretch sloping mountainsides emptying into the ocean, and on the other drops the magnificent Waimea Valley. You can get different perspectives on the valley from numerous roadside clearings, but I suggest you wait until you reach the **Puu Ka Pele Lookout.** There, below you, is the Grand Canyon of the Pacific, a 10-mile-long, mile-wide gorge, the result of an ancient crust fault that split miles of solid stone into a maze of jagged ridges. A rainbow of colors dances along the peaks, spiraling and cascading down the mountain slopes.

Before you reap the full gift of the canyon at **Kalalau Lookout** further up, relax for a few minutes at the **Kokee Museum,** right next to the **Kokee Lodge Restaurant.** Just after you pass this point, follow the signs to Kalalau Lookout. Driving the winding road for these last few miles, you will pass the Kokee tracking station, now world-famous for its part in the success of the Apollo 11 mission to the moon. It was from this site that a laser beam was flashed to reflectors that Neil Armstrong had set up on the lunar surface.

At the end of the road is a sight that may make you forget the moon and stars and your own petty concerns as you stand at the edge of the world: suddenly, 4000 feet below you, past long-abandoned cliffs that once supported ancient villages, the turquoise ocean crashes noiselessly on faraway beaches. White birds glide to and fro on gentle breezes. It is rumored that a wise man once lived here in a cave by the sea; he never came back to civilization again. You may not want to, either; if you must, your drive from Kalalau Lookout to the highway will be about an hour's worth of concentrated driving.

THE NORTHERN AND EASTERN ROUTE: As you start out on your second exploratory tour of Kauai—this time along its eastern and northern shores—you might keep one thing in mind: if there is something spectacular to see, the Menehunes made it. And if they didn't, the gods did. In any case, you will find this end of the island steeped in a mythology that lends an aura of mystery to the breathtaking sights.

Again, plan on a full-day trip, and be sure to take along your bathing suits and perhaps a picnic lunch. Head out of Lihue and past the airport on H-56 until you go through the little village of **Kapaia** just a mile away. If you go too fast you might miss the sign for **Wailua Falls,** four miles mauka of the main highway. Don't attempt to drive up the road past the falls; just enjoy the peacefulness of the area.

Heading down the road, you'll pass the Wailua Golf Course on your right, just before the entrance to **Lydgate Park,** a beautiful beach area that is open to the public and snuggles right up to the grounds of the Kauai Resort Hotel. The beach is safe and great fun for children; restrooms and showers are provided. Just up the road from this spot you approach the Wailua River. Turn left before you reach the bridge over the river and drive to the **Wailua Marina,** where you can hop a boat to the magnificent **Fern Grotto,** where ferns form a frame for a cave under a waterfall. An hour-and-a-half cruise is $5 for adults, $2.50 for children.

Just behind the marina (take the access road on the Lihue side of the bridge) you'll find **Paradise Pacifica,** a 31-acre botanical park filled with plants and trees from all over the Pacific region. A three-car, open-air, battery-powered tram with a lovely island girl as engineer and commentator takes you through the grounds, making its way down the path past African tulip trees, ironwood, poinciana, lauhala, and a peaceful Japanese garden. You'll stop at a Filipino village, a Polynesian village, and a replica of an ancient Polynesian place of sacrifice. Then it's back to the train past scary Tongan tikis, through an extensive collection of members of the ti-leaf family, and the fruit orchards. The trip takes just under an hour, and a friend of mine who has lived in Hawaii for ten years said even she learned things from it (our eight-year-old companion was spellbound). Admission is $3.75 for adults, $2 for children. For details on their evening show and luau, see "After Dark in Kauai," above.

After this little diversion, make your way back to H-56 and turn left just before the sign for the Coco Palms Hotel. Now you're on the **King's Highway,** upon which the corpulent *alii* of old Hawaii were borne by their servants (their feet were too holy to tread common ground). Just up the road is the **Holo-Holo-Ku Heiau,** where human sacrifices were offered up to the gods, and not too long ago. Up a skinny stairway on the right side of the *heiau,* you'll discover an old Japanese graveyard, bespeaking the settlement of Orientals that grew up in this area many years back. Continue on the road to its conclusion at the head of **Opaekaa Falls,** where white birds soar in silence above the steaming, rainbowed waterfalls. Shrimp used to gather at the foot of the falls to spawn, and the tumbling motion that the churning waves put them through suggested the name—Opaekaa, rolling shrimp. A restored Hawaiian village may be opening on this site.

Once you turn around and head back to H-56, you can take the one-way fork off the King's Highway that leads, as the signs indicate, to the **Bellstone,** just beyond the place where the king's home and temple were once located. One of the rocks here is supposed to respond with a clear, bell-like tone when you hit it with another rock. I've never figured out which one, but you're welcome to try your luck. The rock was once used to signal news of danger from the sea—possibly in the form of enemy canoes—or to ring out the news of a royal birth.

At the base of the King's Highway now, you'll be passing the beautiful grounds of the **Coco Palms Hotel.** If it's early, stop in for the lovely $6 breakfast buffet. This has always been a very special area. Long before the days of tourists, Hawaiian royalty lived here, and the lagoon was a series of fishponds. The old days are recalled each night in torchlight ceremonies at 7:30 p.m.

You'll certainly want to make a stop at **The Market Place** at Coconut Plantation, coming up now on the ocean side of the road, and the temptation will be not to stay *too* long here; what with something like 60 shops, about a dozen restaurants or tempting ethnic snackbars, a twin-movie theater, and even colored fountains and an irrigation system that the kids can have fun playing with, it may be hard to tear yourself away—especially if you sink into one of those oh-so-comfy "net-chairs" (swinging hammock seats) they have at **High as a Kite and Toy Company.** You'll recognize a number of places from Honolulu, like **Liberty House, Andrade,** and **Crazy Shirts.** But don't miss some local favorites like **The Pottery Tree,** whose wares, all created by Kauai craftspeople, include beautiful batik wall hangings, batik clothing, pottery, planters, and the like. **Happy Kauaian** has attractive island clothing for everyone, including children and petite sizes; **Garden Island Casuals** has some distinctive women's clothing; **Waves of One Sea** is the place for international gift items, many from Indonesia, Bali, and the Orient; and **Konakope Coffee & Nut Roasting Center** will pour you a free cup of one of their wonderful Hawaiian coffees or native teas. If you can, come back to the Market Place on a Thursday, Friday, or Saturday around 4 p.m., when they present free Polynesian shows. Bring the cameras.

Back on the highway, you'll soon notice an HVB marker indicating the **Sleeping Giant** rock formation, and you can pull off the side of the road to figure this one out. It's my favorite rock formation in the state, since, unlike others, very little imagination is needed to see that it does indeed resemble a reclining Goliath. He was, in fact, the giant Puni, who befriended the Menehunes. Once, while he slept, enemy canoes threatened the shoreline, and the little men threw boulders onto his stomach to wake him up. He swallowed a few and died in his sleep, but a few stones ricocheted off his belly and destroyed the invaders' canoes.

Past the little town of **Kealia** (where once the Waipahoe Slide beckoned visitors but is now closed) you go, and perhaps stop at **Anahala Beach Park** for a picnic. Beyond the beach turn-off point you can get a good view of the **Anahola Valley,** and further on you can pull off the side of the road and try to discover the **Hole-in-the-Mountain** natural wonder. It's easier if you let yourself believe the story of Kapunoho, the chief of Kohala, Hawaii, who challenged the chief of Kauai to a spear-throwing contest. He was so good at it that his spear pierced the mountain and landed near the beach at Hanalei.

A possible side trip is in Kilauea, to the **Kilauea Lighthouse.** The lighthouse is now fully automated, but the view from a high bluff overlooking the sea is spectacular.

It seems hard to believe that **Kalihiwai Bay,** which you come upon next, was once the scene of savage tidal waves that twice, in 1946 and 1957, destroyed its little village. All is peaceful here now, and the road continues along, winding upward until it affords one of the most splendid views in the island of **Hanalei Valley.** Neatly terraced and squared off for irrigation purposes, with its rice paddies, taro patches, and the Hanalei River far below, it looks remarkably like a bit of the Orient.

Now you might want to take a few minutes out to visit **Princeville at Hanalei,** a luxurious resort complex described in the hotel section (above). Join the sporting set at the **Bali H'ai** or the **Princeville Lanai Restaurant** for lunch, perhaps, or wander around the **Princeville Shopping Center,** where our favorites are the **Princeville Plantation Store,** a real "general store" stocked with everything from needlepoint and bluejeans to children's toys and locally made pottery, **Red Hibiscus** for jewelry and fine art, and **Waialea Trading Company,** full of imaginative imports in clothes, jewelry, baskets, and such.

Now proceed to quaint Hanalei Valley itself, maybe have a look at the 1837 **Waioli Mission House,** a small historical house-museum (open Tuesday through Saturday, 9 a.m. to 3 p.m.), perhaps stop in at **Hanalei Garden and Gifts** (handicrafts made on Kauai) or **Hanalei Shell House and Gift Shop** (which has tasty homemade food in addition to shells and beads at low prices). If it's summer, the swimming will be very good at lovely **Hanalei Beach Park.**

Continuing on, you'll skirt a cliffside road that looks out over the much-photographed **Lumahai Beach.** It's one of the most beautiful in the islands, but just to look at. Rocks and currents make it unsafe for swimming, which may be the reason for its untouched appearance. Don't attempt to thread the path down the mountainside to the beach. There's great swimming coming up ahead.

Now your drive takes you through the enchantingly beautiful Haena region, over narrow one-lane bridges, into country that is truly unlike anything else in the islands. Soon, on the left side of the road, you'll see the Manini-holo **Dry Cave** and, a little bit past that, two wet caves, **Waikapale** and **Waikanaloa**. Both figure in the mythology of Kauai, and sometimes the islanders swim in them. But that's a bit dangerous and besides, you're practically at Ke'e, one of the most serene of island beaches. Park where the Na Pali trail begins (devoted hikers claim it is unforgettable). Here, under the towering Na Pali cliffs, once the scene of Hawaiian religious rituals, you can bask in the sun, swim in safe waters, let the rest of the world go by and not miss it a bit.

Hawaiian Fishermen

HOW TO SAVE MONEY
ON ALL YOUR TRAVELS

Saving money while traveling is never a simple matter—which is why, almost 18 years ago, the **$15-a-Day Travel Club** was formed. Actually, the idea came from readers of the Arthur Frommer Publications, who felt that such an organization could bring financial benefits, continuing travel information, and a sense of community to economy-minded travelers in all parts of the world. They were right.

In keeping with the money-saving concept, the membership fee is low, and it is immediately exceeded by the value of your benefits. Upon receipt of U.S. $12 (U.S., Canadian, and Mexican residents), or U.S. $14 (other foreign residents) to cover one year's membership, we will send all new members by return mail (book rate):

(1) The latest edition of any *two* of the books listed on the following page.

(2) A copy of ARTHUR FROMMER'S GUIDE TO NEW YORK.

(3) A one-year subscription to the quarterly Club newspaper—THE WONDERFUL WORLD OF BUDGET TRAVEL (see below).

(4) A voucher entitling you to a $5 discount on any Arthur Frommer International, Inc. tour booked by you through any travel agent in the United States and Canada.

(5) Your personal membership card, which, once received, entitles you to purchase through the Club *all* Arthur Frommer Publications for a third to a half off their regular retail prices during the term of your membership.

These are the immediate and definite benefits which we can assure to members of the Club at this time. Even more exciting, however, are the further and more substantial benefits which it has been our continuing aim to achieve for members. These are announced in the Club's newspaper, THE WONDERFUL WORLD OF BUDGET TRAVEL, a full-size, eight-page newspaper that keeps members up-to-date on fast-breaking developments in low-cost travel in all parts of the world. The newspaper also carries such continuing features as "Travelers' Directory"—a list of members all over the world who are willing to provide hospitality to other members as they pass through their home cities; "Share-a-Trip" —requests from members for travel companions who can share costs; "Readers Ask . . . Readers Reply"—travel-related queries from members, to which other members reply with firsthand information. It also offers advance news of individual, group, and charter programs operated by Arthur Frommer International, Inc., plus in-depth articles on special destinations (most recently, Cyprus, Eastern Europe, and Costa Rica).

If you would like to join this hardy band of international budgeteers and participate in its exchange of information and hospitality, simply send U.S. $12 (U.S., Canadian, and Mexican residents), or $14 (other foreign residents) along with your name and address to: $15-a-Day Travel Club, Inc., 380 Madison Ave., New York, NY 10017. Remember to specify which *two* of the books in section one above you wish to receive in your initial package of members' benefits. Or tear out this page, check off any two books on the opposite side, and send it to us with your membership fee.